CHEAP
SLEEPS IN LONDON

SECOND EDITION
**The Savvy Traveler's Guide to
the Best Accommodations at
the Best Prices.**

SANDRA A. GUSTAFSON

CHRONICLE BOOKS
SAN FRANCISCO

Printed in the United States of America.

SECOND EDITION
ISBN 0-8118-2781-X (pbk.)

Cover design: Robin Weiss
Cover photograph: Mark Snyder
Book design: Words & Deeds
Original maps: Françoise St. Clair

Distributed in Canada by Raincoast Books,
112 East Third Avenue, Vancouver, B.C. V5T 1C8

10 9 8 7 6 5 4 3 2 1

Chronicle Books
275 Fifth Street
San Francisco, CA 94103

For
Mary Gregg Misch

CONTENTS

To the Reader 6

General Information 9

    Tips for Cheap Sleeps in London 9

    When to Go 11

    Holidays 11

    What to Wear 12

    About Money 12

    Staying in Touch: The Telephone 15

    Transportation 16

    Student and Senior Citizen Discounts 19

    This and That: Helpful Hints 20

    Practical Information: Useful Addresses and Telephone
        Numbers 22

How to Use Cheap Sleeps in London 25

    Crown Classifications 25

    Accommodations 25

    Reservations, Deposits, and Cancellations 26

    Rates: Paying the Bill 28

    Hotel Breakfasts 28

    Facilities 29

Hotel Listings by Postal Code 31

    W1 32

    W2, W8, W11 44

    WC1, WC2 72

    SW1 96

    SW3 118

SW5, SW7   124

NW1   146

Other Options   150

  Bed and Breakfast in a Private Home   151

  Camping   156

  Renting a London Flat   159

  Strictly for Students   172

  Staying in a University Dormitory   174

  Ys   184

  Youth Hostels   188

Quick Reference   192

  Big Splurges   192

  Glossary   193

Shopping: Cheap Chic   196

  Cheap Chic Shopping Tips   197

  What Size Is That in American?   199

  VAT Refund   200

  Shopping Areas   201

  Store Listings   203

  Do China in a Day   223

  Department Stores   224

  Markets   227

  Museum Shops   230

Index   234

Reader's Comments   239

To the Reader

When a man is tired of London, he is tired of life; for there is in London all that life can afford.

—Dr. Samuel Johnson

The British hold a unique place in the hearts of Americans for we are bound together and influenced in our daily lives by ancestral ties; shared language, laws, literature, customs, and traditions; and by strong social and religious values. When we look back, most of us began our lifetime love affair with London as children, listening to nursery rhymes, singing songs, reading about the Queen and the royal family, and pretending to be a part of it all. For many of us reared in the English-speaking world, a trip to London is like coming home.

The largest city in Europe, London's metropolitan area comprises more than 625 square miles. Intriguing, invigorating, exciting, London is full of fascinating contrasts. Whether you're making your first or twentieth visit, whatever you are looking for is here: history, tradition, pomp and pageantry; the bright lights of the theater; wonderful music and famous art; fine shopping; and food from around the globe.

London is host to more than twenty-four million visitors every year from more than forty countries. Besides being one of the most appealing destinations, London has the unfortunate reputation as one of the most expensive cities. It is now listed in the top five cities with the highest per-diem rates, right up there with Tokyo and New York City.

Many London hotels can easily top $250 or $300 per night, with breakfast extra. But travelers who want their money's worth need not pay such high prices. Instead, they must be creative. It is important to look for weekend packages that can trim this cost in half, throwing in not only breakfast, but often dinner. In smaller places, offer to pay cash instead of using credit cards, and if your stay will be a week or longer, negotiate the seventh night and get it free. Savvy travelers also look closely at airline deals that include air travel and hotel rooms in a wide range of prices. Just remember not to be intimidated by the first quoted price, and *negotiate.*

Travelers are also learning that bigger hotels with fancy price tags are not necessarily better. The sad fact is that to many Americans so-called budget accommodations in London are not "cheap." The average London budget hotel room runs from £45–80 per night for two and offers little in the Olde English charm department.

In these mom-and-pop operations, don't look for many frills except on the lampshades and curtains. Most have ten or twelve rooms done in a combination of styles and colors. The bathrooms are usually down the hall, or in an effort to please American guests, an airless portable unit has been wedged into a corner of your room.

Despite some drawbacks, you will usually be treated as a welcome family guest by your hosts. The owner will call you by name, take your phone messages, and collect your mail. On your next visit, you won't have to tell him how to fix your bacon and eggs, and you will get your same room if you request it.

This edition of *Cheap Sleeps in London* is *not* about where to find the cheapest beds in London. It *is* about where to find the best value for your money, from campsites to small, antiques-filled doll-house hotels. What are the guidelines I used for selection? The primary concerns, naturally, were value and cleanliness. Next, I looked at location.

All Cheap Sleeps in London, except for campsites, are located within the Circle Line on the London Underground (tube), which means you are never more than a thirty-minute tube ride from your hotel into central London. There is no reason to stay far from the action just to save a few pounds. You will quickly spend the difference in time and energy to reach all the places you want to visit. Finally, the hotel management must be helpful and friendly. While you cannot expect uniformed porters to carry your bags in budget digs, you can expect and insist on getting a clean room in a hospitable place. With *Cheap Sleeps in London* in hand, you will.

During my research in London, I visited hundreds of hotels and other accommodation alternatives, finally narrowing the selection to include bunks in dorms, family-run bed and breakfasts, full-service apartments, rooms in private homes, and hotels of all the types you will find listed. A few fall into the Big Splurge category for those with higher expectations and more flexible budgets. There is a place for every taste and pocketbook, each with the vital ingredient of making your London stay more pleasurable.

When inspecting places, I tried to anticipate your needs and foresee as many disasters as possible lurking in corners. I have ridden in elevators that were short prison sentences, and have felt as though I were on an Outward Bound course as I climbed twisting stairways and groped my way down gloomy hallways. I checked out the hall toilets, showers, and bathtubs, and noted the type of toilet tissue: (i.e., No. 1 sandpaper, waxed, acceptable).

I examined thin towels, opened closets and dresser drawers, dealt with rude owners and indifferent managers, and strange cleaning staff.

I found dustballs under the beds, food under mattresses, mice in the kitchens, mold in too many bathrooms, and much more I won't go into. I walked more than 350 miles, wore out my shoes, and took notes seven days a week, rain or shine. Endurance was a necessity, not an option, but I loved every minute because it never seemed like work.

It is important for you to know that one of my listings can never be bought or solicited. I do all the research for my books myself. I recheck every hotel and shop for each edition of *Cheap Sleeps* and if they still measure up, I consider them for inclusion. Nothing is ever automatically "in." If I like a hotel, I consider it. But if I find it dirty, unfriendly, or otherwise unacceptable, it is out no matter how cheap it is or how many others think it is great.

If a hotel has some snags, is fraying a bit around the edges, has wild colors and limited facilities, but does offer value for your battered Yankee dollar, I will tell you about the bad right along with the good.

My goal is to give you enough information so you can know what to expect and make a realistic choice based on your needs and your budget considerations, so your stay in London will be one you will look back on fondly. Wherever your dreams may take you, if you remember to always take a big smile, lots of patience, and above all a positive attitude, your trip will be successful. If I have been able to help you succeed, I have done my job well. I wish you good luck and a safe and wonderful journey.

General Information

TIPS FOR CHEAP SLEEPS IN LONDON

The good traveler has the gift of surprise.
—W. Somerset Maugham

1. Unless you are a nomad backpacker who does not care where you lay your head, do not even consider arriving in London without confirmed hotel reservations. Why waste precious vacation time standing in lines at tourist offices or railway stations hoping to land something in your price range, only to wind up spending more money for a fringe or marginal location because nothing else was available?

2. Be sure you understand the rates and what they include at the beginning of your stay. Don't wait until the end. Check-out time is not when you want to discover the rates did not include the VAT (17½ percent value-added tax) or those huge breakfasts you enjoyed every morning.

3. To get the best hotel price, go in the off-season from November through March.

4. You would be surprised at the discounts you can get if only you ask. For instance, ask that the price of breakfast be deducted from your room rate. If you are staying a week or more in a small B&B or offer to pay cash, chances are you can get a price break. If you are booking through a toll-free 800 number from the States, these operators are seldom authorized to grant discounts. While it always pays to ask if they have special weekend deals, you usually have to speak directly with the hotel to get special rates. The one exception is the Forte hotel chain, which has fantastic weekend rates and bargain breaks, some as much as 50 percent off the standard rate. The price you pay will include a full English breakfast, and in some cases dinner and theater tickets.

5. Another way to save money is to find a plan combining your airfare with your hotel stay.

6. If you have prepaid a large portion of your trip, and especially if you have rented a flat and prepaid a big chunk in advance, buy

cancellation and trip-interruption insurance. London hoteliers are merciless when it comes to cash refunds, especially the independents.

7. *Always* inspect the room before you check in.

8. In lower-priced hotels and B&Bs with a combination of rooms with and without private toilet and bath facilities, you will save money and gain precious space if you request a room *without* a private toilet and shower or bathtub. These so-called "private" bathrooms are often little more than airless portable units squeezed into a corner of the room. In most cases, hall facilities are far superior.

9. If you are susceptible to cold and visit London during the winter, ask whether your room will be constantly heated or if the central heating will be turned off at certain times during the day and night, leaving you in icy discomfort.

10. The cheapest room will be one facing the back of the hotel, without private facilities. A room with a double bed and shower will cost less than one with twin beds and a bathtub.

11. Do your own laundry or take it to the neighborhood laundromat. If you do wash out things in your hotel bathroom, please be considerate and do not let your things drip dry onto the carpeting.

12. *Always* change money at a bank, at American Express, or a Thomas Cook office, *never* at your hotel. The rates at the hotel will never be in your favor (see About Money, page 12).

13. Be sure you understand the house rules. How late will someone be on the desk to let you in or to take telephone messages? When is check-out time, and can you store your luggage at the hotel if your flight leaves later in the day?

14. When calling home, use USA Direct. Hotel surcharges can be wildly expensive if you place an overseas call through the switchboard (see Staying in Touch, page 15).

15. If you plan to stay in youth hostels or bunk in large dorm rooms in some of the lower-priced hotels, invest in the best lock you can find for the locker you will be assigned. Wear a money belt, don't flash cash or jewelry, and lock up valuables in the hotel safe.

16. If you receive unacceptable service at your hotel, complain to the manager or owner, not to a desk clerk who has no authority to make changes. If the situation cannot be resolved to your satisfaction, report your problem to the London Tourist Board. Then,

let me know (see Reader's Comments, page 239). I cannot be your go-between, but I want to know if an entry of mine does not live up to your expectations. I will report all complaints (and compliments) to the management personally on my next visit to inspect that hotel.

WHEN TO GO

For most of us, a trip to London is not a spur-of-the-moment decision made one day and acted on the next. It is usually part of a carefully planned trip anticipated for some time. If you are really serious about having the most economical trip possible, you must plan to go during the low season. Low season generally runs between November and March, with the week around the Christmas and New Year's holidays excepted. Airfares and hotel rates are lowest at that time, but the low-cost university dormitories open for tourists are full of regular students then and unavailable.

The weather can be cold, damp, and rainy, but on the plus side, tickets to your favorite shows will be easier to get, and you will not have to face crowds in the museums. If you are a shopper, don't forget the January sales, when prices are slashed to their lowest point of the year.

From late spring into early summer, visitors can look forward to beautiful flowers in all the parks and gardens, the Chelsea Flower Show, the Derby and Royal Ascot horse races, and the colorful Trooping of the Colors ceremony with most members of the royal family in attendance. The Wimbledon tennis tournament draws crowds in late June and early July. In August, you will share your London vacation with fellow travelers from around the world and few Londoners, because most of them have escaped to the country for their summer holiday.

During the summer, hotel prices will be at their highest; if there is a heat wave, you will swelter because few small hotels have any sort of air-conditioning. Fall is my favorite time in London. The weather is nice, the colors are magnificent, and tourists are few. As Christmas approaches, London is a fairyland of lights, and the beautifully decorated stores are filled with tempting presents.

HOLIDAYS

Public holidays in England are referred to as "bank holidays," because the banks are closed and so is almost everything else. If a holiday falls on a weekend, the following Monday is also a legal holiday.

New Year's Day	January 1
Good Friday	Friday before Easter
Easter Sunday	Varies
Easter Monday	Monday after Easter
May Day Bank Holiday	First Monday in May
Spring Bank Holiday	Last Monday in May
August Bank Holiday	Last Monday in August
Christmas Day	December 25
Boxing Day	December 26

WHAT TO WEAR

Naturally, you will leave your down-filled coat and lined mittens at home in August. But, what kind of coat makes sense in late April or September? *USA Today* has a weather hotline (1-900-370-USAT) that gives you the weather forecast for 490 cities around the world.

We all know comfortable, well broken-in shoes are musts on everyone's packing list. So is an umbrella, the collapsible kind you can tuck into a purse or totebag. Other essentials include sweaters for layering and a raincoat with a zip-out lining. If you accept only one piece of advice from me on packing, let it be this: *travel light.*

Porters are almost relics of the past, especially in airports and train stations, and dragging heavy bags up and down stairs in a B&B is no fun—believe me. Take half what you think you will need, color coordinate it, and keep in mind you are going to London, not Pluto, so you will be able to wash, throw out, or buy more while you are there.

Leave your diamonds, emeralds, gold bracelets, and other valuables at home. If you do bring something of value and are not wearing it, put it in the hotel safe. Don't hide it in your room, because hotel thieves know about every hiding place you can think of and probably some you cannot.

ABOUT MONEY

It doesn't seem to cost a lot of money to go away.
—Lewis Carroll, *Alice in Wonderland*

If you carry traveler's checks, charge most items on your credit card, and use ATMs for incidental cash, you will come out on top. Be sure to carry a few of your own personal checks. If you suddenly run out of money, you can use them to get cash advances, provided the credit card you have allows that. Try to have a few pounds on hand when you arrive. They'll get you out of the airport faster because you will avoid getting off a long flight only to spend another hour in line to get enough pounds to pay your way into London. True, you will pay for that convenience, but if you change only $100 or $200 before you leave home, you will never miss the few cents extra it may cost. Most U.S. banks supply foreign currency by order. If yours does not, contact Deak International, 29 Broadway, New York, NY 10006 (212-757-6915) to find their office nearest you.

CURRENCY EXCHANGE

Since you lose money with every exchange, it is smart to convert large sums, provided the exchange rate is constant or deteriorating in your favor. Check the *Herald Tribune* for daily exchange rates. Banks are usually less, but at least you will get a ballpark figure to go on.

Traveler's Checks You will always get a better exchange rate for traveler's checks than for cash. The Automobile Club of America (AAA) offers no-cost American Express traveler's checks to its members. Many banks also offer courtesy traveler's checks for customers maintaining certain balances. Check before you get them, however, to be sure they are not some off-brand that will cost you more to convert. American Express, Thomas Cook, and Barclays/Visa will cash their own traveler's checks without charging a commission, but you must handle the transaction in one of their offices. If you don't cash your checks there, your next-best rate of exchange will be at a London bank. Banking hours are Monday through Friday, 9 A.M.–3:30 P.M. Banks are closed on weekends, holidays, and often the afternoon before a holiday and sometimes the day after. After banks, exchange rates go from bad to worse: hotel, airport, and money changers. Chequepoint and other exchange businesses have offices throughout London. They have long hours, but their rates are *very* deceptive . . . even if they say they take no commission. The exchange rate may seem in your favor, but it never is. Someone is making money on the deal and it is *not* you. Avoid these places unless you are desperate.

American Express traveler's checks can be cashed commission-free at any Lloyds Bank or at American Express offices. Some of the more central London American Express locations are 6 Haymarket (tube: Piccadilly); 78 Brompton Road, almost across from Harrods (tube: Knightsbridge); 147 Victoria Street (tube: Victoria Station); 12 Regent Street in the British Travel Center (tube: Piccadilly). Telephone: U.S.: 1-800-221-7282; U.K.: 0800-52 13 13.

MasterCard traveler's checks can be cashed commission-free at any Thomas Cook office in London. Their 24-hour toll-free telephone in England: 0800-62 21 01. In U.S.: 1-800-223-7373.

Visa and Thomas Cook traveler's checks can be cashed at any Barclay's Bank for free. Of course, Thomas Cook traveler's checks can be cashed commission-free at any of their offices. Visa U.S.: 1-800-227-6811; London: 071-937-8091

Credit Cards For the most part, I recommend using a credit card. The benefits are many. It is the safest way to spend because it eliminates carrying large sums of cash that must be obtained by standing in long lines at an American Express office or a bank. You have a record of your purchases, and best of all, you often get delayed billing of from four to six weeks after your purchase, whereas if you pay cash, the money is gone immediately. With a credit card, the money stays in your bank account, hopefully drawing interest, until you need it to pay your final bill. The credit card company will give you the best rate of exchange on the day of your purchase, and that can also be to your advantage.

Every *Cheap Sleeps in London* listing tells you whether credit cards are accepted and which ones are. If you lose a credit card, report its loss to the police immediately, then call one of the following 24-hour hotlines. They will instruct you from there on.

American Express: Call collect 212-477-5700 or 202-544-2639, both in the U.S. You can also contact any American Express office and they will help you.

Diners Club: 0252-51 62 61, or collect in the U.S.: 303-790-2433.

MasterCard: Collect in the U.S. at 609-987-7300 or the 24-hour toll-free number in England: 0800-62 21 01.

Visa: Call collect in the U.S. at 415-574-7700.

CASH ADVANCE AND ATMS

Cash Advance Having funds sent to you abroad is a complicated and expensive process that can be fraught with peril. Instead, use your American Express, Diners Club, MasterCard, or Visa card to get cash advances, either by writing a personal check and presenting your card at one of the offices or by presenting your card and filling out some forms.

American Express If you have an American Express card, you can get money. Green card holders can cash a personal check and receive a $1,000 advance. For gold cards, the limit is $5,000, and for platinum, $10,000. For all these cards, to get your money all you need is your personal check. If the card already has a cash reserve built in, you won't even need the check. In London, call collect 202-544-5639 to the U. S. to get in touch with the American Express Global Assist department. For more information on this service, call 1-800-333-2639 before leaving home.

Diners Club For Diners Club card holders, a cash advance of $1,000 is easy. You can get it with your card only; no personal check is required. For larger sums, verification of your credit must be established with the issuing office. For more information, call (U.S.) 1-800-525-9135.

MasterCard or Visa Cash advances are available through any bank displaying the MasterCard or Visa sign. There is no additional cost for the advance, other than the interest rate charged to your account along with the amount at the time of the advance.

ATMs (Automatic Teller Machines) What did we do before ATMs? These electronic wonders of convenience are now available in Europe, provided your bank belongs to one of the London networks. Before you race to the nearest ATM and punch in your PIN, there are some things you should know. Commissions and fees could cost you up to 10 percent of your transaction. If your ATM card works in the Cirrus or Plus networks at home, you can use it abroad to withdraw cash from any bank that belongs to the same network. Check with your bank to find out if you will need an international PIN number, and to learn how much commission and interest will be charged. You can use your American Express card in Bank of Scotland or Lloyds Bank cash machines in London, but only if before leaving you have your card coded with a PIN number tied in with your checking account. The charge is 2 percent per transaction. Because interest rates begin to accrue the minute of your withdrawal, I do not recommend relying on your ATM for all your foreign-exchange needs, but it can be a lifesaver when the banks are closed and you are down to your last pound.

TIPPING

How much is too much, and what is enough? Here are a few guidelines:

Hat and coat check in theater	25p per item
Men's hairdressers	15–20%
Porters	50p to £1 per bag, depending how heavy and how far carried
Restaurants	15% *if* the tip is not already added onto the bill; *never* tip at a bar pub
Taxi drivers	10–15%
Washroom attendants	15% if personal attention is given
Women's hairdressers	15% to stylist; 5% to shampooer

STAYING IN TOUCH: THE TELEPHONE

If you pick up the phone in your hotel and make an international call through the hotel operator, you could be charged an astronomical 100 percent surcharge. To avoid it, use USA Direct. By calling USA

Direct, you will be connected with an American international operator, who will put through your call to the United States. You pay only the normal operator-assisted American international calling rates. You can also do this from any pay phone. If you have an AT&T calling card, your call will be billed automatically to your home telephone number. For placing multiple USA Direct calls, don't hang up after your first call, just press the # sign and dial your next area code and number. That way, you will only be charged one connection fee to your long distance carrier. To dial London from the U.S.: 011-44-71 plus the local number. To dial the U.S. from London: 080-089-0011, then the local number. The cheapest time to call is between 8 P.M. and 8 A.M. Monday through Friday, and all day Saturday and Sunday. For further information and to get an AT&T calling card (they are free), call (U.S.) 1-800-874-4000.

If you don't use your hotel phone for local or long distance calls, your options are coin-operated booths (which are few and far between) or those that accept only phone cards. Phone cards are available at post offices, any British Telecom office, or at shops and newsagents displaying a green Telecom sign. These cards come in denominations up to £20. You can use the cards for any local or long distance call, up to the limit on the card.

Note: The 071 prefix for telephone numbers in this book is the inner London area code; the outer London area code is 081. As of April 1995, these numbers will change to 0171 and 0181, respectively. If you are calling from within the prefix, you do not need to dial it to get your party. You use the prefix if you are *out* of the prefix area, from the U.S. or somewhere outside central London. All telephone numbers in this book list the prefix first, then the number.

TRANSPORTATION
GETTING INTO LONDON FROM THE AIRPORT

Gatwick, Heathrow, and the new Stansted airports all serve London. Stansted is served by British Rail's Stansted Express to Liverpool St. Station. From either Gatwick or Heathrow, getting into the city is easy, too. From Heathrow, public transportation is slightly more difficult, but the cab fare is less. Taxi fare from Heathrow to your London hotel will run around £30 without tip or baggage handling, which is £1 per bag. If there are several in your party, a taxi makes economic sense. You can also take the Piccadilly Line tube from Heathrow or ride a green airport bus. With either of these, you will still have to hail a cab from the drop-off point to your hotel. Gatwick is farther out, but the

Gatwick Express train into Victoria Station is a breeze. Taxis are always lined up and waiting, so you will not have to stand on a corner and try to flag one down, or look for a tube or bus station to complete the journey. If you go by taxi from Gatwick to London, count on £40 plus tip and baggage fees.

If you are flying British Airways, departing passengers leave from London Gatwick airport. Ticketholders can check in at Victoria station, which eliminates waiting at the airport and dragging heavy luggage all the way from London. You must arrive at the British Airways check-in desk at Victoria Station at least two hours before departure to get your seat assignment, check baggage, and purchase Gatwick Express train tickets. Trains leave for the airport every fifteen minutes. Once there, you walk to your gate and board the plane. It is a breeze and oh, so convenient.

TRAINS

All of Britain is serviced by British Rail. If you plan to do much train travel, by all means look into an economical British Rail Pass, available for purchase *only* in the United States. These passes are issued for both first- and second-class travel and for specific time periods. For more information, contact British Rail at (U.S.) 1-800-677-8585.

If you do not have a British Rail Pass, you can purchase train tickets at the British Travel Center at 4–12 Lower Regent Street (tube: Piccadilly) for all rail travel in Great Britain and the Continent. These tickets are not cheap. In order to save something, ask about "blue days," Cheap Day Return Tickets, and special fares for students and senior citizens. Children under 16 pay half price and those under 5 ride free. To get a Young Person's Railcard, you must be under 24 or a full-time student in the U.K. A Senior Citizen Gold Pass for women over 60 and men over 65 enables you to save a third on off-peak travel for one year (see Senior Citizen Discounts, page 20).

LONDON TRANSPORTATION

The Tube and Double-Decker Buses Be sure to buy *The Guide to London by Bus and Tube,* Nicholson, or pick up a copy of *How to Get There,* a booklet put out by London Regional Transport. These booklets will tell you more than you ever will need to know, and they will save you time and confusion when you want to get from the Tate Gallery to Buckingham Palace and do not know how. They give all the bus and tube routes, including those for late-night buses, so you can avoid getting stuck in the sticks after most public transportation has stopped. You should also pick up a pocket tube map of the entire

Underground network. These are free from most hotels and from Underground ticket counters.

The cheapest way to get around London is to master the Underground and bus systems. The Underground (tube) will be faster, but the bus is much more scenic and fun. The view of London from the top of a red double-decker bus is unbeatable. Bus stops are marked with red signs with *Request* written in white letters. Buses do not always stop automatically; you must flag them down. To get off, ask the conductor to tell you when your stop is next, and be sure to ring the bell to notify the driver that you want off. The most scenic bus routes are No. 11, King's Road to St. Paul's Cathedral; No. 53, Regent Street to the Imperial War Museum; and No. 88, Bayswater and Hyde Park to the Tate Gallery and Vauxhall Bridge.

To save travel money, buy a Travel Card that allows you to ride on the tube or bus for less money than you would spend for single-purchase tickets. Depending on the type of card you buy, it will be good for one to seven days and can be purchased at any tube station. Travel Cards are sold by zones, so be careful; you probably don't need one that will include Wimbledon and/or Richmond. Get the card for Central London.

Taxis The only thing that has changed over the years about London cabs is the price: it has gone up, way up. The 13,500 London cabbies are highly skilled professionals, rated among the best in the world. These drivers spend two years learning the ins and outs of London streets and traffic patterns, and must know how to get from one place to another in peak traffic in the most efficient way. If you have problems, get the number of the cab and report it to 071-278-1744. The usual tip for a taxi driver is 15 percent of the fare. To pay, you get out of the cab, rain or shine, and pay the cabbie through the window. If you want to be assured of a taxi at a specific time, call a 24-hour radio taxi. You will pay from the minute the driver gets the call, but you will avoid the worry of being late because you could not flag down a taxi during rush hour or at some odd hour of the night.

Mini-cabs are *not* black cabs; they are ordinary cars available for hire by telephone. Often, concierges use them if you ask them to book you transportation to the airport. There is usually a kick-back from the mini-cab company to the concierge, but it is built into the price and you never will know what it is. Be sure to establish the price and confirm it when your driver arrives.

Driving Your Own Car or a Rental In London! What for? Driving in London is hazardous to your health. It is a hair-raising experience only for the very, very brave, or foolish. Parking is impossible. There is never anything within walking distance to where you want to be, unless it is an expensive car park. But, if you insist, check with your airline for a fly-drive package. Otherwise, shop the major car rental companies carefully, because rates and deals vary greatly.

Walking One of the best ways to experience London is on foot. You can venture forth with the express purpose of wandering and seeing what you can along the way. Don't worry about getting lost; you can always jump on a bus or hail a cab if you get too far from your base. I think one of the best ways to learn about London is to go on a guided walking tour. On these two-hour tours, you will be guided by well-informed leaders to any number of interesting places you would probably not discover on your own. You can peek into the haunts of Shakespeare, Dickens, and Sherlock Holmes. You can explore the inner workings of legal London and sit in on an actual trial at Old Bailey, go on a late-night pub crawl, or see where Jack the Ripper stalked his prey. You will probably see brochures on these walking tours in your hotel, and please try to make enough time to take in at least one. If you do not see a brochure, call the London Tourist Board at 071-730-3488 or one of the walking tour offices directly: London Walks Ltd., tel & fax 071-624-3978; Historical Walks of London, tel & fax 081-668-4019; City Walks, tel 071-700-6931; Dockland Tours, tel 071-252-0742; Thameside Ventures, tel 081-317-7722; and Stage by Stage (backstage tours of London theaters), tel 071-328-7558.

STUDENT AND SENIOR CITIZEN DISCOUNTS

STUDENT DISCOUNTS

The International Student Identity Card (ISIC) offers access to over 8,000 discounts on transportation, accommodations, and cultural events. You must present the card when you go, and always ask about a discount, even when none is mentioned. If you purchase this bargain in the U.S., you will also get limited medical insurance and access to a hotline. You must have iron-clad proof of your student status and provide a 1½-by-2-inch photo with your name printed on the back in pencil. To obtain the card, you must be at least 12 years old, and it remains valid until the end of the calendar year in which you bought it. To get a card, contact the Council on International Educational Exchange (CIEE), 205 E. 42nd Street, New York, NY 10017, tel 212-661-1414. They have many offices throughout the States.

Council Travel and Council Charter are two budget subsidiaries of CIEE. Council Travel sells discounted flights, Eurail and individual country passes, guidebooks, travel gear, ISIC cards, International Teacher Identity Cards (ITIC), and Youth Hostel Cards (IYHF).

Other budget travel organizations geared toward students are STA Travel, 17 E. 45th Street, New York, NY 10017, tel 1-800-777-0112 or 212-986-9643; and Educational Travel Centre (ETC), 438 N. Frances Street, Madison, WI 53703, tel 608-256-5551.

SENIOR CITIZEN DISCOUNTS

Sometimes it pays to get older. Significant savings are available to visiting senior citizens, and with some of these offers you have to be only 50 years young to qualify. Interested? Read on.

British Airways offers special discounts on their regular airfares and their full range of tours in Great Britain to those 60 or over and to any companions traveling with them who are 50 or older.

Men who are 65 and women who are 60 qualify for the Senior Citizen Gold Pass on British Railways. These passes cost around £20. They are available at all mainline British Railway stations and at British Rail Travel Centers in London, at 4–12 Lower Regent Street (tube: Piccadilly) and The Strand (tube: Charing Cross). You must show your passport as proof of age. The card is valid for one year from date of purchase and offers one-third off on all British Rail fares and half price on off-peak Cheap Day Return Tickets. In addition, it trims 50 percent off the one-day Travel Cards for tube and bus travel in London and one-third off the weekly passes. For more information call the toll-free British Rail office in the U.S. at 1-800-677-8585.

If you are a member of AARP (the American Association of Retired People), you can get free American Express traveler's checks. If you cash them at an American Express office in London, you will not pay a commission.

Very often, if you show your passport, you will get reduced-entry tickets to many London attractions and theaters. Always take your passport; you never know where you will get lucky and be able to save.

THIS AND THAT: HELPFUL HINTS

1. Unfortunately, important things are sometimes lost or stolen. If you lose your passport, not only must you replace it immediately, but you must show absolute proof of citizenship. This is not easy when all of your documents citing proof are gone. To be prepared for such disasters, take a xeroxed copy of your passport, airline and/or train tickets, and any other papers crucial to your trip and a safe and sane return home. Also, take at least four extra passport-sized color pictures. These are necessary if you have to replace a passport or want to buy a Travel Card for tube and bus transportation (see Transportation, page 16).

2. Even though all Britishers are eligible for free medical care, visitors are not. Check with your health insurance agent to see what coverage you will have, and perhaps take out a supplemental policy to cover the trip.

3. Carry a copy of your prescriptions plus a letter from your physician giving the generic names of the drugs you are taking. Sometimes American brands may not be available.

4. Look to the *right* when crossing the street.

5. British current is 240 V AC. If you are bringing a hair dryer, hair curler, or electric razor, you will need both a transformer and an adapter that will plug into the British wall socket and convert it to 110 V AC, the standard in the U.S.

6. What's happening? To find out the latest word on films, theaters, concerts, shows and exhibitions, museums, galleries, and much, much more, buy the weekly publication *Time Out* from any corner newsstand.

7. If you will be in London for more than a day or two, you will need to have two important publications: (1) *London A-Z* (pronounced "a" to "zed"). I like the super-scale version of this street map of London because it is possible to read the fine print without a high-powered magnifying glass. (2) In order to get around efficiently, get the booklet put out by London Regional Transport called *How to Get There*. It details the tube and bus systems and will save you time and high anxiety when you can't get from A to B because you are going in the wrong direction and don't know it.

8. Attending a session of Parliament is not easy, but if you are interested, it is worth a try. Here's how: You can write directly to a Member of Parliament and ask to be given one of his/her allotted tickets for a specific day. Address: MP (name), House of Commons, Westminster, London SW1. Contact your embassy and ask for same-day passes; you will be able to jump the queue, but not necessarily get a seat. Wait in the long queue and hope for a miracle: that you will not only get in, but get a seat. For more information once you are in London, call 071-219-4273 or 071-219-3574.

9. You can receive mail for up to three months at this London post office if the letters are addressed as follows:

Your name
Poste Restante, London
London Chief Post Office
King Edward Street, London EC1
To collect your mail, you must show up and present your passport as identification. Hours for collection are Monday through Friday, 9 A.M.–5:30 P.M., and Saturday, 9 A.M.–noon.

10. If you forgot your camera, Kodak offers a free camera loan service at the British Travel Center, 12 Regent Street (tube: Piccadilly). There is a £30 deposit.

PRACTICAL INFORMATION: USEFUL ADDRESSES AND TELEPHONE NUMBERS

American Embassy
24 Grosvenor Square, London W1
Tel: 071-499-9000
Tube: Bond Street
Hours: Mon–Fri 9 A.M.–6 P.M.
Passport Office: Mon–Fri 8:30 A.M.–noon
U.S. Citizen Services: Mon–Fri 8:30 A.M.–noon and 2–4 P.M.

American Express
6 Haymarket, London W1
Tel: 071-930-4411
Tube: Piccadilly
Other offices: see About Money, *Traveler's Checks,* page 13

British Tourist Authority (U.S. offices)
551 Fifth Avenue
New York, NY 10019
Tel: 212-986-2200
Branches in Chicago, Dallas, Los Angeles, Atlanta

British Tourist Authority (U.K. offices)
Victoria Station Forecourt, London SW1
Tel: 071-730-3488
Tube: Victoria
Other offices at Heathrow Airport, Harrods (third floor), Selfridges (basement), Tower of London, and British Travel Center (see below)

British Travel Center
4–12 Lower Regent Street, London SW1
Tel: 071-730-3400
Tube: Piccadilly
Full information on all parts of Britain; British Rail office; travel agency; theater bookings; American Express office; hotel bookings; gift and book shop.

Canadian High Commission
MacDonald House
1 Grosvenor Square, London W1
Tel: 071-629-9492
Tube: Bond Street
Hours: Mon–Fri 9 A.M.–5 P.M.

City of London Information Center
St. Paul's Churchyard, London EC4
Tel: 071-606-3030
Tube: St. Paul's
Information and advice with emphasis on the City of London. Be sure to pick up a copy of the monthly *Diary of Events,* listing a wide choice of free entertainment in London.

London Regional Transport
Tel: 24-hour hotline 071-222-1234
Tube: Centers located at Euston, Victoria, King's Cross, Oxford Circus, and Piccadilly Circus.
These offices have information on London transportation via tube and bus. Their booklet *How To Get There* is essential for mastering bus and tube routes. The centers also provide information for disabled travelers, places of interest, guided tours, and free maps.

TELEPHONE NUMBERS

Emergencies   999 (medical, police, fire)

Chemist (pharmacist)
  Bliss the Chemist   071-723-6116
  5 Marble Arch, London W1
  Tube: Marble Arch
  open daily 9 A.M.–midnight

Children's London   071-246-8007
  Recorded information Mon-Sat
  7 A.M.–6 P.M., Sun 9 A.M.–11 P.M.
Dentist (emergency care)
  24-hour number   071-937-3951
Disabled Traveler's Information
  Disability advice   081-870-7437
  RADAR   071-637-5400
  Greater London Ass'n for Disabled   071-274-0107
Doctor
  24-hour service   071-935-9535
  Medical advice   081-944-9874
Lost or Stolen Items
  Report the loss or theft to police,
  then call
  Lost on tube   071-486-2496
  Lost on bus   071-222-1234
  Lost in a taxi   071-278-1744
Police   071-230-1212
Telephone
  Inner London area code   071 (will change in April
                                            1995 to 0171)

  Outer London area code   081 (will change in April
                                            1995 to 0181)

  International operator   155
  International directory inquiries   153
  London directory inquiries   142
  Operator   100
  Outside London inquiries   192
  USA Direct (from London)   080-089-0011
  U.S. to London   011-44 plus number
                                            minus first zero (if number is
                                            071-237-0876, dial 011-44-
                                            71-237-0876)
Time   123
Weather   089-850-0401

HOW TO USE CHEAP SLEEPS IN LONDON

CROWN CLASSIFICATIONS

Hotels in Great Britain are not controlled by a government rating system as they are in many other countries. The English Tourist Board operates a voluntary registration and optional grading system for all tourist accommodations from The Ritz down to the grubbiest B&B. Note the words *voluntary* and *optional.* Many good hotels refuse to take part in this classification system because it does not mean that quality, cleanliness, or value go along with the rated hotel. In fact, many hotels displaying two and three crowns are filthy, without redeeming decoration or friendly management. They may have the required number of lights by the bed, the right number of toilets and showers in order to qualify for a certain number of crowns, but there it stops. A word to the wise is to consider the crowns, but not to bank on them. *Cheap Sleeps in London* ignores them altogether.

ACCOMMODATIONS

In London, the hotel day begins and ends at noon. If you overstay (without prior arrangement), you will probably be charged the price of an extra day. If your flight is leaving later in the afternoon, most hotels will let you use the lobby and will keep your luggage in a safe place. If your flight arrives early in the morning, your room may not be ready for immediate occupancy. Most hotels will try their best to let you in your room as soon as possible, but if you absolutely *must* have the room early in the morning, you should consider booking it for the night before. You will pay for an unoccupied room, but it will be yours from the minute you arrive.

The lobby or reception area of a hotel is usually one of the most attractive parts of the hotel both because first impressions are important, and because this is where the owner and manager spend their day. When you arrive at your hotel (especially in a B&B), ask to see your room. This is normal and expected practice. If you are dissatisfied, ask to see another room. After approving the accommodation, reconfirm the rate, making sure there are no hidden extras.

RESERVATIONS, DEPOSITS, AND CANCELLATIONS

RESERVATIONS

Are reservations necessary? Positively! Confirmed reservations are essential to the success of any trip to London or any other world capital if you want to be in charge of how much you spend. With the electronic age, it is easy to telephone or fax reservation requests and in most cases to guarantee them with a credit card. In budget hotels, you will probably be asked to guarantee your room with an international money order in pounds.

No matter how you make your reservation, the following points should be included in your inquiry:

1. The dates of stay, time of arrival (including flight number), and number of persons in your party.

2. The size and type of room you need: double or twin, with or without private facilities, quiet, with a view, and so on.

3. The rates: Determine what the nightly rate will be and whether or not the VAT (value-added tax of 17½ percent and going *up*) is included as well as what sort of breakfast the hotel serves. This is the time to negotiate any rate discounts.

4. The kind of deposit required and the form of payment.

5. *Important:* Request that the hotel send you a confirmation of your reservation and the amount of deposit and carry this with you to the registration desk when you check in. This avoids a multitude of snafus when you arrive.

6. Always send a fax or letter to the hotel (and keep a copy) confirming *your* end of the reservation, noting the time of your call, the name of the person with whom you spoke, and the rates. This can be crucial if you arrive and, heaven forbid, the hotel has "lost" your reservation . . . . and believe me, that happens more often than you think.

Now that you are convinced reservations are necessary, what is the best way to make them? A few suggestions follow on the four ways to make hotel reservations in London.

Fax Faxing is the easiest way to reserve. From the U.S., to fax a message to London, dial 011-44 plus the hotel fax number minus the first zero.

Telex Today, the fax has replaced the telex as the most efficient and least costly way to send messages, but some hotels still have telex numbers. If you or your travel agent prefer this method, it is still a reliable way to reserve.

Telephone A good method for do-it-yourselfers without access to a fax. Always make the call during the hotel's weekday business hours (London is six hours ahead of Eastern Standard Time and nine hours ahead of Pacific). That avoids talking to a night clerk who has no authority to negotiate rates or to offer you a deal. Before calling, write down all your requests and questions. Be sure to ask for a confirmation in writing from the hotel. To dial direct from the States to London, dial 011-44 plus the number of the hotel minus the first zero.

Letter In this day of electronics, why anyone would resort to letter writing is a mystery to me. Many hotels let reservation letters stack up and deal with them when they have time. Transatlantic mail can take as long as two weeks one way, and if there is a strike, who knows how long the letter could be in transit. When you consider the entire cost of your trip against the cost, convenience, and speed of a fax, telex, or phone call, the letter option seems behind the times and woefully inadequate.

DEPOSITS

After accepting your reservation, most hotels require at least a one-night deposit, and more if you are renting a flat. This is smart insurance for both parties. The easiest way to handle all deposits is with a credit card. If the hotel does not accept them, and many budget B&Bs do not, there are other ways of sending money to London. Deak International has offices in most major cities in the United States (call 212-757-6915 to find the office nearest you). If you cannot get to a Deak International office, find out if your hotel will accept an American Express money order in dollars. This can be converted into pounds by the hotel at the exchange rate on the day they deposit it. You will pay a commission to have it converted when they deposit it. (It cannot be cashed.) For more details, call American Express at (U.S.) 1-800-999-9660.

CANCELLATIONS

If you need to cancel or to cut your stay short, be prepared for some anxious moments when it comes to getting back any prepaid monies. When you reserve a hotel room you are entering into a legally binding contract with the proprietor of the establishment. This means that if you have to cancel or leave early, for *any* reason, the proprietor may be entitled to compensation if he cannot re-let your room or flat. If a deposit has been paid, count on forfeiting it if you cancel at the last minute. This whole area has the potential of creating many Maalox moments, so know the hotel, B&B, or flat rental cancellation policy *before* you tie up a big chunk of your vacation money.

As I have stressed throughout *Cheap Sleeps in London,* the best way to circumvent this cancellation nightmare is to buy cancellation and/or trip-interruption insurance before you leave home. Your travel agent or the American Automobile Association can advise you on companies who deal in this insurance. If you only have a one-night deposit invested, it is probably not worth it, but if you have a half-month deposit on a flat, it certainly is.

RATES: PAYING THE BILL

All hotels in Britain are required by law to plainly display their minimum and maximum overnight rates. The price must include service and may or may not include the VAT (value-added tax), which is currently at 17½ percent and scheduled to rise. British hotel rates are in a state of flux, especially in London. Because of the decline in tourists and the world recession, hoteliers are willing to *deal.* In other words, always ask for a discount and be ready to negotiate the rates.

Many hotels offer low seasonal rates, and you would be surprised at the tremendous discounts the high-end hotels will give. All it takes is *you* to *ask.* All rates given in *Cheap Sleeps in London* are for the full price and do not reflect special discounts. Where discounts are available, they are noted. But, and this is important, even if no discounts are mentioned, that does not mean they will not be available.

Every hotel listed gives credit card information. In most Cheap Sleeps, payment is required to secure your first night. Very few lower-priced hotels or youth hostels take any sort of credit cards. They accept only cash up front in British pounds. Hotel exchange rates are terrible, no matter what the front desk may claim. If you are paying your bill in cash, change your money into pounds *before* check-out time (see About Money, page 12). Be sure to go over your bill carefully and get a receipt marked "paid."

HOTEL BREAKFASTS

All London hotels and private B&Bs serve either a Continental breakfast or a full English breakfast. In most cases, the meal is included in the cost of the room. However, if you are trying to save as much money as possible, ask that the cost of the breakfast—per person—be deducted from your hotel rate. Remember this is a per-day deduction and must be arranged *before* check-in. The hotel will probably not allow you to eat there one morning and somewhere else another. You will have to make up your mind and stick to it.

Unfortunately, London hoteliers are very reluctant to deduct breakfast, and many will not . . . period. Actually, a full English breakfast enables many to skip lunch and to save money that way. A full English breakfast can be anything from the addition of an egg and a slice of bacon to the regular Continental breakfast of toast and marmalade, to a full-blown meal of hot or cold cereal, eggs any style, meats, beans, fried bread, mushrooms, tomatoes, and all the tea you can drink. Many smaller hotels and private B&Bs pride themselves on their generous home-cooked breakfasts, a tradition in England you must try at least once.

FACILITIES AND ROOMS WITH OR WITHOUT PRIVATE BATHS

Each hotel listing gives the number of rooms and whether they have private baths, and if so how many. This is coded **W/BST**, with bath or shower, and toilet; and **W/OBST**, without bath or shower, and toilet. At the end of each listing a brief summary describes hotel facilities. The better the hotel, the more services offered, and the higher its room rates. Check each listing for those amenities you consider essential for a comfortable stay.

NW1

Regent's Park

W2
Hyde Park

W11

W1

W<1   E<1

W<2   E<2

E<4   E<3

W8

SW7

SW5

SW3

SW1

SW10

Green Park

E1

THAMES

SE1

RIVER

○ Buckingham Palace
◆ The Tate Gallery
● Tower of London
◇ National Theatre
▬ National History Museum

HOTEL LISTINGS BY POSTAL CODE

> London is chaos incorporated.
> —George Mikes, *Down with Everybody*

London is one of the largest cities in the world. With over 625 square miles of area and 9.5 million inhabitants in the metropolitan area, it is twice as big as Paris or New York City. Originally, London was a collection of small villages. In a sense, it still is, each area having its unique character and atmosphere.

One of the great allures of visiting London is that you never completely see it all. There is always one more pub, a special museum, or a historic street or neighborhood left to explore. It is beyond the scope of *Cheap Sleeps in London* to go into detail about all the sightseeing possibilities in each area that await you. The following sketches of the highlights, organized by postal code, are designed to give you a quick idea of what is around your hotel. For the best in-depth description of what to see in London, the green Michelin *Tourist Guide to London* is a must.

As Paris is divided into arrondissements, London is divided into postal codes. You will see them included in all street addresses and on most street signs. Knowing which postal code is which is important when booking your hotel accommodations. The letters stand for compass directions, with reference to the central district, divided into WC and EC for West Central and East Central. All districts bordering the central districts are numbered "1," and continue to increase in number as they get farther from the center. If you see W8, you will know you are not in the heart of Piccadilly. All hotel and shop listings in *Cheap Sleeps in London* provide the postal code and are arranged according to it. This system parallels the arrangement of the restaurants in *Cheap Eats in London*. If you are staying in W1, trying to decide where to eat dinner close to your hotel, refer to the W1 section in *Cheap Eats* for a listing of nearby restaurants.

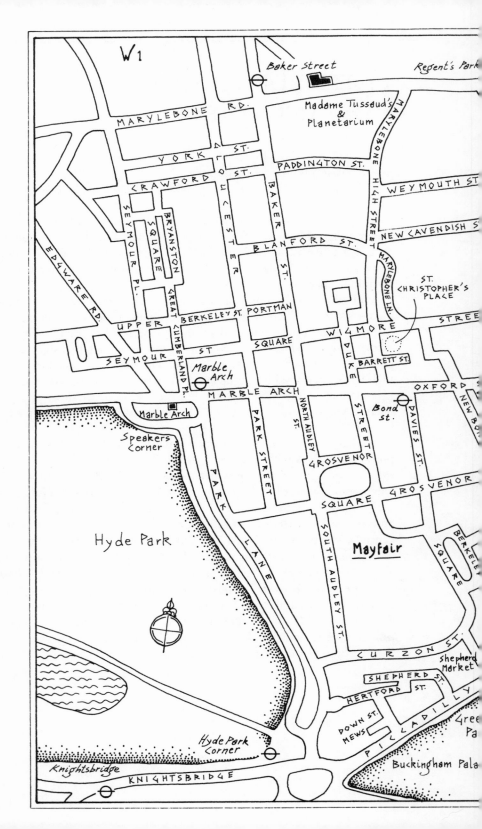

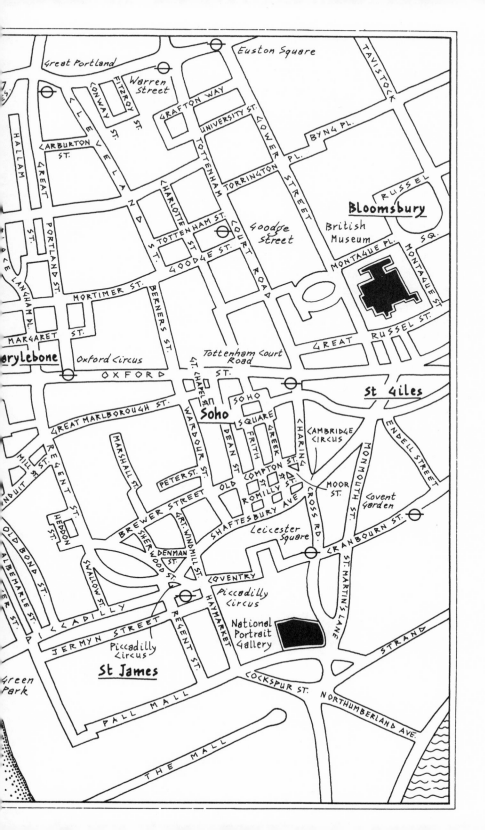

W1 ♣ MAYFAIR, ST. JAMES'S, PICCADILLY, SOHO, MARYLEBONE, MARBLE ARCH

Mayfair and St. James's are characterized by gentlemen's clubs, expensive shops, plush hotels, royal residences, and parks. The tailoring standards of the world are defined on Savile Row, and the finest shopping is found along Jermyn, South Molton, and New and Old Bond streets. St. James's Park and Green Park offer good views of Buckingham Palace. If you see the royal standard (flag) flying, you will know the Queen is in residence.

Piccadilly is London's equivalent of Times Square, with incessant traffic, crowds, noise, and general confusion for the uninitiated.

Soho is full of character and characters. Bustling by day and exciting by night, this is London's entertainment center. Here are the West End theaters, a great selection of cinemas, and hundreds of restaurants catering to every taste and budget. Chinatown hums until the wee hours, drawing many after-theater diners and other night owls.

Marylebone is a residential area with many lovely squares. Doctors' offices line Harley Street, and all Sherlock Holmes fans know about 221B Baker Street. If you are in Marylebone (pronounced Mar-lee-bun), you will be able to visit the Planetarium and stand in the interminable queue for Madame Tussaud's Wax Museum.

HOTELS

Bryanston Court Hotel	35
Hotel Concorde	36
Forte Hotel Leisure Breaks	37
Georgian House Hotel	38
Hallam Hotel	39
Hart House Hotel	40
Hazlitt's	41
The Ivanhoe Suites	42
Regent Palace Hotel	42

OTHER OPTIONS

Strictly for Students

International Students House	172

University Dormitory Accommodations
London School of Economics—Carr Saunders
   Hall & Fitzroy and Maple Street Flats   178
Middlesex Hospital Medical School   183
Nutford House   182
Ramsay Hall—University College London   181
Youth Hostels
Oxford Street Youth Hostel   191

Bryanston Court Hotel
56–60 Great Cumberland Place, W1

The Bryanston Court Hotel is a small, central London hotel affiliated with Best Western. It offers modern services while maintaining the friendly and efficient service of a family-owned and operated hotel. On the ground floor, an attractive bar at the back of a pleasing lounge is dominated by a roaring winter fire. The tufted leather chairs and couches are perfectly arranged so guests can talk, quietly read the morning papers, or plot their evening out in London. The redecorated mauve and pink dining room, where a Continental buffet breakfast is served every morning, has linen-covered tables and comfortable chairs. A conference room with fax and telex facilities makes the hotel an appealing choice for those in London on business. The compact bedrooms have contemporary furnishings, and neat, small bathrooms with all the amenities to ensure a pleasant stay. For those who tend toward claustrophobia, room No. 99 should be avoided: it is a subterranean room with absolutely no view. All major points of interest, whether for sightseeing or business, are easily accessible from the Marble Arch tube station, less than five minutes away.

Note: The Hotel Concorde (next page) is under the same management and ownership. They offer a few luxury flats for those interested in a longer stay.

Facilities and Services: Bar, direct-dial phones, telex and fax services for guests, lift, office safe, room service, TV with cable, radio, tea and coffeemakers in rooms, 1-day cleaning and laundry service

TELEPHONE
071-262-3141

FAX
071-262-7248

TELEX
262076

TUBE
Marble Arch

CREDIT CARDS
AE, DC, MC, V

NUMBER OF ROOMS
54

W/BST
All

RATES
Single £76; double £100; triple: extra bed £15; weekend rates available; Continental breakfast included; English breakfast £7

Hotel Concorde
50 Great Cumberland Place, W1

TELEPHONE
071-402-6169

FAX
071-724-1184

TELEX
262076

TUBE
Marble Arch

CREDIT CARDS
AE, DC, MC, V

NUMBER OF ROOMS
27

W/BST
All

RATES
Single £68; double £80; triple: extra bed £17; Apt: 1-bedroom £95; 2-bedroom £105; 3-bedroom £115; Continental breakfast included for both hotel and apartment

Once a private home, the Concorde is now a 27-room hotel owned by the Theodore family, who also operate the nearby Bryanston Court Hotel. As you enter the hotel, you will see handsome carved woodwork from a demolished London church facing the reception desk and a tiny five-seat bar on the left. The inviting main sitting room has a large brown leather sofa, a convenient writing desk, and stacks of current magazines available for guests. The rooms have good carpets, attractive bedspreads, and few color flaws. Single travelers will want to avoid room 41, a back location with a very small bathroom and creaking floors. In the morning, a Continental buffet breakfast is served in a downstairs wood-paneled dining room decorated with country pine furniture and an old-English plate collection.

A bonus at the Concorde is their selection of furnished flats and town houses, all located no more than a block or two from the hotel. As with most flat rentals in London, price breaks are given for longer stays. Most of these are nice, but a few are rather worn and in need of a dose of TLC. Some are subterranean, which means windowless, so be wary of these. No. 3 is the most spacious, with a large lounge and kitchen opening onto a dining area that could be converted to a second bedroom. The upstairs bedroom has a great marble bath, plenty of closets, and double-glazed windows to buffer street noise. No. 4 is a two-bedroom flat with stairs to climb, an eat-in kitchen, and a view onto the pretty mews houses in back. The hotel has converted some of these 200-year-old houses into town houses. They are especially suitable for families because the whole house is yours, so there is little worry of bothering your neighbors or vice versa.

Facilities and Services: Bar, central heat, direct-dial phones, hair dryer, 1-day laundry and cleaning from Mon–Fri, lift, office safe, room service for light snacks, TV with cable, radio, fax and telex services available, tea and coffeemakers in rooms

Forte Hotel Leisure Breaks

Leisure Breaks: Forte (UK) Limited, Gatehouse Road, Aylesbury, Bucks HP19 3EB; Theater and Rail Breaks: Gardner Merchant Keyline Travel, Arndale House, Arndale Center, Manchester M4 3AE

If you can schedule your London visit around one of the Forte hotel "Leisure Breaks," you will experience one of the best hotel values in the capital. Briefly, the plan works this way. You are required to book a minimum of two consecutive nights, including a Saturday, at your choice of 14 centrally located London hotels. The rates for these incredible Cheap Sleeps are *half* the regular rates and include a room with a private bath (Regent Palace, page 42, excepted), a full English breakfast, and a three-course dinner with coffee. In some cases you can use your dinner voucher at another participating hotel, or have lunch or afternoon tea instead. Children under 16 sharing their parents' room are free. No cancellation charges are made if you cancel up to 4 P.M. the day of arrival and no deposit is required. If you are traveling anywhere else in the U.K., try to take advantage of these "Leisure Breaks" in the other Forte hotels throughout the country. Many are tied to travel on British Rail and offer significant savings all around. If you are a theater buff, ask about special rates in London connected to a hotel stay and tickets to first-run stage performances. For complete details and a price breakdown, call the toll-free number and ask that a brochure be sent to you.

FORTE HOTELS PARTICIPATING IN THE LONDON "LEISURE BREAKS":

Mayfair and the West End
Brown's Hotel
Albemarle Street & Dover Street, W1
071-493-6020

The Cumberland
Marble Arch, W1
071-262-1234

TELEPHONE
Leisure Breaks 0345-40-40-40; Theater & Rail Breaks 0345-543-555; Toll-free in the U.S. 1-800-225-5843

FAX
913-831-1523

CREDIT CARDS
AE, DC, MC

RATES
Start at £45 per person and include English breakfast, 3-course dinner and coffee

Forte Crest Regent's Park
Carburton Street, W1
071-388-2300

Grosvenor House
Park Lane, W1
071-499-6363

Regent Palace Hotel
Piccadilly Circus, W1
071-734-7000

St. George's Hotel
Langham Place, W1
071-580-0111

The Westbury
Bond Street at Conduit Street, W1
071-629-7755

Georgian House Hotel
87 Gloucester Place, W1

TELEPHONE
071-935-2211, 071-486-3151

FAX
071-486-7535

TELEX
266079 GLAD G

TUBE
Baker Street

CREDIT CARDS
AE, MC, V

NUMBER OF ROOMS
20

W/BST
All

RATES
Single £50; double £65; triple £75; four £85; Continental buffet included

For a good hotel value near Baker Street within walking distance of Oxford Street, Hyde Park, and Regent's Park, the Georgian House Hotel receives my vote of confidence. It is obvious from first glance that owner Sam Popat continues to spend time, money, and effort to maintain the consistently high standards of his hotel. The bedrooms are done in a monochromatic modern style that is totally unoffensive. Good lighting, luggage racks, and individually controlled central heating add to their appeal. The bathrooms are exceptionally nice, with heated towel racks and collapsible laundry lines, so handy for those quick overnight laundries. The only drawbacks are the ground-floor rooms, which open directly onto the street, thus offering limited security, and some of the back rooms, which face a wall. Naturally, these back rooms are quiet, and the opposing wall has been painted and a few potted plants scattered around in an effort to break the monotonous view. A few rooms have the bathrooms outside, but these are never shared with any other rooms. Best bets in my opinion are the streetside rooms from the second floor up.

A delicious Continental breakfast includes ham, cheese, hard-boiled eggs, fruit juice, cereals, toast, jam, and coffee or tea. It is served in a mirrored dining room decorated in soothing beige. Special weekend and off-season rates make this hotel even better.

Facilities and Services: Central heat, direct-dial phones, hair dryer available, lift, office safe, TV, tea and coffeemakers, telex and fax for guests Mon–Fri 8 A.M.–5 P.M., desk open for reservations from 7 A.M.–11 P.M.

Hallam Hotel
12 Hallam Street, Portland Place, W1

For a decade, Grant and David Baker have owned this hotel, which is just far enough from the crowded central part of London to make it a good choice for those who want a tranquil place. Situated immediately behind the BBC Broadcasting House, it is only a ten-minute walk to Oxford Circus with all the neon lights and glitz the West End has to offer. The hotel was completely redecorated in 1991. All the rooms are now alike with attractive mahogany built-in furniture, soft green carpeting, and matching floral bedspreads and drapes. Room sizes range from minuscule singles known as "cabins," which are nothing more than a built-in bed squeezed into a five-by-ten-foot space, to large twins with ample closets and nice window seats. For solo travelers, No. 23, or "The Crow's Nest," is an attractive top-floor choice with a tub bath and a commanding view of the British Telecom Tower. A plus for most will be the nonsmoking rooms. Breakfast is served in a cheery garden atrium

TELEPHONE
071-580-1166

FAX
071-323-4527

TUBE
Great Portland Street

CREDIT CARDS
AE, DC, MC, V

NUMBER OF ROOMS
25

W/BST
All

RATES
Single £64; double £84; Continental breakfast included

on tables set with pink cloths and fresh flowers. Good lighting makes the morning papers easy to read, and the no-smoking policy pleases all but a few.

Facilities and Services: Central heat, direct-dial phones, hair dryer, lift, mini-bar, office safe, TV, radio, tea and coffeemakers

Hart House Hotel
51 Gloucester Place, Portman Square, W1

TELEPHONE
071-935-2288

FAX
071-935-8516

TUBE
Marble Arch, Baker Street

CREDIT CARDS
AE, MC, V

NUMBER OF ROOMS
17

W/BST
15

W/OBST
2

RATES
Single £41–47; double £57–71; triple £75; four £85; English breakfast included

Hart House is a seventeen-room bed-and-breakfast hotel run superbly by Andrew Bowden, who took it over from his parents about ten years ago. The building was part of an original terrace of Georgian mansions occupied by French nobility during the French Revolution. It is conveniently located for West End theaters, shopping, Hyde Park, Regent's Park and the Zoo, the Planetarium, and Madame Tussaud's.

Everything in the hotel is always in perfect order and spotlessly clean. In addition, most of the rooms have that hard-to-find commodity in London—*space*. Number 7 is a front-facing triple with a large bath and shower and two floor-to-ceiling windows. On the back of the hotel, number 6 has leaded windows, a good bathroom with shelf space, and neutral decor. Number 11 is a sunny top-floor perch for two. All the rooms are nicely fitted, with mahogany furniture that includes an armoire, desk, comfortable chair, and chest of drawers. The lower-floor breakfast room has three skylights and a coal-burning fireplace, making it a cheerful spot for guests to enjoy the traditional English breakfast included in the price of a room. Andrew Bowden's warm hospitality and reasonable rates make this one a favorite, so get your reservation in the minute you know your dates.

Facilities and Services: Central heat, direct-dial phones, hair dryer available, no lift, office safe, TV, radio, tea and coffeemakers, fax service, desk open for reservations from 7:30 A.M.–10:30 P.M.

Hazlitt's
6 Frith Street, Soho Square, W1

I must be frank, I think Hazlitt's is one of London's best small hotels. The unique surroundings, warm hospitality, and personal service all in a super location have made the hotel a stand-out from the moment it opened its doors in 1986. It is within walking distance of more than thirty West End theaters, twenty cinemas, the Royal Opera House, and dozens of restaurants in every price category (see *Cheap Eats in London*). Named for essayist William Hazlitt, who wrote his last essay here, the hotel occupies three eighteenth-century town houses built in 1718. The twenty-three rooms are named after the many famous occupants of the original houses and those who lived in Soho during that time. The entire hotel is a study in tasteful decorating, dominated by a sensational collection of more than 2,000 original prints, hung throughout the hotel, including all of the guest bathrooms. The individually done bedrooms have high ceilings, comfortable beds—many of which are four-posters—and classic bathrooms with the original Victorian claw-footed bathtubs and brass hardware lovingly polished by the chambermaids.

The ground-floor Baron Willoughby Suite is magnificent, with a massive four-poster, ornamental wood-burning fireplace, and an armoire with deep drawers. The William Hazlitt has a fireplace, a huge four-poster, and a mahogany wardrobe flanked by plant stands. The Earl of St. Albans has a half-canopy bed, mirrored armoire, and a beautiful collection of bird prints in the bathroom. Because the original character of the building has been so well kept, some floors may lean a little, there might be a ray or two of light under the doorway, and there is no elevator. *Please* do not let these minor inconveniences deter you a minute from staying in this charming hotel.

Facilities and Services: Central heat, direct-dial phones, hair dryer available, room service for coffee

TELEPHONE
071-434-1771

FAX
071-439-1524

TUBE
Tottenham Court Road, Leicester Square

CREDIT CARDS
AE, DC, MC, V

NUMBER OF ROOMS
23

W/BST
All

RATES
Single £105; double £130; suite/apt £167. All rates subject to 17½% VAT. £5.95 extra for Continental breakfast served in the room

and tea, office safe, TV, no lift. Desk closed from 11:30 P.M.–7:30 A.M.; no incoming calls, but guests can call out; keys for the front door given to guests

The Ivanhoe Suites
1B St. Christopher's Place (take Gees Court off Oxford Street), W1

TELEPHONE
071-935-1047
FAX
071-722-0435
TUBE
Bond Street
CREDIT CARDS
AE, DC, MC, V
NUMBER OF ROOMS
8
W/BST
All
RATES
Single £58; double £68; Continental breakfast included
MISCELLANEOUS
Must reserve in advance. No walk-ins accepted.

One of the best Cheap Sleeps in London is the eight-room Ivanhoe Suites atop Plexi's Restaurant (see *Cheap Eats in London*). Located on a pedestrian walkway, this simple hotel consists of attractive singles and doubles, each with its own sitting area and private bathroom. The white-glove test will never be necessary, as the rooms are nothing short of antiseptically clean and tidy. I like No. 6, a sunny double with a large closet, plenty of shelf space in a nice bathroom, and an interesting view of the square below. For shoppers, this hotel almost qualifies as Mecca. Besides the interesting boutiques along cobblestoned St. Christopher's Place, you are only minutes from New and Old Bond streets and all the temptations of their elegant shops. A Continental breakfast is served in the Plexi's Restaurant, and, of course, you can dine here for either lunch or dinner and save the hassle of the tube or the cost of a taxi. There are also several other restaurants on the street as well as a corner pub.

Facilities and Services: Electric room heat, hair dryer available, no safe, no lift, no direct-dial phones, TV, desk open 7:30 A.M.–midnight

Regent Palace Hotel
P.O. Box 4BZ, Piccadilly Circus, W1

TELEPHONE
071-734-7000; toll-free in U.S. 1-800-225-5843
FAX
071-734-6435

No hotel could be nearer the bright lights and bustle of Piccadilly Circus than the Regent Palace Hotel, part of the Forte Hotel group (see page 37 for those hotels participating in their bargain "Leisure Breaks"). The Regent Palace is one of the largest in Europe and the perfect point from which to sample London entertainment life. While none of the 880 rooms have private showers or toilets, they are well-furnished in typical tailored-hotel style. All have a sink with hot and cold running water. The spotless hall facilities are large and remind me of my health club. A maid opens the door to the shower or bath on request and cleans it immediately after each use. The hotel has every service you can imagine, including two restaurants, one of which is the Original Carvery (see *Cheap Eats in London*). There is also a hairdresser, several shops, a coffee shop, and two bars.

Facilities and Services: Two bars, central heat, phone calls go through switchboard, lift, office safe, two restaurants, room service, hairdresser, shops, tea and coffeemakers, TV and radio, concierge, porter, theater booking agent

TELEX
23740

TUBE
Piccadilly Circus

CREDIT CARDS
AE, DC, MC, V

NUMBER OF ROOMS
880

W/BST
None

RATES
Single £68; double £83; triple £90; English breakfast included

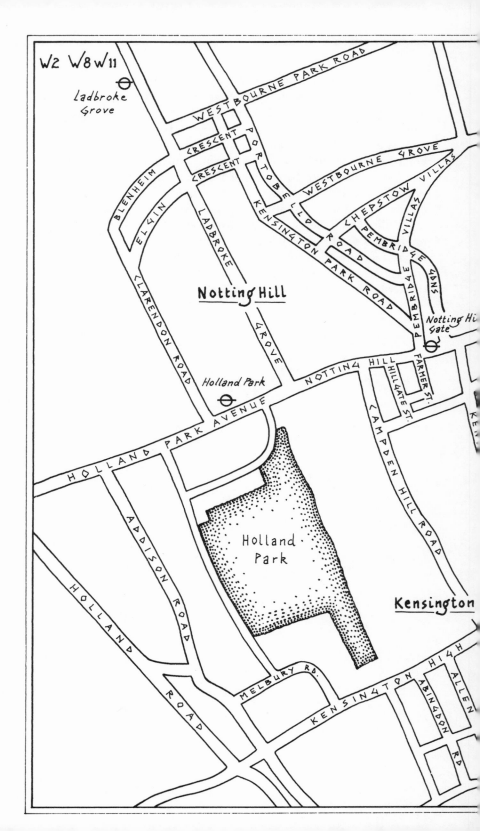

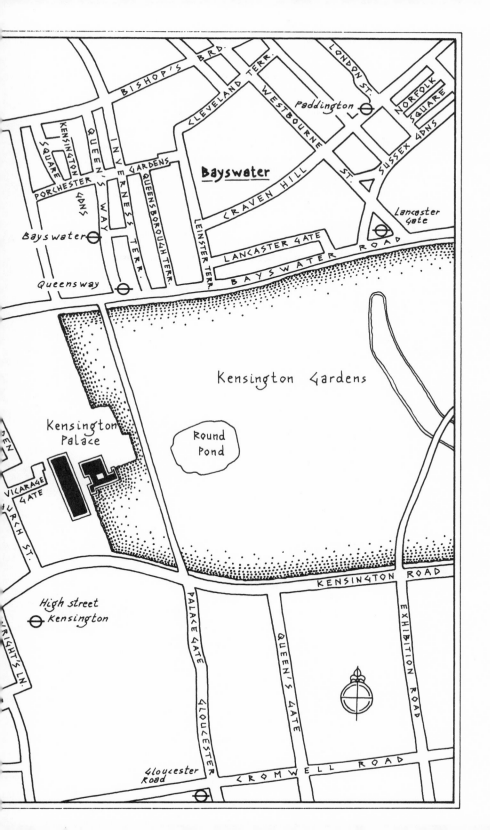

W2 ✢ PADDINGTON AND BAYSWATER

Paddington is a good choice if you are on a budget and traveling with children or by car. It is close to Hyde Park, where your children can run off some of their pent-up energy. If you have a car, parking can be a nightmare, but not if you stay in one of the hotels on Sussex Gardens where *free* parking is part of the deal. Restaurants in the area are budget conscious. Most of the hotels are dull, geared for tourists spending one or two nights near the Paddington train station. However, by consulting *Cheap Sleeps in London,* you have a choice of the best the area has to offer. Transportation is superb. The area is served by four Underground lines: Metropolitan, Bakerloo, District, and Circle.

Bayswater lies north of Kensington Gardens and is known as an area of contrasts. Queensway, its main thoroughfare, has everything from the large Whiteley's of Bayswater indoor mall—housing stores, restaurants, cafés, and cinemas—to 24-hour sleazy luggage shops and greasy-spoon restaurants serving a multitude of ethnic and local foods. On Sunday, it is pleasant to walk along Bayswater Road where artists and craftspeople display works for sale (see Shopping, page 196).

HOTELS

Adare House	47
Ashley Hotel	47
Balmoral Hotel	48
Border Hotel	49
The Byron Hotel	50
Camelot Hotel	50
Dean Court Hotel	51
The Delemere Hotel	52
Europa House	53
Fairways Hotel	53
Garden Court Hotel	54
The Gresham Hotel	54
Kensington Gardens Hotel	55
Mitre House Hotel	56
Mornington Hotel	56
Norfolk Court and St. David's Hotel	57
Palace Hotel	99
Pembridge Court Hotel	58
The Phoenix Hotel	59
Queensway Hotel	60
Royal Norfolk Hotel	60
Westbourne International Residence	99

OTHER OPTIONS

Renting a Flat
Two Hyde Park Square   170
University Dormitory Accommodations
Centre Français de Londres   176
Ys
Lancaster Hall Hotel (German YMCA)   186

Adare House
153 Sussex Gardens, W2

I was first attracted to the Adare House in Sussex Gardens by the pretty blooming flower boxes at the windows and the shiny blue door. Owners Mr. and Mrs. O'Neill have worked hard for 23 years to keep their fourteen-room hotel one of the top budget picks in the area. The hallways have just been redone in lush red carpeting with Regency-striped wallpaper above white wainscoting. Rooms are scrupulously clean, and most have pleasing decor that won't incite nightmares. Six private baths have been added, but if you want to save money and gain space, book a bathless room.

Facilities and Services: Central heat, public hall phones, hair dryers in rooms with private baths, no lift, TV, office safe, children under 12 half price, tea and coffeemakers

TELEPHONE
071-262-0633

FAX
None

TUBE
Paddington

CREDIT CARDS
None

NUMBER OF ROOMS
14

W/BST
9

W/OBST
5

RATES
Single £28–35; double £44–48; triple £22 each; English breakfast included

Ashley Hotel
15–17 Norfolk Square, W2

Many hotels around Norfolk Square are leased to managers and show very little pride of ownership. But not the Ashley, the star hotel in a series of three joined together at the same address. The Ashley has been proudly owned for over a quarter century by two Welsh brothers, John and David George. The sign on the front door of the hotel reads: "This is a highly respectable hotel, and the management reserves its legal right to refuse admission to anyone of dubious or untidy appearance, or without visible luggage. The management also reserves the right to ask

TELEPHONE
071-723-9966, 071-723-3375, 071-723-5442

FAX
071-723-0173

TUBE
Paddington

CREDIT CARDS
None

NUMBER OF ROOMS
52

W/BST
32

W/OBST
20
RATES
Single £27–39; double £25–27 per person; triple £27 per person; family room £25–28 per adult. If the stay is for only one night, add 50p per person. Reduced rates available for children sharing parents' room. English breakfast included

for positive ID." You get the message right away: this is a no-nonsense hotel that does not tolerate a hint of hanky-panky. The brothers cater to repeat visits from couples, families, and businesspeople. They even have guests who spent their honeymoon with them 24 years ago and come back now with their children.

A genuine personal interest is taken in each of the guests. One of the brothers is always at the hotel during the day, and a family member presides over breakfast. Near the breakfast room is a bulletin board with helpful hints and tips on what to see and do in London, from street markets and river cruises to day trips in the country, unusual shopping advice, and what to do on Sunday.

On my last visit, I was happy to see the rooms had improved. Gone for the most part are the pattern and fabric mixes and rump-sprung chairs. In their place, you will find sweet wallpaper, coordinated fabrics, and better furniture. Many of the rooms now have private facilities, which is appealing to most travelers today.

Facilities and Services: Central heat, public hall phones, TV and radio, office safe, tea and coffee-makers, no lift, desk open 8 A.M.–10 P.M.

Balmoral Hotel
156–157 Sussex Gardens, W2

TELEPHONE
071-723-7445, 071-402-0118
FAX
071-402-0118
TUBE
Paddington
CREDIT CARDS
MC, V
NUMBER OF ROOMS
18
W/BST
All
RATES
Single £25–27; double £36–42; triple £18 per person; English breakfast included

Sussex Gardens is a noisy double boulevard not far from Hyde Park and Marble Arch in an area that once offered countless cheap hotels geared to long-term stays of those down on their luck. Definite improvements are underway and the area is on the upswing. One of the better budget addresses is the Balmoral Hotel, run for 20-odd years by the Vieitez family. When you reserve your room, ask to be in the building at 156 Sussex Gardens. Unless you like wild wallpaper and crossing a busy street for breakfast (served only at 156), you don't want to be sleeping at 157 Sussex Gardens. The rooms at 156 have been redone with coordinated colors, fabrics, and carpeting. Unfortunately, some rooms have overhead TVs with no remotes and those facing the street are noisy, but other than these drawbacks, they are nice. Above all, every room in both locations is spotlessly clean, thanks to the daily vigilance of Mrs. Vieitez, who lets nothing escape her sharp eyes. The bottom line is the good price, and for Cheap Sleepers in London, there will be few complaints, I am sure.

Facilities and Services: Central heat, hair dryer in room, TV, radio, no lift

Border Hotel
14 Norfolk Square, W2

"We don't offer fancy rooms, just a clean hotel and friendly service," said Mrs. Davies, who with her Welsh husband has been greeting guests for a quarter century in their spic and span hotel on the edge of the Paddington hotel ghetto. The location is great for public transportation convenience, less than five minutes from the airbus stop for Heathrow Airport, one minute from Paddington Station, and another three from Lancaster Gate. Five bus routes service the area, and if all else fails, taxis are easy to come by. When calling for reservations, ask for a room facing the square. Some of the back rooms face walls, and one in the basement has no view at all. Rooms 5 and 6 have the original 120-year-old doors and 6A has beautiful stained-glass windows. The old marble hall sinks and wood around the public WCs have been kept and add character to this sweet hotel. Mrs. Davies sees to it that the rooms are all clean, and she never allows them to fall into the deferred maintenance category. Each room is outfitted with matching fabrics and color-coordinated paint. Breakfast is served on blue china in a wood-paneled dining room with light-blue cloths on the tables. Photos of her family are proudly displayed, and you will see one of her husband's choir—a well-known Welsh men's chorale. If you like this type of music, tapes are for sale.

Facilities and Services: Electric room heat, public phones, hair dryer available, office safe, TV, no lift, desk open 7 A.M.–10:30 P.M.

TELEPHONE
Guests 071-723-2968;
reception 071-402-8054

FAX
None

TUBE
Paddington, Lancaster Gate

CREDIT CARDS
None

NUMBER OF ROOMS
18

W/BST
None

RATES
Single £30; double £48; triple £60; four £70; English breakfast included

The Byron Hotel
36–38 Queensborough Terrace, W2

TELEPHONE
071-243-0987; toll-free in the
U.S. 1-800-448-8355

FAX
071-792-1957

TELEX
263431

TUBE
Queensway or Bayswater

CREDIT CARDS
AE, DC, MC, V

NUMBER OF ROOMS
42

W/BST
All

RATES
Single £80; double £90–100;
triple £115; suite/apt £145;
English or Continental
breakfast included

For those willing to spend a little more, the Byron Hotel, owned by Mr. and Mrs. Andrews, is one of my favorite choices. Located on a quiet street only 200 yards from Kensington Gardens, the hotel has the atmosphere of a charming country house where you would like to spend considerable time. All of the rooms are named after stately English country homes and each has a picture of the home. They offer such extras as air-conditioning, VCRs, and trouser presses. If I did not splurge and book the penthouse suite, I would stay in one of the ground-floor patio rooms or in No. 21, with a view of a huge green tree filling the window. This sunny yellow room offers built-in luggage space, good closets, and a marvelous tiled bath with plenty of sink space, a basket of pretty English toiletries, and excellent lighting. The downstairs public rooms have large windows looking onto brightly blooming flower boxes. Guests of the hotel can take advantage—free of charge—of a conference room and office facilities. There is a minibus available for airport transfers and an automatic 10 percent discount on the hotel bill upon presentation of your business card. For breakfast, you will be seated in a mirrored room with silk wallpaper and botanical prints on the walls and served on Royal Doulton china.

Facilities and Services: Air-conditioning and central heat, bar, direct-dial phones, hair dryers, lift, office safe, TV with video and cable, tea and coffee-makers, trouser press, mini-van available for airport transfers (nominal charge), conference room, fax and telex available, porter, room service for light snacks

Camelot Hotel
45–47 Norfolk Square, W2

TELEPHONE
071-262-1980, 071-723-9118

FAX
071-402-3412

TELEX
268312 Westcom G Central

Built in 1850, the Camelot is a beautifully restored hotel full of character and distinction, combining classical English elegance with the best in modern facilities. Ideally positioned on a quiet garden square just west of Hyde Park, the hotel is renowned for offering all guests, but especially those with children, a warm and friendly welcome.

To start the day, an all-you-can-eat breakfast is served in two connecting country-style dining rooms with the original wood-burning brick fireplaces still in use. The meal consists of a help-yourself buffet of cereals, fruits, pastries, and exotic jams, jellies, and honeys. Waitresses take your order for the hot portion which could be any or all of the following: eggs with bacon, sausage, tomatoes, beans, and toast. If you can finish all of this and are still hungry, just say so and you can have more. While eating your breakfast, you will have a chance to admire the display of charming pictures of London drawn by some of the young visitors from around the world who have stayed at the hotel. The pretty lobby is dominated by a massive gold-framed mirror above a marble fireplace that was uncovered during the 1989 restoration project. All the rooms have soft pastel colors, oak built-ins, and bright modern geometric quilted bedspreads. The rooms on the first floor facing the front have their own balconies, and three have fireplaces. Unusual prints of early scenes from the London Underground hang in each room, and an interesting collection of advertising posters for the Underground is hung throughout the hotel's hallways.

The Camelot would be a perfect ten if it were not for the four twin-bed rooms on the top floor. The only windows in these rooms are ceiling skylight windows that are lovely to look at, but next to impossible to open. Unless you are a contortionist, the best advice is to avoid these rooms.

Facilities and Services: Central heat, direct-dial phones, hair dryer available, lift to fifth floor, office safe, TV with in-house films, radio, clock, desk open from 7 A.M.–11 P.M.

Dean Court Hotel
57 Inverness Terrace, W2

This Bayswater neighborhood is a haven for run-down hotels that, in a last-ditch effort to stay afloat, accept social security recipients. Believe me,

TUBE
Paddington

CREDIT CARDS
MC, V

NUMBER OF ROOMS
44

W/BST
40

W/OBST
4 singles

RATES
Single £41–55; double £80; triple £95; four £125. Discounts for stays over 4 days; English breakfast included

TELEPHONE
071-229-2961

FAX
071-727-1190

TUBE
Bayswater

CREDIT CARDS
None

NUMBER OF ROOMS
40

W/BST
None

RATES
No singles; double £38; triple £45; dorms £15 per person BYO towels and soap; English breakfast included

no matter how cheap they may be, you do not want to get caught in one of these flea-bag palaces where the world of London on the cheap will take on an undesirable new meaning. The Dean Court and its next-door annex, the New Kent, offer beds and bunks to backpackers and students on shoestring budgets. No social security recipients are accepted. Kitchen privileges, weekly rates, and a friendly international crowd compensate for the tired, but still habitable rooms. If you land in a dorm room, please bring your own towel and soap because they are not provided.

Facilities and Services: Central heat, hall phones, no lift, office safe, TV lounge, kitchen privileges, iron available

The Delemere Hotel
130 Sussex Gardens, W2

TELEPHONE
071-706-3344

FAX
071-262-1863

TELEX
8953857

TUBE
Paddington or Lancaster Gate

CREDIT CARDS
AE, DC, MC, V

NUMBER OF ROOMS
40

W/BST
All

RATES
Single £75-85; double £95; suite/apt Crown room with jacuzzi and king-size bed £100. See below for Weekend Break rates; Continental breakfast included, English breakfast £7 extra

MISCELLANEOUS
Weekend Break rates: Prices are per person and include a Continental breakfast. A stay must include a Saturday night. Two nights £72; extra night £36; single-room supplement £17; seven nights £235

The Delemere Hotel is a fine town house in Sussex Gardens, part of a legacy of early nineteenth-century design by architect Samuel Pepys Cockerell. One of his star pupils was Latrobe, who built the Capitol in Washington, D.C.

This area of Sussex Gardens was built to provide luxurious homes for fashionable Victorian families. Lord Baden-Powell, founder of the Boy Scouts (see Baden-Powell House, page 137), was christened in St. James's Church. Sir Arthur Conan Doyle's family lived in Sussex Gardens, and at St. Mary's Hospital, Sir Alexander Fleming discovered penicillin.

The hotel is one of the best along this leafy avenue. Downstairs, there is a comfortable sitting room and library stocked with daily papers and current magazines. There is also a bar where cocktails and light snacks are served. For something more, guests can eat at La Perla, which serves Italian and Continental dishes at moderate prices.

The rooms range from spacious to extremely snug, but all are well thought out with built-ins and compact baths offering good towels and bright lighting. Each room has a soft easy chair and comes with an electronic key card for additional security. The hotel has attractive weekend rates that make it appealing to Cheap Sleepers who want the best for less.

Facilities and Services: Bar, central heat, direct-dial phones, same day laundry, lift, office safe, restaurant, TV, radio

Europa House
151 Sussex Gardens, W2

Europa House offers very good value for Cheap Sleepers not willing to give up the comfort and convenience of a private bathroom. All baths are tiled and have only showers, but shelf space is limited and there is no door hook. The rooms are simple in style, but without many homey touches. They are, however, clean and acceptable, especially if you are staying more than five nights, or arriving in the off-season when owner Franco Vales reduces the rates. If you are driving, there is parking space in front of the hotel, *if* you book in advance. If you have a car, take my advice and leave it here for the duration of your London visit. Either walk, ride the bus or tube, or hail a cab to get where you are going. Driving in London is, as the song goes, "for mad dogs and Englishmen."

Facilities and Services: Central heat, public phones, parking if booked in advance, TV, no lift, no safe, desk open 9 A.M.–10 P.M.

TELEPHONE
071-723-7343, 071-402-1923

FAX
071-224-9331

TUBE
Paddington

CREDIT CARDS
MC, V + 4% surcharge

NUMBER OF ROOMS
18

W/BST
All

RATES
Single £36; double £50; triple £22 per person; lower off-season rates and price reduction if stay is longer than 5 nights; English breakfast included

Fairways Hotel
186 Sussex Gardens, W2

Steve and Jenny Adams run the sprightly Fairways Hotel. Their high standards keep this 17-room hotel one of the best B&Bs in London, where you can expect to find an abundance of ruffles and flourishes along with large portions of hospitality. Nothing is modern, but that is part of the charm that keeps regulars coming back. The breakfast room is full of family photos and an interesting thimble and Wedgwood china collection. You will soon feel right at home with all the other guests who gather here each morning to enjoy a hearty home-cooked breakfast

TELEPHONE
071-723-4871

FAX
071-723-4871

TUBE
Lancaster Gate

CREDIT CARDS
AE, DC, MC, V

NUMBER OF ROOMS
17

W/BST
10

W/OBST
7
RATES
Single £35; double £48–55;
English breakfast included

while plotting their day in London. Motorists will certainly appreciate the *free* parking spaces in front of the hotel, and walkers will be able to pace themselves nicely going to Hyde Park and the West End. Bus and tube transportation is within easy reach.

Facilities and Services: Central heat, public phones in the hall, free parking in front, office safe, tea and coffeemakers, TV, desk closed from 10 P.M.– 7 A.M., no lift

Garden Court Hotel
30–31 Kensington Gardens Square, W2

TELEPHONE
071-229-2553
FAX
071-727-2749
TUBE
Queensway or Bayswater
CREDIT CARDS
None
NUMBER OF ROOMS
35
W/BST
14
W/OBST
21
RATES
Single £28–40; double £40–55;
triple £52–60; four £60;
English breakfast included
MISCELLANEOUS
The hotel is closed for one
week between Christmas and
New Year's.

The area is rather run-down, but this simple B&B has kept ahead of its neighbors and continues to provide clean and modest lodgings for value-conscious budgeteers. There are few glaring color schemes or pattern mismatches. The plain rooms are generally large enough, with adequate closet and shelf space, decent lighting, and furniture that is not ready for a garage sale. Most of the rooms have nice views onto the street and square in front, or onto the gardens in back. The private bathrooms are an afterthought, and some are gnome-sized and difficult to walk into unless you are reed-thin or stand sideways. To save the most money, reserve a room without bathroom facilities and walk down the hall. The hotel is not too far from the Whiteley's of Bayswater shopping center and the famous Portobello Road antiques and junk market. There are loads of restaurants nearby, from tasty and cheap Indian to upscale Chinese (see *Cheap Eats in London*).

Facilities and Services: Central heat, direct-dial phones, hair dryer in room, office safe, TV, no lift, desk open 7:30 A.M.–11 P.M.

The Gresham Hotel
116 Sussex Gardens, W2

TELEPHONE
071-402-2920
FAX
071-402-3137
TUBE
Paddington

I will never forget my visit to The Gresham, and I am positive not one of the staff will ever forget the day I was there. In the wee hours of that morning, one of the hotel guests gave birth right in her hotel room to a healthy baby. The staff was brilliant, rising to the occasion with calm determination and swift action. Mother and baby were soon whisked to a nearby hospital and an announcement in the lobby assured the rest of us that they were resting comfortably and doing well. I love my job . . . there is *never* a dull moment!

What about the hotel? In a word, wonderful. It has been totally redone in a tasteful style that will appeal to those who enjoy comfortable living away from home. A professional, uniformed staff oversees the reception desk next to a little bar with a five-seat counter and black-and-white prints of early London on the walls. Each floor has its own color scheme— orange, yellow, blue, and sea green—carried out with designer touches in the rooms. Pickled wood, large bathrooms, and good-sized closets add to their appeal. The garden-style mirrored dining room with pink cloths and green chairs is a nice place to enjoy the large Continental breakfast included in the room rate. Special off-season rates and weekend packages are always available. Be sure to ask.

Facilities and Services: Bar, central heat, direct-dial phones, hair dryer, same-day laundry service, lift, parking, room safe, cable TV, radio, tea and coffee-makers, iron available, secretarial services with conference room, fax and photocopying available

CREDIT CARDS
AE, DC, MC, V

NUMBER OF ROOMS
38

W/BST
All

RATES
Single £60; double £75; triple £95; Continental breakfast included; English breakfast £5

Kensington Gardens Hotel
9 Kensington Gardens Square, W2

Mr. Kazolides, the new owner, spent eight months and thousands of pounds to turn this once-drab dump into an attractive mid-price choice in Bayswater. All of the seventeen color-coordinated rooms have showers, but only four are complete with private bathrooms. A bonus for those living in bathless rooms are the superb hall facilities, some of the best I have ever seen in *any* hotel in London. The newly fitted rooms are snug, with limited luggage space, but do have the extra details that add to a comfortable stay: color TV, hair dryer, mini-bar, and tea and coffee-makers. The best views are in the top-floor perches, but you must be prepared to climb endless stairs to

TELEPHONE
071-221-7790

FAX
071-792-8612

TUBE
Bayswater

CREDIT CARDS
AE, DC, MC, V

NUMBER OF ROOMS
17

W/BST
4

W/OBST
13

RATES
Single £40; double £60; triple £85; Continental breakfast included

get there. A Continental breakfast is served in a nice dining room with skylights, pink tablecloths, and soft green wall coverings.

Facilities and Services: Central heat, direct-dial phones, hair dryer, mini-bar, 1-day laundry, office safe, TV, tea and coffeemakers, no lift

Mitre House Hotel
178–184 Sussex Gardens, W2

TELEPHONE
071-723-8040
FAX
071-402-0990
TELEX
914113 Mitre G
TUBE
Paddington or Lancaster Gate
CREDIT CARDS
AE, DC, MC, V
NUMBER OF ROOMS
70
W/BST
All
RATES
Single £60; double £70; triple £80; family room £90; suite £100; English breakfast included

It is always rewarding to go back to a good hotel and find it getting even better. This was the case when I visited the Mitre House Hotel this spring. Andrew and Michael Chris grew up in the hotel, which their parents ran for thirty years. The two brothers are now in charge and have carried out ambitious plans to improve and expand the facilities. The new 39-room wing has opened and is wonderful. It includes three junior suites with the latest in bathrooms, including jacuzzis. Several of the rooms connect, a real advantage for families with children who also want some privacy. The rooms in the older section are somewhat cramped and have limited luggage space, but the beige color scheme is not bothersome. If you need sunlight and moonbeams, avoid the viewless ground-floor rooms.

The large dining room has had a facelift and the hotel has just been repainted outside. Paddington and Lancaster Gate tube stops are a few minutes away, and several major bus routes are within a one-block walk. Free parking for a few cars in front is a big advantage; so is the youthful and outgoing desk staff who try so hard to please.

Facilities and Services: Bar, central heat, direct-dial phones, hair dryer, trouser press, mini-bar in suites, lift, free parking, office safe, TV with cable, fax facilities from 10 A.M.–6 P.M.

Mornington Hotel
12 Lancaster Gate, W2

TELEPHONE
071-262-7361; toll-free from U.S. 1-800-528-1234

Swedish-owned and -operated, the Mornington i s an exceptional hotel with a delightful staff dressed in bright red tartan in winter and lighter colors in summer. The spotless rooms have some of the best bathrooms in London, and definitely the cleanest. All have wonderful mirrors, lots of space for your things, and a selection of shampoo, soap, and other items you might have forgotten to pack. The bedrooms display a high standard of Swedish-modern comfort with an easy chair, floor lamp, desk, remote-controlled TV, and firm beds with fluffy comforters. I could move right in to room No. 84, a twin split-level with floor-to-ceiling windows, an upstairs bed-room, and a downstairs sitting room. Numbers 103 and 107 are also twin split-level rooms with plenty of light. The rooms to avoid are those facing "the Well." Downstairs is a book-lined lounge where you can order a snack from the bar or afternoon tea. Breakfast is served Scandinavian style, which means a large buffet with meats, cheeses, breads, cereals, and juice. There will be enough here to keep most voyagers going strong until dinner time. If you are tired from traveling or sightseeing, take advantage of the free 24-hour sauna, which is booked ahead in half-hour intervals. In connection with the sauna is a shower room with plenty of big towels. The hotel is part of the Best Western chain in Europe, making reservations a snap via the toll-free 800 number in the United States.

Facilities and Services: Bar, central heat, direct-dial phones, hair dryers in rooms, lift, office safe, snacks and afternoon tea, TV with cable, free sauna

FAX
071-706-1028
TELEX
24281
TUBE
Lancaster Gate
CREDIT CARDS
AE, DC, MC, V
NUMBER OF ROOMS
68
W/BST
All
RATES
Single £85; double £95–115; triple extra bed £15; buffet included

Norfolk Court and St. David's Hotel
16–20 Norfolk Square, W2

These two hotels are run simultaneously by owner George Neokleous. They are less than a minute or two away from Paddington Station, and should be kept in mind by budget seekers who need to be in this vicinity. The main hotel lobby, with its glaring orange and brown bulls-eye carpeting, still has the original Art Deco tinted glass windows with stained glass highlights. As you wander through the hotel, be sure to notice the other original windows and the ceiling details that have mercifully been kept intact,

TELEPHONE
071-723-4963, 071-723-3856
FAX
071-402-9061
TUBE
Paddington
CREDIT CARDS
MC, V
NUMBER OF ROOMS
50
W/BST
6

W/OBST
44

RATES
Single £30–40; double £40–50;
triple £50–65; four £55–65;
English breakfast included

despite years of repainting and redoing. The rooms are comfortable, but lackluster—filled with the usual budget mix of patterns, colors, and outmoded furnishings. In their favor, they are clean, provide more space than most, and the beds are good. Steer clear of those with only a cubicle shower positioned in a corner. Included in the price of your room will be a cooked breakfast.

Facilities and Services: Central heat, public phones, hair dryer available, office safe, cable TV, no lift, 24-hour desk

Pembridge Court Hotel
34 Pembridge Gardens, W2

TELEPHONE
071-229-9977

FAX
071-727-4982

TELEX
298363

TUBE
Notting Hill Gate

CREDIT CARDS
AE, DC, MC, V

NUMBER OF ROOMS
21

W/BST
All

RATES
Single £95–100; deluxe room
at single occupancy £120–130;
double £122–165; family rates
available upon request;
ask about reduced rates on
some weekends; English
breakfast included

People always ask me to tell them about my favorite London hotel. I have several, and the Pembridge Court is a special one. I could occupy any of its twenty-one rooms and be happy. It is hard to know just where to begin telling you about the hotel because everything is so lovely. It has won many certificates of distinction and honors for its excellence in all categories, and after one visit, you will know why.

It has, without question, the most beautiful flower arrangements and outdoor blooming potted-plant displays I have seen in London. I also love the whimsical framed lace collars, Victorian beaded bags, delicate ivory fans, old tortoiseshell combs, frilly baby dresses, and other collectables that owner Paul Capra has ingeniously hung throughout his hotel. No two rooms are alike, but all are beautifully done and display pieces from Mr. Capra's extensive collection of English antiques. On my next visit, I will reserve the Lancaster Room, a deluxe double with a separate sitting area, more wardrobe space than I have at home, and a gloriously feminine pink-tiled bath with brass fittings and enough thick white towels to last almost forever. For extra-special occasions, the Belvedere Room, with a four-poster bed and a sitting area by a sunny window, is a romantic choice.

To gild the lily even further, the hotel has a separate restaurant, Caps, that is getting rave reviews and gaining more devotees every day. Offering a monthly changing menu at very affordable prices, the food is light and imaginative with Thai overtones. After a long day in London, it is nice to return to a wonderful hotel and know you won't have far to go for a delicious dinner.

Facilities and Services: Bar, central heat, hair dryer in rooms, laundry service, lift, free parking, room safe, 24-hour room service, restaurant, TV with video and cable, radio, trouser presses

The Phoenix Hotel
1 Kensington Gardens Square, W2

Most London small hotels began life as family homes of some note; the Phoenix is no exception. It is made up of eight town houses built originally in 1854, refurbished to suit today's modern traveler.

The 125 bedrooms are designed with the guest's needs in mind, providing tiled baths with tub and stall showers, remote-controlled cable television, and hair dryers. All are done in the same mauve color with sea-green accents. Each has a luggage rack, desk, and a framed print on the wall. The split-level suites are recommended for families, or those wanting more room. If you ask to have the mezzanine made into a sitting room, you will have a very pleasing accommodation, especially for a longer stay.

To relax outside your room, you can sit in a chair by one of the fireplaces in the entry, or in the small room off the bar and have a bracing cup of tea, or something stronger. The bar also provides 24-hour room service for beverages or hot and cold snacks. The professional staff is helpful and pride themselves on their history of personal service to each guest. The hotel is affiliated with Best Western International, so booking from your own home won't cost you a penny if you use the toll-free 800 number. If, however, you are looking for a discounted price, you will have to deal directly with the hotel.

Facilities and Services: Bar, central heat, direct-dial phones, hair dryer, lift, office safe, cable TV, 24-hour room service and desk, irons available

TELEPHONE
071-229-2494; toll-free from the U.S. 1-800-528-1234
FAX
071-727-1419
TELEX
298854
TUBE
Bayswater
CREDIT CARDS
AE, DC, MC, V
NUMBER OF ROOMS
130
W/BST
All
RATES
Single £70; double £85; triple £110; suite/apt £140; Continental breakfast included

Queensway Hotel
147–149 Sussex Gardens, W2

TELEPHONE
071-723-7749
FAX
071-262-5707
TUBE
Paddington or Lancaster Gate
CREDIT CARDS
DC, MC, V
NUMBER OF ROOMS
44
W/BST
All
RATES
Single £60; double £70–75; triple £90; lower off-season rates and special rates offered . . . be sure to ask; English breakfast included

The location is good. Both the Paddington and Lancaster Gate Underground stations are close, and so are several bus routes giving excellent service to theaters, museums, art galleries, and historic monuments. This long-established hotel is well done from top to bottom and prides itself on personal service from a friendly and helpful staff. To say it is clean is an understatement. The bedspreads are washed after every guest leaves, all the curtains are taken down fortnightly and washed, and the public areas are scrubbed, polished, and shined daily. If you think a relaxing jacuzzi would revive you after a hard day of London sightseeing and shopping, reserve one of the executive doubles and sample this welcome luxury for yourself.

The dining room, with mirrored walls and Royal Doulton china, is well-lighted and has cushioned chairs. You can help yourself to a first-course buffet of fruits and cereals before being served an individually cooked breakfast. As one guest wrote to me after a stay here, "It is hard to imagine a stay at the Queensway being anything but enjoyable from start to finish." Try it for yourself and I think you will agree.

Facilities and Services: Central heat, direct-dial phones, hair dryer in room, lift, 2 parking spaces, office safe, TV, radio, clock, tea and coffeemakers, trouser presses, desk open from 7 A.M.–11 P.M.

Royal Norfolk Hotel
24 London Street, W2

TELEPHONE
071-402-5221, 071-723-3386
FAX
071-724-8442, 071-723-3505
TELEX
266059STY-AL G
TUBE
Paddington

The Royal Norfolk Hotel is a utilitarian address to remember if you want to be near Paddington Station. It is only a short hike or a quick bus ride to Marble Arch and Hyde Park, and from there easy access to all of London. The hotel reminded me of those in which I have stayed in Eastern Europe; no pizzazz, but most conveniences on hand for a comfortable stay. The rooms are on the small side with no out-of-sight luggage space. Modest redecorating has upgraded the carpets, curtains, and bedspreads. The hall facilities show their age, but are kept clean by the maids. The back rooms are naturally the calmest, and if the huge flowering tree is in bloom, the view is pleasant. Hot coffee and tea can be brewed anytime with the electric kettle in each room, or you can pop downstairs to the Dickens Inn and order a pint or two of beer. Adjoining the hotel is a Deep Pan Pizza restaurant that won't appeal to everyone, but if you have children, this could be a lifesaver.

Facilities and Services: Bar, central heat, direct-dial phones, hair dryer in room, lift, office safe, TV with satellite, radio, clock, tea and coffeemaker in room

CREDIT CARDS
AE, DC, MC, V

NUMBER OF ROOMS
62

W/BST
50

W/OBST
12

RATES
Single £42–62; double £59–83; triple £75–95; four £85; Continental breakfast included

W8 ✦ KENSINGTON

Kensington became an important section of London when William III commissioned Sir Christopher Wren to rebuild Kensington Palace. The palace, where Princess Diana maintains her residence, stands at one end of Kensington Gardens, which along with Hyde Park forms the largest open space in London. Kensington High Street is one of London's best shopping streets, lined with a wonderful variety of shops, several department store branches, and some of the wildest fashions imaginable, displayed in Hyper-Hyper and the Kensington Market (see Shopping, page 196). To the north is Kensington Church Street, famous for its magnificent antiques shops, filled with museum-quality examples that have very high price tags. But, it costs nothing to look and to dream.

HOTELS

Abbey House	62
The Amber Hotel	63
Demetriou Guest House	64
Forte Hotel Leisure Breaks	65
Hotel Lexham	65
Vicarage Private Hotel	66

OTHER OPTIONS

Strictly for Students
Lee Abbey International Students' Club 173
University Dormitory Accommodations
Queen Elizabeth Hall 183
Youth Hostels
Holland House, King George VI Memorial
  Youth Hostel 190

Abbey House
11 Vicarage Gate, W8

TELEPHONE
071-727-2594

FAX
None

TUBE
High Street Kensington

CREDIT CARDS
None

NUMBER OF ROOMS
15

The Abbey House is on a tranquil Victorian square close to Kensington Gardens. The house was built around 1860 for a wealthy businessman and has since been the home of a bishop and a Member of Parliament. Now it is a small hotel and a classic example of what good taste and hard work by a young, enthusiastic couple can do to create an appealing budget B&B. The owners, Albert and Carol Nayach, provide warm hospitality and a genuine value that is not lost on their many regulars who book rooms a year in advance. If you want to stay here in high season, it will never be too early to call for reservations and to secure them with a deposit.

As you enter the front door of the hotel from the wide porch, you will see a beautiful interior staircase that winds up from the entry hall. The rooms are done in a girlish old-fashioned style and are kept up to snuff with yearly painting and decorating when needed. All the beds have orthopedic mattresses, and every room has a live plant and simple, nick-free furniture. No. 12 on the ground floor is a ruffly double with good drawer and hanging space. No. 11 is also on the ground floor and has good all-around space. The large breakfast room has hanging plates and English prints scattered on the white walls. It looks onto a small patio with tubs of green plants.

Facilities and Services: Central heat, hall phones, TV, no lift

W/BST
None

RATES
Single £30; double £52; triple £62; four £72; English breakfast included

The Amber Hotel
101 Lexham Gardens, W8

Dutch hospitality shines at the spanking new Amber Hotel, owned and managed by a Dutch company. This hotel sparkles from its bright yellow exterior right through the forty rooms, the Windsor bar, and welcoming breakfast room. This solid choice puts the guest close to the exhibition center at Earl's Court Olympia and within easy tube or bus reach of the rest of London. Business travelers are well cared for with personal computers, copying, and fax machines available. The petite rooms look posh and feel comfortable. Decor plays it safe with light woods, lavender colors, and good reading lamps. A beautiful breakfast buffet includes the hotel's own baked breads and pastries, platters of cheese and meat, as well as fruit juices, cereals, and hot beverages. At the mezzanine bar, you can order a bottle of Amber beer, imported directly from Holland for the hotel, or try one of their selections of fine malt whiskeys. Another reason to stay here is the attractive Weekend Break

TELEPHONE
071-373-8666

FAX
071-835-1194

TUBE
Gloucester Road, High Street Kensington

CREDIT CARDS
AE, DC, MC, V

NUMBER OF ROOMS
40

W/BST
All

RATES
Single £75; double £80–85; extra bed £10; large Continental breakfast included

rates, which are available only from the hotel, not through the UTELL 800 number.

Facilities and Services: Bar, central heat, hair dryer, lift, office safe, restaurant, cable TV, radio, clock, tea and coffeemaker, trouser press, free newspapers, fax and computer facilities

Demetriou Guest House
9 Strathmore Gardens, W8

TELEPHONE
071-229-6709

FAX
None

TUBE
Notting Hill Gate

CREDIT CARDS
None

NUMBER OF ROOMS
9

W/BST
3

W/OBST
6

RATES
Single £28; double £21–23 per person; triple £20 per person; English breakfast included

MISCELLANEOUS
Hotel is closed from the end of February through second or third week in March.

The Demetriou Guest House is part of a historically preserved square of Georgian row houses dating from the beginning of the eighteenth century. The owners are not allowed to change the exterior of the buildings, so this small gem displays no sign at all. As you walk along Strathmore Gardens, look for No. 9; that will be the door you want. Once inside, you will be greeted by Mr. and Mrs. Demetriou and their two house cats, Louis and Katy-Kate. Louis is a real ham, spending most of his time lounging by the telephone, waiting to be photographed. Katy-Kate is more reserved.

My initial reaction here was that I felt like a family member in a relative's home, and that is just the feeling the Demetrious try to create. They have turned their private home into a guest house, catering to long-staying guests who prefer intimate surroundings at rates that won't send shock waves through their travel budgets. Their home is lovingly maintained, with red-carpeted halls contrasting richly with white walls and a multitude of green plants on the sunny middle landing. The Demetrious not only live here, they do *all* the work themselves in order to keep it exactly the way they want it. Your room will be cleaned by Mrs. Demetriou, and in the morning, Mr. Demetriou will prepare your bacon and eggs and serve them to you on Blue Willow china in their dining room. The spacious bedrooms have the original marble fireplaces, which, unfortunately, do not work and in some instances, are boarded or covered by a piece of furniture. The beds are all firm, there is plenty of natural light, and the tiny floral prints that are used throughout create a home-spun feeling. If you are looking for a sweet B&B run by a lovely couple, you will need to look no further.

Note: During the spring, Palace Garden Terrace, which is off Strathmore Gardens, is lined on each side with spectacular blooming cherry trees. Even if you are not staying at this B&B, it is worthwhile to make a special trip, with your camera, to see and photograph this lovely sight.

Facilities and Services: Central heat, hall phones, TV, hair dryer in public bathrooms, no lift

Forte Hotel Leisure Breaks

See description of these money-saving hotel deals on page 37.

The Kensington Close
Wrights Lane, W8
071-937-8170

Hotel Lexham
32–38 Lexham Gardens, W8

A well-managed hotel, reasonably near the center of things, but not too expensive—how many times have we all wished for this? The Hotel Lexham is all this and more. It is a family-run hotel providing on-the-spot supervision and operating expertise in a welcoming atmosphere. Both the family and their long-term staff understand that cleanliness, courtesy, comfort, and good food are basic necessities in any hotel stay. In the restaurant, which overlooks a small walled garden, the à la carte snack menu changes often and offers bargain prices that run from £2–4 for soups, salads, sandwiches, and sweets. The three-course dinner, served for the breathtakingly low price of £9, is a welcome bonus for those who cannot face going out again after a long day. If you want wine or beer, you will have to bring it, but there's no corkage fee.

The bedrooms are limited in the inventive style department, but every one is 100 percent acceptable, even the bathless singles. What would be considered big elsewhere is billed as small here. The beds are made up with crisp white sheets, soft comforters, and

TELEPHONE
071-373-6471

FAX
071-244-7827

TUBE
Earl's Court

CREDIT CARDS
AE, MC, V

NUMBER OF ROOMS
64

W/BST
46

W/OBST
18

RATES
Single £39–53; double £50–77; extra bed, child 3–9 £12, child 10–13 £15; weekly rates including meals available on request; English breakfast included

thermal blankets. The front rooms face the small, private Lexham Gardens. All guests are provided with a key, so on a slow day, you can spend a leisurely hour or so with a good book in a pretty, private garden.

In the public portion of the hotel are two lounges and a separate meeting room. The front desk will also arrange for sightseeing tours around special events; seats for the theater, concert, and sporting events; and rental cars.

Facilities and Services: Central heat, direct-dial phones, hair dryer available, same-day laundry service, lift to most floors, office safe, restaurant, TV and video, radio, baby cots, iron and ironing board available

Vicarage Private Hotel
10 Vicarage Gate, W8

TELEPHONE
071-229-4030

FAX
None

TUBE
High Street Kensington

CREDIT CARDS
None

NUMBER OF ROOMS
19

W/BST
None

RATES
Single £34; double £58; triple £74; four £79; English breakfast included

For the money and value it represents, the Vicarage Private Hotel is one of the best hotel buys in this part of London. The hotel is situated in a splendid turn-of-the-century mansion in a quiet section of the Royal Borough of Kensington. The impressive entry hall, with red carpeting and dark, red-flocked wallpaper, has a grilled staircase leading up to the nineteen practical bedrooms, all of which have hot and cold running water, but no private bathrooms. A few of the rooms have color televisions. The large hall showers and WCs are above average and have attractive touches like framed prints or playbills on the walls. Room No. 6 is a front-facing double with new wallpaper and forties-style furniture. For the sturdy solo traveler, No. 19 is a top-floor nest with a pretty oak armoire and beveled mirror. The triple or quad rooms make sound budget sense, especially if you consider that a family of four can stay for around $125 a night, and that includes a he-man breakfast for each of you. The hotel is close to Kensington High Street and its many trendy boutiques and surrounding antiques shops (see Shopping, page 196).

Facilities and Services: Central heat, hall phones, hair dryer available, TV in lounge, desk closed for incoming calls 10 P.M.–7:30 A.M., office safe, no lift

W11 ✦ NOTTING HILL, PORTOBELLO ROAD

Notting Hill is a mixture. Its most interesting feature, from a visitor's point of view, is around Portobello Road, the famous outdoor flea and antiques market that is best on Saturday morning when stalls and shops display a bewildering array of goodies (see Markets, page 227). On the August Bank Holiday Monday and the Sunday before, the Notting Hill Carnival, Europe's biggest outdoor festival, is celebrated with nonstop music, dancing, and thousands of revelers.

HOTELS

Gate Hotel	67
The Portobello Hotel	68
Ravna Gora	69

OTHER OPTIONS

Books for Cooks Flat	162

Gate Hotel
6 Portobello Road (Pembridge Road end), W11

The Gate Hotel is one of my favorite Cheap Sleeps in London. It is also the favorite of many Cheap Sleep readers who have enjoyed their stay and recommended it to friends. I found the hotel by accident. I was on my way several years ago to the Saturday morning antiques market on Portobello Road (see Shopping, page 196), when I took a wrong turn and wound up in front of this six-room B&B. Before it was renovated, it would have been the type of place I would never even have slowed down for. Now that owner Brian Watkins and his right-hand manageress Debbie Fletcher have redone it from stem to stern, it is the type of place that once found, people want to keep secret for fear it will be booked when they want to stay there.

The bright single and double rooms all offer a good measure of space, comfort, and practicality. Each has a built-in wardrobe, a full-length mirror, an orthopedic mattress, a small refrigerator, some desk space, and tea and coffeemakers. There are no random styles; everything is coordinated in shades of gray, peach, and pink with multifloral prints on the

TELEPHONE
071-221-2403

FAX
071-221-9128

TUBE
Notting Hill Gate

CREDIT CARDS
DC, MC, V

NUMBER OF ROOMS
6

W/BST
3

W/OBST
3

RATES
Single £38; double £52–62; triple £72; Continental breakfast included; English breakfast £4 extra

comforters and curtains. Original paintings depicting the early days of the Portobello Road market and its famous habitués add a touch of local character to each room. A Continental breakfast will be brought to your room, or for a few pounds more, you can go downstairs to the living room, where you will be greeted by Sergeant Bilko, the resident parrot, and served a full English breakfast.

It sounds perfect, doesn't it? But a cautionary word *is* in order. For those of you who do not like stairs, the ones here are quite steep and there are many to climb, especially if you have a room above the ground floor. The hall bathrooms are on alternating floors, so if you land in one of the three bathless rooms, you may have even more stairs to negotiate. However, for most of us, Debbie's enthusiastic welcome and hospitality, and the above-average rooms more than make up for the stairs or the extra walk to the showers.

Facilities and Services: Central heat, direct-dial phones, hair dryer available, mini-bar, office safe, TV, tea and coffeemakers, no lift

The Portobello Hotel
22 Stanley Gardens, W11

TELEPHONE
071-727-2777
FAX
071-792-9641
TUBE
Notting Hill Gate
CREDIT CARDS
AE, DC, MC, V
NUMBER OF ROOMS
25
W/BST
All
RATES
Single cabin £75, regular single £90; double £110–130; suite/apt £180; Continental or English breakfast included

Staying at the Portobello can be the next best thing to sampling life in the Upstairs-Downstairs era, but with twentieth-century plumbing. The owners of this sophisticated hotel did not miss a trick in adapting their hotel from two side-by-side town houses. The lovely collection of art, armoires, rich antiques, oriental rugs, and goose down duvets are only a few of the nice touches that carry you back to an era when graciousness and lovely surroundings mattered. If all of this plus rooms overlooking well-tended private gardens, four-poster beds, and impeccable service is your style, things don't get much better than the Portobello.

The entry and ground-floor sitting room are almost an English stage setting with lush fabrics on overstuffed furniture and masses of fresh flowers and green plants. It looks like an American idealization of what a London drawing room should be. The twenty-five individually decorated rooms are inviting with just a dash of whimsy and flamboyance. No. 42, a junior suite, has a marble bathtub with gold fittings separated from the bedroom by an ornate scrolled screen. The room has an oriental feel to it, created by bamboo wall covering and delicate furniture. No. 22, a two-room suite, has an inlaid desk, old-fashioned wash basin, and four large windows overlooking the gardens. For something unusual, book No. 16, a round room with a round bed, gauzy curtains, and a bathtub on claw feet. Top-floor rooms are referred to as "cabins" and that they are, miniscule havens with bathrooms to match. If you are at all claustrophobic, these are not for you.

Besides all the amenities you would expect to find in a fine hotel, there is a restaurant and bar reserved for hotel guests only; fax, copy, and courier service; theater bookings; and health club facilities within a four-minute walk including a swimming pool, sauna, steam room, massage, hairdresser, and Nautilus gym. For guests not wishing to eat at the hotel, preferential reservations are given at Julie's Restaurant, an upmarket and very popular establishment also owned by the hotel, only a few minutes away.

Facilities and Services: Bar, central heat, direct-dial phones, hair dryer, laundry service, lift to third floor only, office safe, restaurant and room service, cable TV, business services, theater bookings, health club privileges

Ravna Gora
29 Holland Park Avenue, W11

For a no-frills Cheap Sleep, the Ravna Gora is a smart address to remember. In its heyday, this palatial mansion set back from busy and noisy Holland Park Avenue must have been something. Standing in the rotunda and looking up at the sweeping staircase, I can just imagine the grand parties and balls that were staged here. Since 1956, it has been a B&B—for the last 15 years, managed by a hard-working Yugoslavian couple, Mr. and Mrs. Jovanovic. If you are at

TELEPHONE
071-727-7725
FAX
071-221-4282
TUBE
Holland Park
CREDIT CARDS
None
NUMBER OF ROOMS
21

W/BST
3
W/OBST
18
RATES
Single £28; double £44;
triple £53; four £66; English
breakfast included

all behind in your Yugoslavian history, a word or two with Mr. Jovanovic will bring you right up to date. Just ask him about one of the Yugoslavian freedom fighters whose pictures hang in the lounge, or about General Mihailovic, and he will do the rest. He is a virtual encyclopedia of his native country's history, especially the period dating from World War II.

The back-to-basics rooms are geared for students and the backpacking crowd. They are generally snag and tear-free and offer dependably clean beds for as many as six in a room. New hall showers were installed last year and most of the rooms repainted. Even though the hotel is off the beaten tourist track, the Holland Park tube stop is across the street, and if you are driving, plenty of free parking is available in a locked lot right by the hotel.

Facilities and Services: Central heat, public phones in hall, free parking, desk open from 7 A.M.–midnight, no messages after hours, no lift

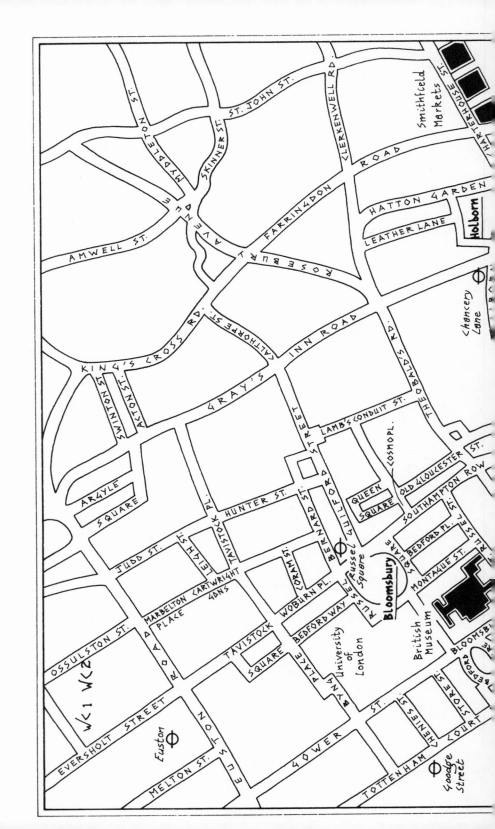

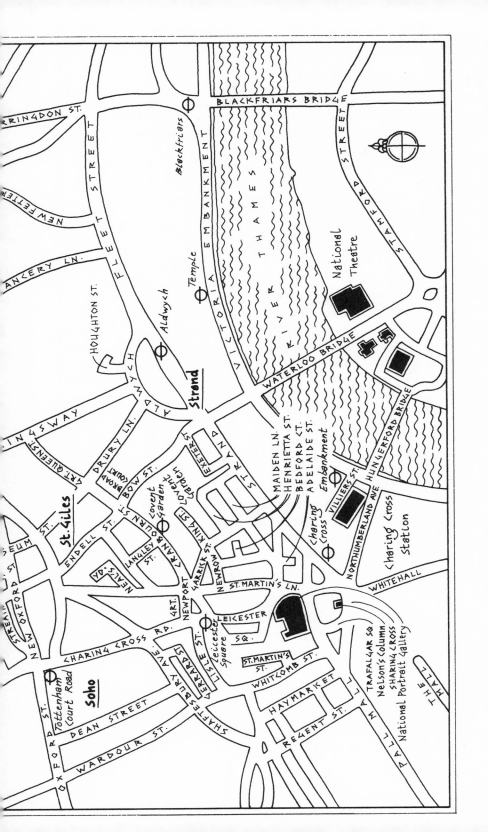

WC1 ✦ BLOOMSBURY

Bloomsbury is one of the most popular areas to stay in London, and for good reason. Transportation is excellent and it is within walking distance to West End theaters, Soho, shopping on Oxford and Regent streets, and many good restaurants (see *Cheap Eats in London*). Consisting of elegant leafy squares and parks surrounded by lovely Georgian town houses, Bloomsbury is the home of the British Museum, the University of London, and many well-known hospitals. In the early 1900s, it was the base of the Bloomsbury Group, an intellectual, liberal group whose members included Virginia Woolf, E. M. Forster, D. H. Lawrence, John Maynard Keynes, and others.

HOTELS

Academy Hotel	75
Arran House Hotel	76
Avalon Private Hotel	76
Bonnington	77
Cambria House	78
Celtic Hotel	78
Crescent Hotel	79
Elmwood Hotel	80
Forte Hotel Leisure Breaks	80
Harlingford Hotel	80
Imperial London Hotels Limited	
Bedford Hotel	82
Imperial Hotel	82
Royal National Hotel	83
Tavistock Hotel	83
Jenkins Hotel	84
Mabledon Court Hotel	84
Morgan Hotel	85
The Portland Bloomsbury	86
Ridgemount Private Hotel	87
Ruskin Hotel	88
Russell House Hotel	88
St. Margaret's Hotel	89
Thanet Hotel	90

OTHER OPTIONS

University Dormitory Accommodations
Canterbury Hall	182
Commonwealth Hall	182

Connaught Hall	182
Hughes Parry Hall	182
International Hall	182
London House for Overseas Graduates	183
University College, Campbell Hall	183
Ys	
Indian Student YMCA	185
YMCA Central Club	187

Academy Hotel
17–21 Gower Street, WC1

The hotel management and staff at the Academy Hotel provide the type of personal service so often lacking in today's small hotels. Whether it is securing a seat for a popular stage production in advance of your arrival, or reconfirming ongoing reservations, they are only too happy to be of service. Located on Gower Street, in the heart of London's publishing world and very close to the British Museum, the hotel was once a series of Georgian houses built in the late 1700s. The original colonnades, the intricate plaster on the facade, and the delicate glass paneling are still in place today, despite several major remodelings. Public areas feature attractive trompe l'oeil murals leading to the restaurant and pastel bird prints by Barbara A. Wood. The library, with a coal-burning fireplace, writing desk, and selection of good books, opens onto a walled garden where drinks, snacks, or dinner can be served. The rooms are softly decorated in beige with handsome dark furniture that offers a nice contrast. The hotel bar and restaurant have proven to be very successful with businesspeople who entertain clients, as well as with other guests who want a secluded place for a quiet cocktail or dinner. The Continental menu features two- and three-course lunches and dinners ranging from £13–18.

Facilities and Services: Air-conditioning in studios, bar, central heat, direct-dial phones, hair dryer in rooms, office safe, restaurant, room service, TV with Sky channels, tea and coffeemakers, 24-hour desk, no lift

TELEPHONE
071-631-4115; toll-free from the U.S. 1-800-678-3096

FAX
071-636-3442

TELEX
24364

TUBE
Goodge Street

CREDIT CARDS
AE, DC, MC, V

NUMBER OF ROOMS
33

W/BST
25

W/OBST
8

RATES
Single £77–85; double £95–100; suite/apt, studio £120–124; extra bed in room £20; ask for special American Friends rate; Continental breakfast £8 extra per person; English breakfast £10 extra per person

Arran House Hotel
77–79 Gower Street, WC1

TELEPHONE
071-636-2186
FAX
071-637-1140
TUBE
Goodge Street, Warren Street
CREDIT CARDS
MC, V
NUMBER OF ROOMS
28
W/BST
9
W/OBST
19
RATES
Single £28–35; double £40–52;
triple £52–70; four £62–80;
five £63; English breakfast
included

John and Brigitte Richards head an outgoing and friendly staff at this simple hotel in the central Bloomsbury area of London. Yes, the floors dip here and there, the top-floor rooms have mismatched curtains, hall carpets need redoing, and the private showers in the rooms resemble portable units found in campgrounds and parks. Once past these negatives, things *do* pick up. The hall facilities are clean, the lounge has been redone, and so have many of the rooms. There are also three other stellar features one seldom sees in a hotel of this type: a coin-operated laundry, a microwave oven with free use of the kitchen, and a rose garden with table and chairs and barbecue for guest use. If you are a World War II buff, you will be fascinated by the owner's extensive war memorabilia collection displayed in the breakfast room.

Facilities and Services: Central heat, phone downstairs, office safe, TV, tea and coffeemakers, coin-operated laundry, microwave and kitchen privileges, desk open 7:30 A.M.–11 P.M., no lift

Avalon Private Hotel
46–47 Cartwright Gardens, WC1

TELEPHONE
071-387-2366
FAX
071-387-5810
TUBE
King's Cross or Euston
CREDIT CARDS
MC, V
NUMBER OF ROOMS
28
W/BST
4
W/OBST
24
RATES
Single £36 (none with private
facilities); double £44–50;
triple £60–67; lower rates for
long stays; English breakfast
included

There are several hotels on Cartwright Gardens (see the Harlingford Hotel, page 80, and the Jenkins Hotel, page 84), forcing keen competition that keeps each one on its toes. The prices and easy-going management are the biggest draws at the Avalon. Discounts are offered for longer stays and the rates will be reduced if you eat your breakfast elsewhere. Rooms on the top floor are reached by some incredibly steep stairs. These rooms are lower in price, kept mainly for those on long stays or for students. If you have much laundry, there are drying lines next to the boiler room, and an iron and ironing board are available if your clothes have developed that slept-in look. Some of the halls have been redecorated, but the sagging lounge chairs and many of the rooms still need attention. The wildly mismatched decor of brown and beige carpets, fuschia-colored spreads that don't quite fit, orange drapes, and patterned wallpaper—all in the same room—may give some guests nightmares. On the other hand, dedicated Cheap Sleepers will find the big rooms spotless and owners Peter and Rosanna Taylor easy to get along with. As with all the hotels on Cartwright Gardens, a key is available if guests want to use the garden or play a set or two of tennis (small fee charged for the use of courts).

Facilities and Services: Central heat, public phones downstairs, hair dryer available, office safe, TV, tea and coffeemakers, no lift

Bonnington
92 Southampton Row, WC1

The Bonnington is a 215-room business hotel useful for Cheap Sleepers if they are able to take advantage of their "Getaway Weekend" bargain rates that include bed, breakfast, and dinner. These rates are good for a stay of one, two, or three nights on any Friday, Saturday, and Sunday. It is nice as well for those who want a choice location within two miles of almost forty of London's top attractions, ranging from Bond Street and the High Courts of Justice to Madame Tussaud's and Trafalgar Square. Excellent tube and bus connections are minutes away.

The well-kept, but basically boring, rooms are seeing gradual improvement. The newer ones are efficient and practical, with neatly designed bathrooms and better color schemes—if you like browns and pink chenille. Many of the doubles offer a small sitting area, a built-in wardrobe with shelf space and a full-length mirror. The large lounge is filled with comfortable seating and the corner bar offers a buffet lunch and early-evening meal handy for those racing to a 7:30 or 8 P.M. curtain. For more leisurely meals, there is a full-service restaurant.

Facilities and Services: Bar, central heat, direct-dial phones, hair dryer, laundry service, lift, office safe, restaurant, room service, TV, rooms for disabled, trouser press, tea and coffeemakers in rooms, conference room

TELEPHONE
071-242-2828
FAX
071-831-9170
TELEX
261591
TUBE
Russell Square
CREDIT CARDS
AE, DC, MC, V
NUMBER OF ROOMS
215
W/BST
All
RATES
Single £90; double £110–145; triple £150; four £175; suite/apt £190; children under 3, no charge; children from 3–14 sharing parents' room, £35. Getaway Weekends (includes breakfast & dinner): single £55; double £95–145; triple £127; four £155; suite £190; children 3–14, £25; English breakfast included

Cambria House
37 Hunter Street, WC1

TELEPHONE
071-837-1654

FAX
071-837-1229

TUBE
Russell Square

CREDIT CARDS
MC, V

NUMBER OF ROOMS
37

W/BST
3

W/OBST
34

RATES
Single £25 per night, £145 per week; double £31–45 per night, £230–291 per week; children under 3, £4 per night, £25 per week; children 3–14, £12 per night, £75 per week; English breakfast included

If you like the Vandon House (see page 114), you will *love* Cambria House. Both of these squeaky-clean sites are owned and operated by the Salvation Army. This means no smoking, no boozing, and no fooling around with management and/or the rules. Wait a minute, this is not a prison with impossible standards, but rather an extremely safe bet for those in the slow lane who want value for money in a pleasant Bloomsbury location. Most of the hotel was refurbished about two years ago, and the 37 rooms are uniformly simple in style with gray carpet, floral duvet covers, and light blue and mauve curtains. The hall facilities are old, but clean, so you can leave the Lysol spray in the suitcase for another time. Rooms can be booked for a maximum 28-day stay and must be paid for upon arrival. Special rates for children from 3–14 apply. For guests' convenience, there is a cafeteria serving breakfast, lunch, and dinner.

Facilities and Services: Central heat, public phone, no lift, office safe, restaurant, TV lounge, tea and coffeemaker, £5 key deposit for front door, desk open 7 A.M.–11 P.M.

Celtic Hotel
61–63 Guilford Street, WC1

TELEPHONE
071-837-9258, 071-837-6737

FAX
None

TUBE
Russell Square

CREDIT CARDS
None

NUMBER OF ROOMS
40

W/BST
None

RATES
Single £35; double £47; triple £65; four £75; five £90; English breakfast included

The success of the Celtic Hotel is not due to the exceptional look of the facade or to its interior decorating scheme, neither of which is particularly impressive. Its charm lies in the warmth of the welcome and friendly service offered by the Gerra family who, along with Arnie, their cocker spaniel, do their best to make staying here a pleasant experience. Their hospitality is duplicated by Mr. Gerra's sister and her family who run St. Margaret's Hotel (see page 89). Plans have been on the drawing board for some time to redo the Celtic and add some private bathrooms. But, since the building is listed, renovations require even more red tape and hassle than normal. Hopefully, by the time of your visit, progress will be made.

For now, the rooms are dated and without much dazzle, but they are always clean, and in an inexpensive hotel, a clean bed and friendly owner count for a great deal. There is some traffic and street noise and none of the rooms have private facilities, but for those who measure a stay by the small size of the final bill, the Celtic is a good Cheap Sleep in London.

Facilities and Services: Electric or gas heat in each room, phone on main floor, office safe, desk open 7 A.M.–1 A.M., no lift

Crescent Hotel
49–50 Cartwright Gardens, WC1

The Crescent Hotel occupies a quiet position directly on Cartwright Gardens, a private square owned by the City Guild of Skinners and looked after by the University of London, whose residence halls are across the street. Keys to the garden and the four tennis courts are available to hotel guests, and if you forgot your tennis racket and balls, they are available on loan.

What sets this family-owned hotel apart from dozens like it? Aside from the well-kept, nicely furnished rooms, the lovely sitting room with a fireplace, and the immaculate hall facilities, the key to success here is the warmth and genuine hospitality of Mrs. Bessolo and her daughter, Mrs. Cockle. Mrs. Cockle admits she was not formally trained in hotel management, but she did not need to be. She grew up in this hotel and inherited her mother's charm and graciousness. The word-of-mouth clientele has been returning for almost forty years, and are welcomed each time as family. As Mrs. Cockle said, "The hotel is an extension of our home and we treat our guests accordingly."

Note: If you are interested in small antiques that tuck into a suitcase, be sure to look carefully at the curio cabinet outside the dining room. Mrs. Cockle's young daughter scouts around and picks up little treasures and displays them here for sale. I found some wonderful pieces and I hope you will too. Prices are very, very reasonable.

TELEPHONE
071-387-1515

FAX
071-383-2054

TUBE
Russell Square, King's Cross

CREDIT CARDS
MC, V

NUMBER OF ROOMS
28

W/BST
7

W/OBST
21

RATES
Single £38 (none with private facilities); double £55–65; triple £70–80; four £80–90; English breakfast included

Facilities and Services: Central heat, public phones, hair dryer available, no lift, office safe, TV, tea and coffeemakers, iron available

Elmwood Hotel
19 Argyle Square, WC1

TELEPHONE
071-837-9361

FAX
None

TUBE
King's Cross

CREDIT CARDS
None

NUMBER OF ROOMS
12

W/BST
None

RATES
Single £22; double £30; triple £16 per person; English breakfast included

If you want to be within shouting distance of King's Cross or St. Pancras railroad stations, stay here. It is definitely miles ahead of the competition in this iffy hotel area. No two rooms look alike and goodness knows, nothing matches, but things are trim and tidy and provide what you need . . . a place to land at a terrific Cheap Sleeping price. Green plants, carefully tended by Mr. and Mrs. Ronchetti, the owners, add a pleasing touch throughout the hotel, especially in the downstairs dining room, which doubles as the owner's eating area when guests have finished their breakfasts. Each room has its own television, but you will have to share a bathroom with others in the hall.

Facilities and Services: Central heat, public phones, TV, no lift, no safe, 24-hour desk

Forte Hotel Leisure Breaks

See description of these money-saving hotel deals on page 37.

Forte Crest Bloomsbury
Coram Street, WC1
071-837-1200

Hotel Russell
Russell Square, WC1
071-837-6470

Harlingford Hotel
61–63 Cartwright Gardens, WC1

TELEPHONE
071-387-1551

FAX
071-387-4616

TUBE
King's Cross or Russell Square

The Harlingford Hotel is an attractive B&B on the Cartwright Gardens crescent in Bloomsbury. The caring management of the Davies family is reflected in the many repeat customers who value consistency, not only in the hotel and its upkeep, but in its reasonable rates for the area and the little added touches that make a difference. For instance, at Easter you will find Easter candies on your pillow, and at Christmas, little mince tarts. All rooms are generally light and pleasing, with floral-print wall coverings, small tiled baths, and double-glazed windows. The best ones are on the second and third floors facing front or on the top floor with views over the gardens. These perches on the top do require endless stairs because there is no lift. The rooms to avoid are those in the basement or on the ground floor with no security. The exception is No. 4, popular because it has a nice bathroom. Keys are available for the tennis courts in front of the hotel, and the small fee goes to the University of London, which maintains them.

Facilities and Services: Central heat, direct-dial phones, hair dryer available, office safe, TV, no lift, desk open for calls from 7 A.M.–midnight

CREDIT CARDS
MC, V

NUMBER OF ROOMS
43

W/BST
All

RATES
Single £48; double £60; triple £70; four £80; English breakfast included

Imperial London Hotels Limited

The Imperial London Hotels Limited is a group of six centrally located hotels with over 4,500 beds. For Cheap Sleepers in London, only the Bedford, Imperial, Royal National, and Tavistock are recommended. The other two, the President and the County, do not offer enough value. All these hotels deal mainly with tour groups and as a result are big, bustling, and impersonal. They offer loads of amenities, all have restaurants, and they are in Bloomsbury, which puts the visitor close to the British Museum, theaterland, and all the best tube and bus lines.

Lower rates are available on request for groups, and their weekend "Let's Go" packages are bargains well worth checking into. Rates for these packages are good from Friday through Sunday and include two nights in room with private bath and television; daily English breakfast and one lunch or dinner in any of the four hotel restaurants in the group; free parking space in underground garage; welcome cocktail in hotel bar on arrival; no supplement for single room; first child under 14 occupying cot or mini-bed in parents' room, no charge; other children in parents' room, half price.

Weekend "Let's Go" Package rates:
Bedford: £95 per person
Imperial: £100 per person
Royal National: £90 per person
Tavistock: £75 per person
Optional supplements: Sunday dinner, bed and breakfast, and parking when booked together with the two-night weekend: £42 per person.

Bedford Hotel
Southampton Row, WC1

TELEPHONE
Reservations 071-278-7871,
guests 071-636-7822

FAX
071-837-4653

TELEX
263951 Rusimp London

TUBE
Russell Square

CREDIT CARDS
AE, DC, MC, V

NUMBER OF ROOMS
180

W/BST
All

RATES
Single £60; double £73;
English breakfast included

The Bedford offers uniformly nonthreatening rooms with mahogany furniture, luggage racks, and good closet space especially in the twin-bedded rooms at the back with pretty views over the hotel garden and row houses beyond. The rooms are in soft blues, mauve, greens, and gray with built-in furniture and two chairs. Those on the busy street have double glazing to reduce traffic noise. In warm weather, tables are arranged in the back garden patio, which has a wading pool and a fountain.

Facilities and Services: Bar, central heat, direct-dial phones, lift, car park, office safe, restaurant, coffee shop, room service, satellite TV, radio, same-day laundry and cleaning service, conference room

Imperial Hotel
Russell Square, WC1

TELEPHONE
Reservations 071-278-7871,
071-837-3655

FAX
071-837-4653

TELEX
263951 Rusimp London

TUBE
Russell Square

CREDIT CARDS
AE, DC, MC, V

NUMBER OF ROOMS
450

W/BST
All

RATES
Single £65; double £77; triple
£90; English breakfast included

The Imperial has everything from a car park to a casino next door. The rooms from the fourth to the ninth floors have been redecorated and these are the ones you definitely want to request. The quietest rooms overlook the entry and fountain area. If you are here on a weekend (you must arrive on Friday and stay two nights) and participate in one of their packages, you will get free parking, a cocktail on arrival, and either lunch or dinner on Friday or Saturday.

Facilities and Services: Bar, central heat, direct-dial phones, satellite TV, radio, trouser press, tea and coffeemakers, lift, office safe, restaurant, room service, conference room, hair salon, bank, laundry and dry cleaning service, tours, theater tickets, florist

Royal National Hotel
Bedford Way, WC1

At the Royal National, the utilitarian rooms are clean and reasonably large, with only a few dings here and there. The refurbished rooms are, of course, better, but all face the other wing of this large complex and you will be viewing floor upon floor of windows clad in life-boat-orange-colored curtains. You will find everything you need, from an underground car park and a money changer (poor rates unless you're desperate), to a bar, gift shop, theater booking agency, and a coffee shop and restaurant that serve predictable English fare.

Note: The corridors are endless; be sure you learn the fire escape route from your room.

Facilities and Services: Bar, central heat, direct-dial phones, hair salon, car park, lift, money changer, office safe, several restaurants, room service, satellite TV, radio, VCRs, conference room, handicapped room w/wheelchairs available, tea and coffeemakers, same-day laundry and dry cleaning, trouser presses

TELEPHONE
Reservations 071-278-7871

FAX
071-837-4653

TELEX
263951 Rusimp London

TUBE
Russell Square

CREDIT CARDS
AE, DC, MC, V

NUMBER OF ROOMS
1,150

W/BST
All

RATES
Single £60; double £70; triple £83; English breakfast included

Tavistock Hotel
Tavistock Square, WC1

The Tavistock is impersonal, and with three hundred rooms catering to large tour groups, one could hardly expect more. Like all the others in this group, the rooms are bigger than average and every possible convenience is offered within the hotel, from a wine bar to laundry services. Best rooms are those that overlook the park.

Facilities and Services: Bar and wine bar, car park, central heat, direct-dial phones, lift, restaurant, room service, satellite TV, radio, office safe (50p per day), theater booking

TELEPHONE
Reservations 071-278-7871, guests 071-636-8383

FAX
071-837-4653

TELEX
263951 Rusimp London

TUBE
Russell Square

CREDIT CARDS
AE, DC, MC, V

NUMBER OF ROOMS
500

W/BST
All

RATES
Single £52; double £64; extra bed £15; baby cot £6; special weekend "Let's Go" rates; English breakfast included

Jenkins Hotel
45 Cartwright Gardens, WC1

TELEPHONE
071-387-2067
FAX
071-383-3139
TUBE
Euston
CREDIT CARDS
MC, V
NUMBER OF ROOMS
15
W/BST
6
W/OBST
9
RATES
Single £35; double £46–60;
triple £65–75; English
breakfast included

Cartwright Gardens is one of the most beautiful crescents of Georgian town houses in London. Owing to high property values and taxes, individual owners have been replaced by small B&Bs. The family-run Jenkins is one of the best. Guests return year after year, drawn by the tranquil location and the outgoing manner of the young owners, Felicity Langley-Hunt and Sam Bellingham. The home-like rooms are not fancy and some are small for storing shopping loot or bulky suitcases, but the basic comforts are here and the colors are feminine and frilly. When I visited the hotel I could not help admiring the delicately hand-embroidered silk flowers framed with a poem that are hung throughout the hotel. In the 1920s, these flowers came in cigarette packages, along with seeds, instructions on how to grow them, and a poem describing each variety. The owner found a large collection of these in a box belonging to his grandfather and had them framed for the hotel. They are a special touch that everyone seems to appreciate and enjoy.

There is no downstairs reception or sitting room, so you will be received in a large kitchen with a big table in the center. Guests gather each morning in the adorable blue-and-white breakfast room with lacy white table covers and fresh flowers on the tables. Keys to the gardens opposite the hotel are available for anyone who wants to use the private tennis courts or just to relax on a sightseeing or shopping break.

Facilities and Services: Central heat, direct-dial phones, hair dryer available, mini-bars, office safe, TV, tea and coffeemakers, no lift

Mabledon Court Hotel
10–11 Mabledon Place, WC1

TELEPHONE
071-388-3866
FAX
071-387-5686
TUBE
Euston or King's Cross

The Mabledon Court is an oasis in a real desert for nice hotels, just on the edge of Bloomsbury and close to Euston and King's Cross rail stations. The Davies family, who own the Harlingford Hotel (see page 80), purchased and redid this hotel about five years ago. They tossed out the terrible furnishings and dismal color schemes and put in good beds, comfortable seating, and private showers or baths. There are no twin-bedded rooms, but the simple and direct colors include beige walls, salmon spreads, and brown and beige mottled carpeting. A basement lounge with bright chintz floral love seats leads to a dining room with pink and beige marbleized wallpaper and plants along the windowsill. Breakfast is served on tiny tables with crisp paper table coverings. The Davies' professionalism and hospitality have made their new hotel very popular, especially with business travelers.

Facilities and Services: Central heat, direct-dial phones, hair dryers, office safe, tea and coffeemakers, lift

CREDIT CARDS
MC, V

NUMBER OF ROOMS
33

W/BST
All

RATES
Single £44; double £55; English breakfast included

Morgan Hotel
24 Bloomsbury Street, WC1

Once people find the Morgan Hotel, they *never* consider staying anyplace else in London. Reservations for this B&B jewel in Bloomsbury are absolutely vital as far in advance as possible, and a year ahead is not *too* soon to begin making your plans.

The Morgan and four adjacent apartments are owned by Joy Ward and her two brothers, John and David. For eighteen years they have worked very hard and spared no effort in creating a marvelous B&B where attention to every detail and consideration of guests' comfort is their number one priority. They are so dedicated to their high level of excellence, that they do all of the work in the hotel themselves, from greeting guests at the door to cleaning the rooms, and preparing a delicious English breakfast each morning.

David Ward is a carpenter and craftsperson par excellence and has done all the fine interior paneling and cabinetry. Everything is well planned, from the blooming flower boxes at the windows to the carefully maintained rooms with their deep red carpets and batik bedspreads. The dining room is comfortably fitted with booths and accented with green plants and fresh and dried flower arrangements. An impressive collection of blue-and-white willowware, toby

TELEPHONE
071-636-3735

FAX
None

TUBE
Tottenham Court Road

CREDIT CARDS
None

NUMBER OF ROOMS
14 rooms; 4 flats

W/BST
All

RATES
Single £42; double £65; triple £80; suite/apt £80 per night (minimum 2-night stay); English breakfast included if staying in the hotel

mugs, and early London photographs adds warmth and interest.

Everything in the four stunning apartments is done in the best of taste with beautiful polished furniture, decorator fabrics, and framed English prints lining the walls. All include a television and video, an eat-in kitchen with a view, a large en suite bathroom with a separate shower and bathtub, a security system, and daily maid service. For a stay of a few nights, a week, or a month or more, the Morgan Hotel and apartments receive my highest recommendation . . . and that of the many Cheap Sleepers who have made this their favorite London B&B address.

Facilities and Services: Air-conditioning in most rooms, central heat, direct-dial phones (coin-operated in flats), hair dryer, office safe, TV with cable in hotel, video in flats, no lift

The Portland Bloomsbury
7 Montague Street, WC1

TELEPHONE
071-323-1717
FAX
071-636-6498
TUBE
Russell Square, Tottenham Court Road
CREDIT CARDS
AE, DC, MC, V
NUMBER OF ROOMS
27
W/BST
All
RATES
Single £85; double £120–130; suite with garden access £220; additional person sharing room £30; weekend rates on request; Continental or English breakfast included

It is new, it is lovely, and it can be a Cheap Sleep if you time your stay to take advantage of the weekend rates. Service and attention to detail are the hallmarks of this appealing hotel with an attractive restaurant and private garden backing up to the British Museum. The staff's willingness to please is admirable. One afternoon while I was in the sitting room, a young family arrived with three tired and hungry children. The kitchen was closed, but the receptionist and porter put their heads together, and within minutes a tray appeared with hot chocolate, a plate of cookies, and a bowl of fresh fruit. It was not a hard thing to do, but it was very thoughtful and caring. The children were soon content, the parents relieved, and the hotel definitely gained points for service beyond the call of duty.

The richly appointed decor throughout is perfect English with silky wall coverings, floral and striped fabrics, antiques, and lovely paintings. The drawing room has comfortable settees, a marble fireplace, and vases of fresh and dry flowers. It is a delightful place to sip a cup of afternoon tea and catch up on the daily papers or current magazines provided for guests. New and old combine in the stylish bedrooms, and each floor is coordinated in pink, salmon, beige, or blue. Each room has period reproduction furniture and original paintings, a comfortable lounge chair, full mirrors, and out-of-sight luggage space. Little extras that count are boxes of chocolates and a bottle of Italian mineral water left daily. If you are hungry and don't feel like going out, you can call room service 24 hours a day, or eat in the garden side restaurant that serves contemporary Italian dishes. All in all, this is an upscale hotel that should appeal to those with more flexible budgets, but who still do not want to spend wantonly.

Facilities and Services: Bar, central heat, direct-dial phones, hair dryer, 1-day laundry, lift, office safe, restaurant, room service, cable TV, radio, porter

Ridgemount Private Hotel
65 Gower Street, WC1

The house was originally built by the Duke of Bedford, who still owns the land and most of the property around Russell Square and the British Museum. You can tell by the carved moldings and elaborate marble fireplace in the sitting room that this was once a very grand residence. Today it is a modern B&B conscientiously run by Mr. and Mrs. Rees.

A year or so ago they bought the hotel next door and doubled their capacity. Just as in the older rooms, these newly refurbished rooms are a mixed lot. All are absolutely spic and span, but some are very small, especially Nos. 3 and 5, which have the beds placed toe-to-toe to allow for walking space. While some have pleasing color schemes, notably Nos. 19 and 20, others have curious glow-in-the-dark pink bedspreads clashing with red carpet and floral wall coverings. On the plus side, the hall facilities are very good and for the price and good location and especially *sympa* owner, this Cheap Sleep is worth considering.

Facilities and Services: Central heat, public phone downstairs, office safe, hair dryers in renovated rooms, desk open 7:15 A.M.–11:30 P.M., no lift

$28

fax 171 636-2558

TELEPHONE
071-636-1141, 071-580-7060

FAX
None

TUBE
Goodge Street

CREDIT CARDS
None

NUMBER OF ROOMS
35

W/BST
4

W/OBST
31

RATES
Single £27; double £40; triple £54; English breakfast included

Ruskin Hotel
23–24 Montague Street, Russell Square, WC1

TELEPHONE
071-636-7388

FAX
071-323-1662

TUBE
Russell Square, Holborn, or
Tottenham Court Road

CREDIT CARDS
AE, DC, MC, V

NUMBER OF ROOMS
34

W/BST
7

W/OBST
27

RATES
Single £38; double £55–68;
triple £68–78; English
breakfast included

An enviable location next to the British Museum and clean rooms are offered by the Spanish family who have run the Ruskin Hotel for almost 18 years. Obviously, their efforts at modernization and careful maintenance have paid off, and the Ruskin enjoys one of the best reputations in a neighborhood full of B&Bs. The clean bedrooms do not all quite mix and match, but nothing is badly worn, and the front windows are double-glazed to help muffle the constant street noise. The rooms on the back are better because they overlook a lovely green private park. There is a lift to every floor and all major credit cards are accepted, two rarities in most small, family-operated B&Bs in London. The prices depend on the amount of private plumbing in your room. For Cheap Sleepers, there is absolutely no need to pay extra to get a cramped private bathroom when the ones on the hall are not only bigger and better, but save you significant money. The owner, Mr. Sedeno, has a green thumb and this is especially evident in the cheerful, mirrored dining room where he displays his many lush plants. When you are in the television lounge you will not be able to miss the beautiful oil painting right on the plaster above the mantle. It was done by James Ward, who painted animals for the Duke of Bedford, and depicts the area around Camden Town in the early 1800s.

Facilities and Services: Central heating, public phone in hall, hair dryers, lift to all floors, office safe, desk open from 7:30 A.M.–midnight

Russell House Hotel
11 Bernard Street, WC1

TELEPHONE
071-837-7686

FAX
None

TUBE
Russell Square

CREDIT CARDS
None

Although basic, the ten-room Russell House Hotel is a clean Bloomsbury Cheap Sleep. Owners Mr. and Mrs. Chiesa and their two sons live on site and oversee every detail. As a result, nothing gets past them, from a lazy maid forgetting to dust well to a guest with too much dripping laundry, or leftover picnic scraps lurking in room corners. Even though the rose-colored chenille spreads do not match the orange floral-print carpet, guests can bank on clean rooms with built-in wardrobes and private bathrooms stocked with facecloths, a good bar of soap, and plenty of towels. A Continental breakfast is served on traditional English china in a dining room flanked by two massive breakfronts displaying a collection of crystal and china.

Facilities and Services: Central heat, phone in the hall, TV, no lift, no safe, desk open from 7 A.M.– midnight for incoming calls

NUMBER OF ROOMS
10

W/BST
All

RATES
No singles; double £50; triple £65; four £75; Continental breakfast included

St. Margaret's Hotel
26 Bedford Place, WC1

For most of their many years at the St. Margaret's, the Marazzi family has served a quiet circle of regulars, the sort of people who would not return if they were not fully satisfied. The keynote of the hotel is friendly, personal service by a dedicated staff that has worked at the hotel for years. As Mrs. Marazzi told me, "My staff changes only when someone retires!"

The eclectically furnished, slightly outmoded rooms are fresh and bright. The views along the back overlook the Duke of Bedford's gardens and are truly magnificent in the spring and early summer when the trees and flowers are in full bloom. Even the tiniest single has a generosity of space and is clean enough to please the most demanding guest. Almost all of the rooms still have their original fireplaces, which in the early days the maids had to stoke several times a day in order to keep the guests warm. With the addition of central heat, stoking the fires is no longer one of the maids' responsibilities, and the fireplaces serve as decorative reminders of a long-lost era in hotel living. For a family, No. 53 is an unusual room with a glassed-in garden along the back and the bathroom just around the corner. No. 23 on the garden is a favorite because it is so light and has excellent closet and luggage space. No. 24, an L-shaped bathless single, is quiet and has enough room to fully unpack and stay for a week or more.

I think the dining room is one of the nicest in Bloomsbury. It is bright and airy with fresh flowers

TELEPHONE
071-636-4277, 071-580-2352

FAX
None

TUBE
Holborn or Russell Square

CREDIT CARDS
None

NUMBER OF ROOMS
64

W/BST
10

W/OBST
54

RATES
Single £40; double £51–60; £2 supplement for one-night stays; English breakfast included

and green plants. I like to sit in the back section by the window that overlooks the beautiful garden below. As you walk from the lounge to the dining room, be sure to take a minute to look at the original hand-painted glass featuring birds, flowers, and plants you might see in the neighborhood.

Facilities and Services: Central heat, direct-dial phones, cable TV, hair dryer available, office safe, tea and coffee served anytime, no lift

Thanet Hotel
8 Bedford Place, WC1

TELEPHONE
071-636-2869, 071-580-3377, 071-323-9053

FAX
071-323-6676

TUBE
Russell Square

CREDIT CARDS
MC, V

NUMBER OF ROOMS
12

W/BST
8

W/OBST
4

RATES
Single £40–50; double £55–65; triple £76; four £90; English breakfast included

Hotels around Russell Square are a dime a dozen. The key is to find one that is not only clean and fairly priced, but without the usual dime-store style of decorating that features clashing colors, patched carpets, shrunken bedspreads, and furnishings that can charitably be called "curbside." If you like Bloomsbury and want to be close to the British Museum, Covent Garden, and the theaters, the Thanet should be a top contender for your London stay. You will recognize the hotel by the bright-blue awning over the door and the colored-tile entry leading up two steps from the street. As you enter, look up to admire the original glass dome in the ceiling that sheds light on a winding staircase. A ground-floor dining room with seven tables and red-flocked wallpaper looks onto the street. There is no formal lounge, but the rooms are nice enough to encourage you to spend more than just minimum sleeping time in them. Be sure to ask for one of the newer rooms, done in subdued beige with yellow and green as accent colors. These all have a small bathroom with a stall shower and two shelves. Believe me, they are nice for the price. Number 7 is a narrow twin that probably wouldn't appeal to everyone, because the beds are placed end-to-end. It is basic, but absolutely okay for two friends traveling together.

Facilities and Services: Central heat, direct-dial phones, some hair dryers, no lift, office safe, TV and radio, tea and coffeemakers, desk open 7:15 A.M.– 11 P.M.

WC2 ✦ COVENT GARDEN, LEICESTER SQUARE, THE STRAND

Covent Garden used to be London's fruit and vegetable market, the place that the legendary Professor Henry Higgins met Eliza Doolittle. Now the market has been converted into a complex of shops, cafes, restaurants, and wine bars that draw crowds every day and night of the week. Street entertainers perform in the plaza, and the narrow streets fanning out from the Market are lined with interesting boutiques that can easily take up an afternoon of browsing. Covent Garden is where you will find some of London's most famous theaters, including Drury Lane. Many of the top restaurants here offer well-priced pre- and post-theater menus (see *Cheap Eats in London*).

Leicester Square, sandwiched between Piccadilly Circus and Charing Cross Road, is perpetually crowded with people standing and milling around, or attending one of the first-run cinemas. Chinatown is close and so are West End stage theaters along Shaftesbury Avenue.

The Strand is a rich assortment of former noblemen's homes occupying the area between The Strand and the River Thames. It is the principal route between the West End and The City.

HOTELS

The Fielding Hotel	91
Forte Hotel Leisure Breaks	92
Manzi's Hotel	92
The Pastoria	93
Royal Adelphi Hotel	94
Royal Trafalgar Thistle Hotel	94

The Fielding Hotel
4 Broad Court, Bow Street, WC2

The building seems to have been here since time began. Some visitors love this hotel, calling it "quaint" and "historical." Others find it dreadfully cramped and lacking in modern amenities. Frankly, I am somewhere in-between, feeling the location and pleasant management save the day.

The hotel is in a small, paved pedestrian walkway next to Bow Street Magistrates Court, site of the world's first police station, and almost opposite the Royal Opera House in Covent Garden. Diamond-paned windows and flower-filled window boxes frame

TELEPHONE
071-836-8305

FAX
071-497-0064

TUBE
Covent Garden

CREDIT CARDS
AE, DC, MC, V

NUMBER OF ROOMS
26

W/BST
24

W/OBST
2

RATES
Single £45–75; double £75–100; triple £110; four £125–130; suite/apt £125; ask for off-season rates; Continental breakfast £3; English breakfast £5

the entrance. Once inside the small reception area you will be met by Smokey, the parrot, who holds court in a tiny adjacent bar.

The rooms are far from spacious, but they do have a certain old-world air that makes them appealing to many. En suite bathrooms are very small, and more than a few rooms have gloomy vistas. Floors can be uneven and some carpeting has seen better days, but for those wanting to be only a heartbeat away from theaters, Soho, Piccadilly Circus, and West End shopping, The Fielding is a popular destination.

Facilities and Services: Bar, central heat, direct-dial phones, hair dryer available, no lift, office safe, TV, radio, 24-hour desk

Forte Hotel Leisure Breaks

See description of these money-saving hotel deals on page 37.

The Strand Palace
372 The Strand, WC2
071-836-8080

The Waldorf
Aldwych, WC2
071-836-2400

Manzi's Hotel
1–2 Leicester Square, WC2

TELEPHONE
071-734-0024, 734-0025

FAX
071-437-4864

TUBE
Leicester Square

CREDIT CARDS
AE, DC, MC, V

NUMBER OF ROOMS
16

W/BST
All

RATES
Single £40–47; double £63; triple £70; four £80; Continental breakfast included

Why in the world would I continue to list a hotel that is noisy 24 hours a day, offers nondescript rooms, and employs a staff in need of charm school? Because, despite these shortcomings, the hotel has several things going for it. For night owls and those who love being in the midst of things, Manzi's is right off Leicester Square only a few minutes from the West End theaters, several large cinema complexes, Piccadilly Circus, Soho night spots, Covent Garden, and all of Chinatown. The hotel is on the second floor over an expensive, well-known Italian fish restaurant. Entering at the ground level, you will meet a non-smiling receptionist who doubles as the hatcheck girl and greeter for the restaurant when she is not handing out keys or settling accounts. The rooms vary in size and style, from big doubles with generous wardrobes to basic, small singles. Everything is clean enough, and the bathrooms have been modernized. A Continental breakfast is served in the Cabin Room, outfitted with brass portholes, ship's steering wheel, lights, and a life raft.

Facilities and Services: Bar, central heat, public phone in hall, lift from second floor up, TV, radio, tea and coffeemakers, office safe

The Pastoria
326 St. Martin's Street, Leicester Square, WC2

Tucked away in a traffic-free side street off Leicester Square is The Pastoria. For those with flexible budgets and more demanding needs who want a key location in the center of the West End, this hotel has a lot to offer. For starters, Piccadilly Circus, Regent Street, Covent Garden, Parliament Square, and Buckingham Palace are all within walking distance; and with Leicester and Trafalgar Squares on the hotel's doorstep, many of London's top theaters and cinemas are only minutes away. If you fly a major airline to London, you may be eligible to receive significantly lower rates, but you must contact the hotel by phone or fax to secure them. The toll-free number for Utell International in the U.S. does not have these discounted prices. The hotel also offers year-long weekend discounted rates, and these are available through the U.S. booking number.

The hotel originally began as a gentleman's private club and restaurant, and it was not converted into a hotel until 1931. All but the sixth floor has been refurbished to reflect the style and feel of the early thirties. Unsolvable plumbing and electrical problems keep sixth-floor rooms considerably less attractive than the rest of the hotel, so these old, viewless rooms should be avoided. Flicks, the hotel's brasserie restaurant, celebrates Hollywood's golden era and pays homage to the stars of that time by displaying their photos and naming most of its dishes after them. The hotel also has two air-conditioned

TELEPHONE
071-930-8641; toll-free in U.S. and Canada 1-800-424-2862

FAX
071-925-0551;
U.S. 301-563-6323

TELEX
25538; U.S.: 401101

TUBE
Leicester Square

CREDIT CARDS
AE, DC, MC, V

NUMBER OF ROOMS
58

W/BST
All

RATES
Single £110; double £120. Weekend rates: single £90; double £110; Continental breakfast £5; English breakfast £9

MISCELLANEOUS
The hotel is closed December 25 and 26. The restaurant (lunch and dinner) is closed Sundays and holidays.

and sound-proofed conference rooms and a full range of secretarial services for business guests.

Facilities and Services: Air-conditioned conference rooms, bar, central heat, direct-dial phones, hair dryers, lift, office safe, restaurant and room service, satellite TV, clock radio, porter and concierge

Royal Adelphi Hotel
21 Villiers Street, WC2

TELEPHONE
071-930-8764
FAX
071-930-8735
TUBE
Embankment, Charing Cross
CREDIT CARDS
AE, DC, MC, V
NUMBER OF ROOMS
49
W/BST
35
W/OBST
14
RATES
Single £35; double £52–66;
Continental breakfast included;
English breakfast £5 extra

Located up steep stairs over an Italian restaurant and next to a Dunkin' Donuts shop, the Royal Adelphi is no "ooh la la" hotel, but a good mid-city choice within walking distance to more than the average visitor will ever be able to see and absorb. The 55-room hotel is an old one that has been modernized with room colors and furnishings circa 1960. Dated baths are clean, and do have heated towel racks, guaranteed to dry a light overnight hand laundry. The higher floors have the best views. Hopefully, the smoking policy in the breakfast room will be rescinded soon . . . otherwise it gets very hot, stuffy, and unpleasant for those of us who do not light up the minute we finish breakfast. The Embankment tube station is at the end of the short street, and Charing Cross station is at the top. Also at the end of the street is the charming Victoria Embankment Garden, full of beautiful spring color when the tulips, daffodils, and crocuses are in bloom.

Facilities and Services: Bar, electric room heat, direct-dial phones, hair dryer, TV and radio, office safe, tea and coffeemakers in rooms, no lift

Royal Trafalgar Thistle Hotel
Whitcomb Street, WC2

TELEPHONE
071-930-4477
FAX
071-925-2149
TELEX
298564
TUBE
Piccadilly, Leicester Square

While the rack rates are high and would discourage most, the weekend deals, holiday packages, half-price children's accommodations, and freebies make this hotel a good bet in the heart of London. A stay here guarantees guests no unpleasant surprises in terms of service or facilities. This predictable hotel is located in a small street behind the National Gallery, between Trafalgar Square and Leicester Square. The conventional rooms are done in pastels with mahogany furniture. If you are a nonsmoker, request something on the fourth floor. You can eat lunch or dinner at Hamilton's Brasserie, featuring Parisian bistro fare, or pop into the Battle of Trafalgar pub for a pint of real ale and a quick snack. The hotel's special weekend breaks are good value, especially in the winter period from November 1 to April 29. Up to two children under 16 who share their parents' room are free. Half-price food portions from adult menus are available to children, or they can pick something from the children's menu.

Facilities and Services: Two bars, central heat, direct-dial phones, hair dryer, 1-day laundry service, lift, office safe, restaurant, pub, 24-hour room service, TV, video, radio, trouser press, tea and coffeemaker, porter, concierge, 24-hour desk

CREDIT CARDS
AE, DC, MC, V

NUMBER OF ROOMS
108

W/BST
All

RATES
Single £99–110; double £115–125. Special weekend break rates include 2 or 3 nights accommodation including Saturday and full English breakfast; rates are per adult in shared room: 2 nights winter £100, summer £120; 3 nights winter £145, summer £170; special holiday rates available directly from the hotel; Continental breakfast £6.90 extra; English breakfast £10 extra

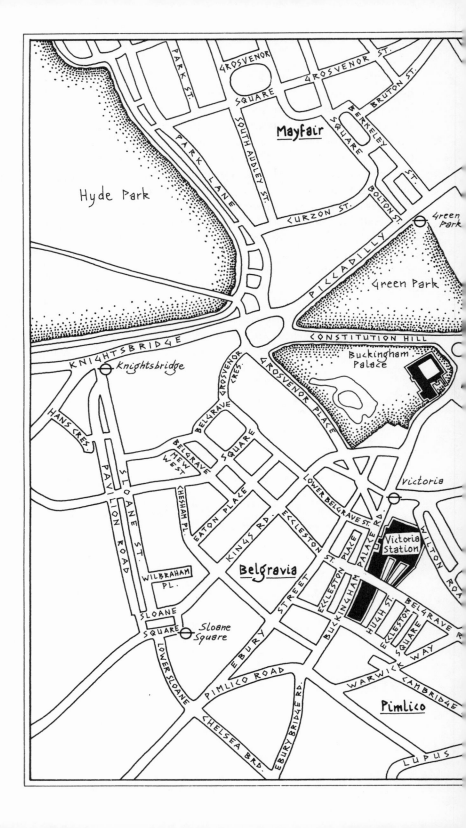

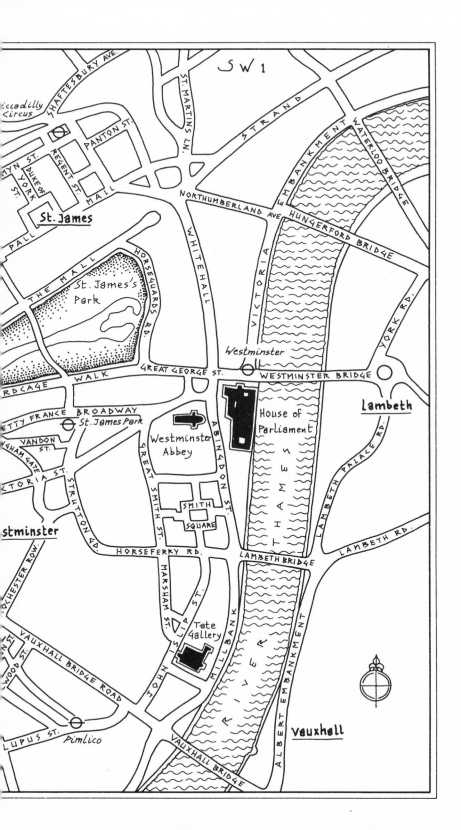

SW1 ✤ BELGRAVIA, KNIGHTSBRIDGE, PIMLICO, VICTORIA, WESTMINSTER, AND WHITEHALL

Belgravia is reported to have the most expensive real estate in London, especially around Eaton Square, where one or two million pounds for a fixer-upper is considered a bargain. Ebury Street, one of London's best B&B hotel streets, in on the edge of Eaton Square. There are some good restaurants and charming small pubs in this area (see *Cheap Eats in London*).

Knightsbridge is another top-drawer address where residents can shop at Harrods, gaze longingly at the designer salons on Sloane Street, and browse through the tempting boutiques along Beauchamp Place.

Pimlico is an area of large terraced town homes. It has a small neighborhood feel to it, probably because it does not have any tourist sites drawing scores of visitors.

Victoria hasn't much to recommend it, other than the massive Victoria Station through which every visitor to London probably passes at least once. Restaurants in this part are geared mainly toward the hungry one-time tourist, so you know they are basically terrible.

Westminster and Whitehall are devoted to running the country. In Westminster you will set your watch according to Big Ben and visit the Houses of Parliament and Westminster Abbey, the burial site of many historical figures.

One of the most famous addresses in the world is here: No. 10 Downing Street, home of the British prime minister. Trafalgar Square, the official center of London, from which all distances to and from London are measured, is ringed by the National Gallery and the National Portrait Gallery. Other must-sees include the beautiful Tate Gallery with its Turner collection, and the Cabinet War Rooms used by Winston Churchill and his cabinet and generals during World War II.

HOTELS

Accommodation Express	99
Collin House	101
Diplomat Hotel	101
Eaton House Hotel	102
Ebury House	102
Elizabeth Hotel & Apartments	103
Enrico Hotel	104
Forte Hotel Leisure Breaks	105
Hamilton House Hotel	105
Harcourt House	106
The James Cartref House	106

Luna & Simone Hotel	108
Melbourne House	108
Oak House Hotel	109
Oxford House Hotel	110
Pyms Hotel	110
Richmond House Hotel	111
Searcy's Roof Garden Bedrooms	111
Tophams Ebury Court	112
Vandon House	114
The Victoria Inn	114
Westminster House Hotel	115
Wilbraham Hotel	116
Winchester Hotel	116
Windermere Hotel	117

OTHER OPTIONS

Renting a Flat

Dolphin Square	163
E & E Apartments	164
The Kensbridge Hotel Group—Flat Rentals	167

University Dormitory Accommodations

Wellington Hall	183

Ys

Elizabeth House	184

Accommodation Express (Palace Hotel, Westbourne International Residence, Sky Star Hotel, Chelsea Hotel)
General offices: 199 Buckingham Palace Road, SW1

If you leave your expectations at the door and do not expect to be pampered, have much privacy, or look for perfection, one of these four hotels offered by Accommodation Express will suit the budget and backpacking set hellbent on a Cheap Sleep in London. The hotels are run by a young, friendly staff, complete with security bouncers to take care of sneaky guests who think they can visit a friend and not pay for an overnight stay. Other than towels and soap, you do get something for your money. The no-

TELEPHONE
071-233-8139

FAX
071-244-6891

TUBE
Victoria

CREDIT CARDS
None

NUMBER OF ROOMS
600 altogether

W/BST
300

smoking dorm rooms (both coed and segregated) all have their own bathrooms and include a Continental breakfast served anytime. To keep your social life active, there is a juke box, pool table, cable TV and video lounge, and scheduled "party nights." In some locations, there is a restaurant serving Cheap Eats along the lines of sandwiches, hot dogs, salads, and daily specials. Check-out time is 10 A.M. sharp, or you stand to lose your £5 deposit.

Facilities and Services: Varies with location, but you can always expect public telephones, lift, safe (50p each day), restaurant, cable TV and video in lounge, social activities, 24-hour desk

Palace Hotel
31 Palace Court Road, W2
Tel: 071-221-5628
Tube: Notting Hill Gate
Dorms only, restaurant, luggage storing

Westbourne International Residence
104 Westbourne Terrace, W2
Tel: 071-402-0431
Tube: Paddington
Dorms only, kitchen facilities, laundry, games room, luggage storing

Sky Star Hotel (least desirable)
22 Collingham Place, SW5
Tel: 071-370-4398
Tube: Earl's Court
Rooms with private facilities, free tea and coffee, video games

Chelsea Hotel
33–41 Earl's Court Square, SW5
Tel: 071-244-7395
Tube: Earl's Court
Dorms and rooms, restaurant

Collin House
104 Ebury Street, SW1

Ebury Street is a busy thoroughfare close to Victoria Station, lined with countless small B&Bs. Welshman Dafydd Thomas and his wife run this straightforward B&B with redecorated spare rooms that offer the necessities required for a basic stay. While others on the street may be cheaper or have more flowers and frills, the Collin House is known for its cleanliness and hospitality. Mr. Thomas is a photographer of note, and stunning photos of his southwestern homeland in Wales hang throughout the hotel. The number of repeat guests makes reservations at least two months in advance a must, especially in the busy summer season.

Facilities and Services: Central heat in some, electric in others, public phone, hair dryer available, no lift, office safe

TELEPHONE
071-730-8031

FAX
None

TUBE
Victoria

CREDIT CARDS
None

NUMBER OF ROOMS
13

W/BST
8

W/OBST
5

RATES
Single £35–40; double £52–60; triple £68–72; four £72; English breakfast included

MISCELLANEOUS
Hotel closed for 2 weeks from Christmas through New Year's Day.

Diplomat Hotel
2 Chesham Street, SW1

Elegance and privacy in one of London's most exclusive and fashionable residential neighborhoods are yours at the Diplomat Hotel. Number 2 Chesham Street is a magnificent corner dwelling built by Thomas Cubbit in 1822, listed as a building of architectural distinction by Her Majesty's Government. The hotel is within a pleasant walk to boutique-lined Beauchamp Place, Harrods (see Shopping, page 196), and many good restaurants (see *Cheap Eats in London*).

A glass-domed stairwell housing a gilded circular staircase leads to the well-appointed rooms and tiled baths. Even though it is partially below street level, the Cromwell is one of the most sought-after rooms with its separate dressing room lined with closets. I like the Cadogan, a large double with floor-to-ceiling windows, a separate sitting room, and a wall of built-ins. Another favorite is the Belgravia, a high-ceilinged suite with a double bed, electric log fireplace, and bay windows overlooking the street. The huge bath has a

TELEPHONE
071-235-1544

FAX
071-259-6153

TELEX
926679 Diplmt G

TUBE
Knightsbridge

CREDIT CARDS
AE, DC, MC, V

NUMBER OF ROOMS
27

W/BST
All

RATES
Single £73-95; double £110–120; executive double or twin £130–150; lower rates if staying more than 3 nights; buffet English breakfast included

shower and tub, heated towel racks, and good lighting over a mirrored marble sink. A generous buffet breakfast is enjoyed by guests in a room with black furniture accenting soft yellow tablecloths and gray carpeting. Three double doors open onto a tiny patio, and a stack of daily newspapers is available for guests to peruse over a second cup of tea or coffee.

Facilities and Services: Central heat, direct-dial phones, hair dryer, lift to 3rd floor, office safe, TV with video, radio, tea and coffeemakers, irons available, trouser presses

Eaton House Hotel
125 Ebury Street, SW1

TELEPHONE
071-730-8781, 071-730-6535
(guests)
FAX
071-730-3267
TUBE
Victoria
CREDIT CARDS
AE, MC, V
NUMBER OF ROOMS
11
W/BST
None
RATES
Single £30; double £42; triple £54; extra bed no charge, except cost of linens; English breakfast included

If you stay in an Ebury Street B&B, chances are you will encounter noise or some uninspiring views in the quieter rooms along the back. Some visitors overlook these minuses in favor of a genuinely friendly owner of a small and tidy B&B who treats her guests like family. A stay at Eaton House means just that. Owner Josephine Belgrano has been treating her devoted guests like long-lost relatives for almost a quarter of a century. All of her well-used rooms are painted white and kept clean, and the hall toilet and bath facilities on alternate floors are more than satisfactory. Each room has its own tea and coffeemaker and color television in case you want to brew a cup of tea and catch up on your British telly programming, which includes "I Love Lucy" reruns. Breakfast is served piping hot each morning in a plain room where guests share tables and swap shopping and restaurant tips and discoveries.

Facilities and Services: Central heat, public phones in hall, TV, tea and coffeemakers, no lift or safe

Ebury House
102 Ebury Street, SW1

TELEPHONE
071-730-1350, 071-730-1059
FAX
071-730-1350

The friendly owner of Ebury House, David Davies, runs his B&B with a great sense of wit, wisdom, and goodwill. More hoteliers should subscribe to his philosophy of running a successful hotel:

"This year's guest is next year's business." Many Canadians, Australians, and Americans consider Ebury House their home in London. It is obvious Mr. Davies really enjoys his guests when you see him joking with them at breakfast or offering helpful tips and sound practical advice about visiting London. He is also an avid golfer and rugby player, so if these are your sports, you will have something in common. Who knows, maybe you can play a round or two of golf with him.

Now that you know how you will be treated by your jovial host, what about the rooms? Not to worry. For a B&B in central London, they are just fine. All rooms and hall bathrooms are in good condition and clean. Every bedroom is decorated with nice wallpaper coordinating with the duvet cover and curtains. It is not surprising that reservations are always at a premium, so if you are interested, get yours in very early.

Facilities and Services: Electric room heating, public phones in hall, hair dryer, office safe, TV, no lift, desk open 6:30 A.M.–10:30 P.M.

TUBE
Victoria

CREDIT CARDS
None

NUMBER OF ROOMS
12

W/BST
None

RATES
Single £40–45; double £50–55; triple £66; English breakfast included

Elizabeth Hotel & Apartments
37 Eccleston Square, SW1

This hotel has a prime location on the west side of Eccleston Square, one of London's finest gardens, with over 5,000 blooming flowers and shrubs. Hotel guests are entitled to use the gardens and tennis courts.

Thomas Cubbit, Queen Victoria's favorite builder, who constructed the east front of Buckingham Palace, was the creator of Eccleston Square. The fine neoclassical society houses surrounding the gardens provided elegant homes for the aristocracy and wealthy professional classes in the mid-nineteenth century. As you can imagine, the square has had some famous residents. Prince Louis of Battenberg, father of Lord Louis Mountbatten who was Prince Phillip's uncle and the Viceroy of India, lived at this address. From 1909 to 1913, Winston Churchill occupied No. 34 a few doors away.

TELEPHONE
071-828-6812

FAX
None

TUBE
Victoria

CREDIT CARDS
None

NUMBER OF ROOMS
40

W/BST
24

W/OBST
16

RATES
Single £36–55; double £58–80; triple £75–80; four £80–100; five £110; English breakfast included; Continental included for early departures; three-month stay required for apartments, rates upon request

Owner Julian Maslinski has made some needed improvements to the hotel. Besides installing a lift, he has added several apartments and redone many of the rooms. Despite redecoration attempts, the rooms would never qualify as glamorous. With some exceptions, they are clean and serviceable, with an interesting piece of furniture in most and a fine vintage English print in every one. No. 32 is a new ground-floor triple, and No. 30 is a small double or single with a nice bath. Unless it has been completely revamped, avoid No. 3 with its exhausted furniture, creaking floors, and bed in a curtained alcove.

If you are a print collector or merely appreciate them, you are in for a rare treat if you stay here. Over the years, Mr. Maslinski has amassed an extensive collection of thousands of English prints, which he has hung throughout his hotel. He is extremely knowledgeable about them all and only too happy to spend time discussing them with any guests who are genuinely interested.

Facilities and Services: Central heat, public phones, lift to 4 floors, no safe, some mini-bars, TV in most rooms, desk open 8 A.M.–midnight, apartments fully furnished and equipped

Enrico Hotel
77–79 Warwick Way, SW1

TELEPHONE
071-834-9538,
071-834-4177 (guests)

FAX
071-233-9995

TUBE
Victoria

CREDIT CARDS
None

NUMBER OF ROOMS
26

W/BST
8 with showers only

W/OBST
16 without showers; all rooms without toilets

There are several hotels on Warwick Way, but the Enrico is one of the best Cheap Sleeps of all. I like it because the prices are low while the standards are high. From the washed steps leading into the red-and-gold-carpeted entry hall, and the television room ringed with red and green leatherette chairs, the hotel offers fundamental rooms with a minimum of jarring bad taste. The rooms without private facilities (i.e., a portable shower) are best. Unless you like showering in a metal phone booth with no air, these rooms with showers are not worth the extra investment. At these prices, you can't expect exotic floral displays and designer chintz on wingback chairs. What you get instead is a reliable Cheap Sleep in a neighborhood in which good ones are in very short supply. If you stay at least two or three nights, lower rates apply.

Facilities and Services: Central heat, public phone downstairs, office safe, no lift

RATES
Single £25–30; double £32–35; English breakfast included

Forte Hotel Leisure Breaks

See description of these money-saving hotel deals on page 37.

Forte Crest St. James's
81 Jermyn Street, SW1
071-930-2111

Hyde Park Hotel
66 Knightsbridge, SW1
071-235-2000

Hamilton House Hotel
60 Warwick Way, SW1

When I first saw Hamilton House a few years ago, I thought, "Oh no, how boring." True, it was at first glance, but things began to get better once I was inside. Actually, the longer I was in the hotel, the better I liked it, despite its rather worn appearance. Now, after a 1991 redecoration, I am happy to report that the unevenness is gone and the rooms have improved in overall appearance, even though they are done in staid hotel fashion. Most have no views to speak of and those on the front are noisy. I think the back side of the third floor has the best rooms in the house because they are quiet. When reserving, ask for a room with a tiled bath, not one with an airless portable metal unit placed in a corner of the room. Solo travelers who do not want to venture out alone at night and tired businesspeople on a budget will appreciate the hotel restaurant's English food at reasonable prices. Room service is also available, an advantage if you are traveling with children.

Facilities and Services: Bar, central heat, direct-dial phones, hair dryer, restaurant for breakfast and dinner Mon–Sat, cable TV, radio, office safe, tea and coffeemakers, no lift

TELEPHONE
071-821-7113

FAX
071-630-0806

TUBE
Victoria

CREDIT CARDS
MC, V

NUMBER OF ROOMS
40

W/BST
25

W/OBST
15

RATES
Single £40–60; double £50–70; triple £70–85; English breakfast included

Harcourt House
50 Ebury Street, SW1

TELEPHONE
071-730-2722
FAX
071-730-3998
TUBE
Victoria
CREDIT CARDS
AE
NUMBER OF ROOMS
9
W/BST
6
W/OBST
3
RATES
Single £42–50; double £50–60; triple £68; four £78; English breakfast included
MISCELLANEOUS
The hotel is closed for 10 days between Christmas and New Year's.

In 1890 it was a gentleman's club. During World War II, an American spy used this house as his London base. Now the glamour and intrigue have been replaced by a family-run B&B competing with all the others on Ebury Street. The owners, David and Glesni Wood, confidently state in writing that "everything possible will be carried out to make your London stay a comfortable one." Judging from their contented guests, they are succeeding.

A calorie-charged breakfast is served in a breakfast room with a collection of plates, ceramics, and miniatures nicely displayed. Upstairs, most of the rooms are uniform in color. The best advice is to opt for a room without a private bath or toilet. You will save money and gain room space in the bargain. Most of the rooms with private facilities offer the toilet and shower in added units that have zero ventilation and redefine *tiny*. If you are athletic, climb the long, steep stairs to the top floor and occupy No. 9, a double or triple (the small sofa makes into a bed) with pink walls and matching comforter covers. It has its own bathroom and if the chair coverings matched and the brown carpet were changed, it would be perfect. The prices overall may be a bit higher than some others on the street, but the nice welcome and earnest service offered by the Woods merit the extra pounds.

Facilities and Services: Radiator electric heating, public phone in hall, hair dryer, office safe, TV, desk open 7 A.M.–10 P.M., no lift

The James Cartref House

The James House and Cartref House across the street merged in 1992. For years, Tom and Iris James had the popular Cartref House and their son, Derek, and his wife, Sharon, ran the James across the street. When the senior Jameses retired, the running of the two hotels was taken over by Derek and Sharon. It would be hard to imagine a better London B&B than the newly merged James Cartref House, which ranks high on my list of top budget B&Bs in London.

These small hotels reflect the family's sense of dedication to the needs of their guests, who receive the kind of attention seldom seen in this busy world. They take tremendous pride in keeping everything in tip-top condition by repainting, refinishing, and redecorating whenever necessary so nothing fails from neglect or wear and tear. Each room is different, and although they are individual in scope and size, they are designed to give guests a sense of cozy comfort. Budget-wise families will appreciate the low rates, large rooms (some with bunk beds), and close proximity to the Victoria train, bus, and tube stations. Everyone is always made to feel right at home by the energetic young hosts, who live at James House with their three children. The large English breakfast is served here in their own dining room, which has family photos on the mantle, an odd toy or doll under a chair, and a computer in one corner. At the Cartref House, the breakfast room was redone last year. It has a lovely collection of plates and more family photos on display. After a stay with the James family, you will be like many Cheap Sleepers who now count themselves in the widening circle of extended family who return each time they are in London.

James House
108 Ebury Street, SW1

TELEPHONE: 071-730-7338
FAX: 071-730-7338
TUBE: Victoria
CREDIT CARDS: MC, V
NUMBER OF ROOMS: 11
W/BST: 2
W/OBST: 9

RATES: Single £37; double £50–60; triple £60–70; four £70–80; five £80–90; lower off-season rates from November to Easter; English breakfast included

FACILITIES AND SERVICES: Central heat on first floors, electric on the rest, public phone in hall, TV, tea and coffeemakers, no lift or safe

Cartref House
129 Ebury Street, SW1

TELEPHONE: 071-730-6176
FAX: 071-730-7338
TUBE: Victoria
CREDIT CARDS: MC, V
NUMBER OF ROOMS: 10
W/BST: 7
W/OBST: 3
RATES: Single £37; double £50–60; triple £60–70; four £70–80; five £80–90; lower off-season rates from November to Easter; English breakfast included
FACILITIES AND SERVICES: Central heat, public phones in hall, hair dryer in some rooms and one available at the desk, irons available, no lift or safe, TV, tea and coffeemakers, desk open from 7 A.M.–10:30 P.M.

Luna & Simone Hotel
47–49 Belgrave Road, SW1

TELEPHONE
071-834-5897, 071-828-2474
FAX
None
TUBE
Pimlico or Victoria
CREDIT CARDS
None
NUMBER OF ROOMS
36
W/BST
15
W/OBST
21
RATES
Single £20–28; double £28–45; triple £33–51; English breakfast included

Belgrave Road is loaded with grubby little B&Bs catering to determined budget-tied travelers of all nationalities. One of the better bets on the street is the Luna & Simone. When you see the prices, you will know your room will not make the lead story on "Life Styles of the Rich and Famous." The beds are hard, the noise from the street will drive insomniacs crazy, and the rooms on the back have uninspiring views. But—and this is important—this friendly family-run hotel has a minimum of scrapes and scratches and will provide a clean bed and a substantial cooked English breakfast to hard-core Cheap Sleepers with strict monetary constraints.

Facilities and Services: Central heat, hair dryer available, TV, desk open 7 A.M.–midnight, no lift

Melbourne House
79 Belgrave Road, SW1

TELEPHONE
071-828-3516
FAX
071-828-7120
TUBE
Pimlico or Victoria

When you look up and down Belgrave Road, all you see are signs for the numerous B&B accommodations that line both sides. These rooms range from cheap and cheerful to down-and-out-dirty and totally out-of-the-question. Melbourne House falls into the cheap and cheerful category, thanks to the enthusiastic young owners, John and Manuela Desira, and their eight-month renovation effort. All rooms are the same with bright, hot pink chenille spreads the only color notes in the notably clean, white-washed rooms. Laminated knotty-pine furniture and tiled baths with stall showers behind glass doors make housekeeping easy. The double-glazed windows help drown out the incessant traffic noise that starts at o-dark-hundred and goes until after midnight, and adequate wardrobes are there for your hanging clothes. The breakfast room is full of guests who return on a regular basis, and at these prices, why not?

Facilities and Services: Central heat, no public phones, no lift, office safe, TV, tea and coffeemakers, desk open 7:30 A.M.–midnight

CREDIT CARDS
MC, V

NUMBER OF ROOMS
16

W/BST
All

RATES
Single £35; double £50–55; triple £70; 2-room suite £80; English breakfast included

Oak House Hotel
29 Hugh Street, SW1

It is small, but oh, so choice! Located close to Victoria Station between the Eccleston and Elizabeth bridges, the Oak House is an absolute jewel, providing you do not mind tiny. Run by a wonderful Scottish couple, Mr. and Mrs. Symington, it is quite simply the best Cheap Sleep in this area. You will notice their Scottish heritage from their lilting accents to the tartan carpeting, and Mr. Symington's striking kilt outfit he wears to perform weekly country dancing. (The rest of the time he is a London cabbie.) There are only six small, but tidy, twin-bedded rooms. Each one is packed with an orthopedic mattress, knife and cutting board, bottle opener, and tea and coffeemaker. Clothes are hung on hooks and possessions are stashed on open shelves. Bathrooms are down the hall. A Continental breakfast of toast and juice is delivered each morning to your room, and you can make your own tea and coffee with the supplies provided. You won't find a lounge or dining room or a careless impersonal staff. Mrs. Symington is definitely in charge of it all and looks after her contented guests with a cheerful intensity. Advance reservations are accepted *only* for long stays,

TELEPHONE
071-834-7151, 071-828-6792

FAX
None

TUBE
Victoria

CREDIT CARDS
None

NUMBER OF ROOMS
6

W/BST
None

RATES
No singles, but will rent a double for single occupancy; double £27; triple £38; four £45, bunk beds; Continental breakfast £2 per person

so if you arrive in London and want to stay here for the short haul, call immediately and hope for the best.

Facilities and Services: Central heat, public phone, hair dryer, TV, tea and coffeemakers

Oxford House Hotel
92–94 Cambridge Street, SW1

TELEPHONE
071-834-6467/9681
FAX
071-834-0225
TUBE
Victoria
CREDIT CARDS
MC, V. Add 10% surcharge if you pay entire bill by credit card. A reservation can be made with a credit card followed by written confirmation.
NUMBER OF ROOMS
17
W/BST
None
RATES
Single one night £30, more than one night, £28; double one night £40, more than one night £38; triple one night £51, more than one night £48; four one night £68, more than one night £64; English breakfast included

If you want a clean place to stay with a minimum of decorating mismatches, this could be your hotel. All rooms have American-style wallpaper color-coordinated with the curtains. The chenille spreads blend in well most of the time and so do the carpets. The owners, Mr. and Mrs. Kader, live at the hotel with their two sons, a pet rabbit named Sable, and a fat cat called Mr. China, who had his tail amputated. Football fans please note that one of the sons is a Chicago Bears fan, and the other, a die-hard fan of the 49ers. Before going to his office in the morning, Mr. Kader prepares breakfast in the open kitchen just off their downstairs dining room. During the day, Mrs. Kader is on the desk, managing the hotel and making sure guests' needs are met. I like their commitment to their hotel and their personal involvement with each guest. If you like this sort of homespun lodging, send your one-night deposit soon. Unfortunately, if you are paying by credit card, there will be a 10 percent surcharge.

Facilities and Services: Central heat, telephone in hall, hair dryer available, no safe, no lift, desk open 7 A.M.–10 P.M.

Pyms Hotel
118 Ebury Street, SW1

TELEPHONE
071-730-4986 (reception), 071-730-9577 guests
FAX
None
TUBE
Victoria
CREDIT CARDS
None

Owner Margarita Farrell will not allow a speck of dust or a dirty dustball to collect in her 11-room hotel. Running a *very* tight ship, she rules the roost over the maids to keep it all right up to her exacting standards and makes sure her guests pay for their stay in cash upon arrival. The rooms are nice and you will never encounter threadbare carpeting, peeling paint, or sagging mattresses. You will find an unfussy place to call your London home, done in beige and brown with white laminated furniture. The hall facilities are sanitary and in top shape. A huge cooked breakfast will start you on your tourist rounds in good order, and when you return in the evening, you can walk to a good selection of *Cheap Eats in London* (see the book and look under SW1).

Facilities and Services: Central heat, public phone, no lift, office safe, TV, desk open 7 A.M.– 9 P.M.

NUMBER OF ROOMS
11
W/BST
2
W/OBST
9
RATES
Single £25–40; double £44–60; triple £65–75; English breakfast included

Richmond House Hotel
38b Charlwood Street, SW1

Cheap Sleepers in London looking for maximum value for their hotel pound should check the Richmond House Hotel, where the twelve rooms have open closets, easy-care bed coverings, one chair, and enough space for you and your luggage. In addition, each has its own TV, hair dryer, and basin with hot and cold running water, but you will have to use the hall toilet and shower. If you stay here, you will not be the first budgeteer to do so. Mr. Goudie and his parents before him have been welcoming guests from around the world for three generations.

An English breakfast with cereal, fresh bread, eggs, bacon, sausage, potatoes, or tomatoes is served in a small downstairs dining room. I hope Mr. Goudie always keeps his San Diego placemats. It is not often when I am in London that I eat at a communal breakfast table covered with lovely views of my home-town.

Facilities and Services: Gas heat in rooms, public phone in hall, hair dryer, TV, tea and coffeemakers, no safe or lift

TELEPHONE
071-834-4577
FAX
071-630-7467
TUBE
Pimlico
CREDIT CARDS
None
NUMBER OF ROOMS
12
W/BST
None
RATES
Single £25; double £40; triple £50; English breakfast included
MISCELLANEOUS
Hotel closed from Christmas through New Year's Day.

Searcy's Roof Garden Bedrooms
30 Pavilion Road (one block below Basin Street; enter off Rysbrack Street), SW1

As the saying goes, you can't tell a book by its cover. Truer words were never spoken about this hidden find only a heartbeat from Harrods, the designer boutiques along Sloane Street, and all of

TELEPHONE
071-584-4921
FAX
071-823-8694

TUBE
Knightsbridge

CREDIT CARDS
AE, MC, V

NUMBER OF ROOMS
11

W/BST
All

RATES
Single £65–75; double
£85–110; three flats on
Brompton Road, rates on
request; Continental breakfast
included

MISCELLANEOUS
Hotel closed December 24–26.

exclusive Knightsbridge. When you arrive, you will be standing in front of a bright yellow building with a green door. Press the buzzer by the door and wait for the voice telling you to step into the freight elevator and ride to the third floor, where you will be met by the manager, Mr. Harris, or one of his family members. Behind that discreet green door lies the comfortable world of Searcy's Roof Garden Bedrooms, a surprisingly peaceful London oasis, owned and operated by Searcy's, one of London's finest catering firms. Each room is elegantly and individually designed, the service is impeccable, and the price considerably less than most nearby hotels. All rooms are beautifully furnished with pretty fabrics and a collection of antiques you wish you could sneak home with you. Some rooms have canopy beds; others, sitting alcoves. Some of the "rooms with baths" are just that: the bathtub is right in the room, not in a separate bathroom. And the red-lacquered toilet seats are something else. But you are just going to have to trust me on this: everything fits right in and you *will* like it. There is a sunny roof garden for guests and the large catering kitchen is open to those who want to brew a cup of tea or store snacks in the refrigerator.

Just this year, they have added several fully equipped flats on Brompton Road, where you can expect to find the same high quality surroundings as at the hotel.

Facilities and Services: Electric radiator heat, ceiling fans, direct-dial phones, hair dryer, use of refrigerator, lift to some rooms, office safe, TV; flats: Fully fitted kitchens, TV, direct-dial phones, no lift

Tophams Ebury Court
28 Ebury Street, SW1

TELEPHONE
071-730-8147

FAX
071-823-5966

TUBE
Victoria

CREDIT CARDS
AE, DC, MC, V

Behind the long success of this lovely and *very* British hotel has been Diana Topham, who came to the hotel to help her brother run it during World War II. She and her husband recently turned over management to their daughter and son-in-law, Marianne and Nicholas Kingsford, who have made some tasteful changes while still keeping the spirit and dignity of the hotel fully intact. Throughout the five adjoining buildings, the rooms have the friendly feel of a country home, with flowery chintz fabrics, little sitting alcoves where guests can take tea or read a newspaper, loads of family antiques, and a dedicated staff who have been with the hotel for decades. Bedrooms are furnished in the genteel style of an old-fashioned home—some with four-poster beds and all with little extra touches like a pretty plate hanging on one wall, a framed lithograph, or a Limoges vase filled with spring flowers. The comfort of each guest is always the primary consideration. For instance, soft terrycloth robes are provided for those using the hall showers, and a night porter is on duty to assist those who arrive after hours. Lunch and dinner are served daily in a new streetside restaurant called Tophams. Daily newspapers and complimentary membership in the private bar, open only to guests of the hotel and members of the Ebury Court Club, a group that gathers for drinks in congenial surroundings, are just two more of the benefits of staying at Tophams.

Another *very* special feature of this charming hotel is Jennifer Dorn, of Oh, To Be in England. Ms. Dorn is a noted travel authority on Great Britain, and runs her own consulting business in New York. As a complimentary service for the hotel to its American guests, the services of Ms. Dorn are included. When your reservation is confirmed, she will telephone you and, if you wish, help you to organize your trip to London or throughout the U.K. Even if you don't stay at the Ebury Court, please consider using her services. When you think of what you could save in lost time, energy, and money on costly mistakes, it is worth the small investment. You can contact her by writing or calling her at Oh, To Be in England, 2 Charlton Street, New York, NY 10014 (212-255-8739).

Facilities and Services: Private bar, electric heat, direct-dial phones, hair dryer, laundry service available, lift, office safe, restaurant and room service, cable TV, tea and coffeemakers

NUMBER OF ROOMS
40
W/BST
20
W/OBST
20
RATES
Single £60–95; double £75–130; triple £150; Continental or English breakfast included

Vandon House
1 Vandon Street, off Buckingham Gate, SW1

TELEPHONE
071-799-6780
FAX
071-799-1464
TUBE
St. James's Park
CREDIT CARDS
AE, DC, MC, V
NUMBER OF ROOMS
40
W/BST
20
W/OBST
20
RATES
Single £35–50; double £55–80; triple £95; four £115. Weekend Bargain Breaks: single £50; double £80–115; triple £145; four £170; Continental breakfast included; English breakfast £3.50 extra

This hotel is owned and run by the Salvation Army. For twenty-five years it served as their headquarters and as a charity for those needing a free bed and a free meal. After a radical floor-to-ceiling facelift a few years ago, it is now an unpretentious hotel and restaurant that I can recommend wholeheartedly (see *Cheap Eats in London*). Because it is under the auspices of the Salvation Army, there are some rules that won't appeal to those determined to vacation in London's fast track. For starters, no smoking or liquor is allowed on the premises, period. The desk is open *only* from 6:30 A.M. until 12:30 A.M., and no front door keys are provided. If you miss curfew, you will sleep elsewhere. The hotel is neat as a pin throughout and meticulously cared for. It is far from lavish, and the rooms will bring back memories of college dorm rooms with their utilitarian furnishings. The downstairs lounge has a bookshelf with many well-thumbed titles for guests to borrow, a CD player for musical interludes, a small television, an aquarium, and two birdcages of finches. The reception desk is staffed by a prim and proper crew with an eagle eye out for anything unbecoming to the hotel and its valued clientele.

If you will be here over a weekend, be sure to inquire about their "Bargain Break Weekends." These are available for two- and three-day stays from Friday through Sunday nights. All prices are per room (not per person, except for a single) and include a Continental breakfast. For three nights, add 50 percent. For English breakfast, add £2.50.

Facilities and Services: Central heat, direct-dial phones, hair dryer in some rooms, lift, office safe, restaurant, TV, tea and coffeemakers, trouser presses in some rooms

The Victoria Inn
65 Belgrave Road, SW1

Belgrave Road is chock-a-block with B&Bs, most falling into the reject pile. Several do, however, stand head and shoulders above the rest, and The Victoria Inn is on that short list.

Well-done and professionally run, it offers many five-star comforts at prices Cheap Sleepers in London cannot ignore. For openers, all rooms are serviced by a lift and have private bathrooms. They are done in nondescript "motel modern" with remote-controlled televisions, tea and coffeemakers, security locks, and direct-dial telephones. Children up to 8 stay free. The hotel has a luggage storeroom, night porter, fax service, and safe deposit boxes. Staying here will put you within walking distance of Victoria Station, Buckingham Palace, the River Thames, Houses of Parliament, and several museums.

Facilities and Services: Central heat, direct-dial phones, hair dryer, lift, safe in reception, TV and radio, iron available, tea and coffeemaker, 24-hour desk

TELEPHONE
071-834-6721, 834-0182

FAX
071-931-0201

TELEX
911619 VICINN

TUBE
Pimlico, Victoria

CREDIT CARDS
AE, DC, MC, V

NUMBER OF ROOMS
49

W/BST
All

RATES
Single £50–65; double £80; triple £35 per person; four £30 per person; Continental breakfast included; English breakfast £4 extra

Westminster House
96 Ebury Street, SW1

Those watching their wallets will be pleased to know about the Westminster House, a no-frills generic place to spend a night or two near Victoria Station. You will know that it is family owned and run when you encounter Kate, Elizabeth, or Alexandra Jones doing their homework in the family dining room, or skipping down the outside stairs on their way to school. Their mother, Mrs. Jones, cooks breakfast for everyone in the morning and serves it in their lower ground-floor dining room, filled with family photos and books. Mr. Jones is on hand at the desk to make sure the hotel is running well. Cleanliness rather than lavishness is emphasized and the rooms bear this out. Yes, there are some wild-colored carpets, but for the most part, the furniture is sensible and fabrics are coordinated. If your room does not have its own bath or toilet, don't worry. Those on the hall are way above par.

Facilities and Services: Electric room heat, public phone in hall, no lift, no safe, TV, tea and coffeemaker, 24-hour desk

TELEPHONE
Reservations 071-730-4302; guests 071-730-7850

FAX
071-730-3267, attention Westminster House

TUBE
Victoria

CREDIT CARDS
MC, V

NUMBER OF ROOMS
11

W/BST
2

W/OBST
9

RATES
Single £35; double £45–50; triple £55–60; English breakfast included

MISCELLANEOUS
Hotel closed Christmas day

Wilbraham Hotel
1 Wilbraham Place, off Sloane Street, SW1

TELEPHONE
071-730-8296, 730-8297, 730-8298

FAX
071-730-6815

TUBE
Sloane Square

CREDIT CARDS
None

NUMBER OF ROOMS
52

W/BST
48

W/OBST
4

RATES
Single £40–56; double £58–78; deluxe twin from £80; crib £5; extra bed £12; Continental breakfast £5; English breakfast £7. All prices exclusive of VAT, so 17½% will be added.

If you can remember visiting your grandmother in a big Victorian home with lots of small rooms, you will be able to picture this bastion of traditional English dignity and decorum. With a staff straight out of central casting, the hotel offers a top location just off Sloane Square. It would be nice if some of the rooms were combined to create more space, but management foresees no more radical changes than adding one or two private baths and redecorating a few rooms each year. The slightly frumpy but well-kept rooms are filled with antiques of varying degrees of quality. Single Cheap Sleepers can ask for No. 45, a bathless second-floor room that shares facilities with two other rooms. If you need a large room, reserve one of the four suites or a deluxe twin. The double-bedded rooms are quite small, especially if you have any large pieces of luggage. No. 1 is my choice for a long stay. It is a ground-floor deluxe twin with lovely wood paneling, a fireplace, sofa and two easy chairs, leaded windows, and a big bathroom with heated towel racks. Breakfast, which will cost extra, is brought to your room, but lunch and dinner are served in a pleasant Victorian dining room on the main floor. The food is not gourmet, but it is honest English cooking that will stick to your ribs.

Facilities and Services: Bar (closed Sundays and holidays), portable electric heaters, direct-dial phones, hair dryer available, 2 lifts, office safe, restaurant (Mon–Sat lunch and dinner, sandwiches on Sun), room service, TV in most rooms or available at no extra charge

Winchester Hotel
17 Belgrave Road, SW1

TELEPHONE
071-828-2972

FAX
071-828-5191

TUBE
Victoria

If you are only looking for a bed for the night with bacon, eggs, and beans on your breakfast plate in the morning, there are myriad choices along this long hotel strip leading from Victoria Station into Pimlico. For those of you who prefer something more, Jimmy McGoldick's Winchester Hotel is a class act, offering all the benefits of a small hostelry that prides itself on the high standards of comfort and service expected by today's world travelers. It is not cute and cozy or filled with English antiques and picture-postcard perfect floral displays, but it is well thought out with coordinated decor and excellent maintenance. All rooms have private tiled bathrooms with high-pressure showers, a real bonus for those tired of holding a limp nozzle with two squirts of water erratically spraying. If you are staying more than a few days, consider reserving one of the three fully equipped apartments displaying the same attention to detail as the hotel rooms. An added extra is the English breakfast included in the reasonable rate.

Facilities and Services: Central heat, public phone in hall, office safe, cable TV, no lift, desk open 6 A.M.–midnight

CREDIT CARDS
None

NUMBER OF ROOMS
18

W/BST
All

RATES
No singles; double £65; triple £75; four £90; apt from £75 per night; English breakfast included

Windermere Hotel
142–144 Warwick Way, SW1

At this top-of-the-line Pimlico B&B, the rooms are painted white and have good-quality fabrics in muted shades of pink, turquoise, and mauve. All are kept up, but the ground-floor rooms facing the street should be avoided due to noise, and so should No. 11, thanks to an airless bathroom. American guests will be happy to discover American-style showers with fixed shower heads, not that wiggly kind on the end of a limp hand-held hose that has little water pressure. An added feature is the option of calling room service for hot and cold beverages or sandwiches. An evening meal is served from 6–9:30 P.M. If you are pressed to make an early curtain call, a quick sandwich or an early supper at the hotel could be very convenient. The cordial staff, headed by owners Nick and Sylvia Hambi, works diligently to make your stay as comfortable as possible.

Facilities and Services: Bar, central heat, direct-dial phone, some hair dryers, trouser presses, minibars, restaurant, room service, TV, no lift or safe

TELEPHONE
071-834-5163, 071-834-5480

FAX
071-630-8831

TELEX
94017182 WIRE G

TUBE
Victoria

CREDIT CARDS
AE, MC, V

NUMBER OF ROOMS
23

W/BST
All

RATES
Single £50–75; double £70–80; triple £75; four £90; English or Continental breakfast included

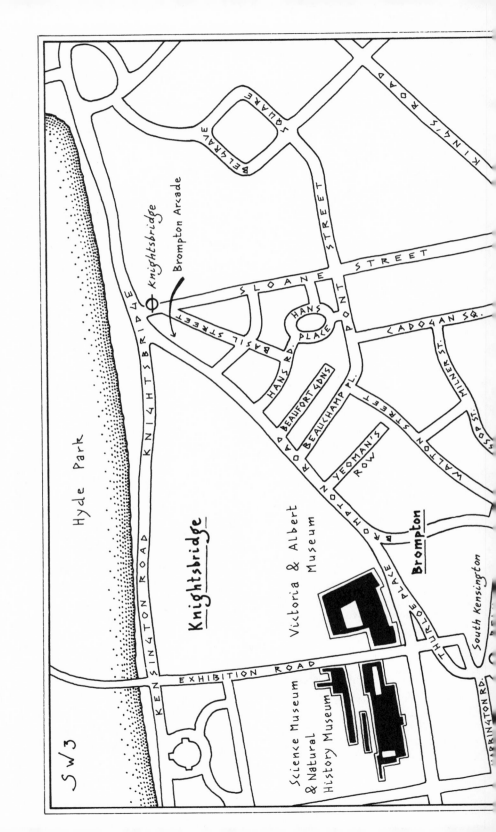

SW3 ✤ CHELSEA

In the nineteenth century, Chelsea gained fame as London's Bohemia where writers and artists lived such as Thomas Carlyle, George Eliot, Henry James, James Whistler, and Oscar Wilde. It is unlikely the area will ever again be an impoverished artists' colony because now it is one of the toniest and most expensive London neighborhoods. King's Road, lined with boutiques and restaurants, runs the length of Chelsea and is a mecca for the youthful and trendy sets. Sir Christopher Wren designed one of Chelsea's loveliest buildings, The Royal Hospital, home to the Chelsea Pensioners, old soldiers who are a familiar sight along King's Road in their blue uniforms trimmed in red and covered with war medallions and medals. In late May, the famous Chelsea Flower Show is held on the grounds of the hospital. Sloane Square, at the top of King's Road, is home to the Sloane Rangers, London's equivalent of preppies. You will find them out in full force, especially on Saturdays, around Peter Jones Department Store and browsing through Justin de Blank's General Trading Company.

HOTELS

Blair House Hotel	120
The Claverly	121
Magnolia Hotel	122
Oakley Hotel	122

OTHER OPTIONS

Renting a Flat

Nell Gwynn House Apartments	168

University Dormitory Accommodations

Allen Hall	175
Lightfoot Hall	183

Blair House Hotel
34 Draycott Place, SW3

TELEPHONE
071-581-2323, 071-225-0771

FAX
071-823-7752

TUBE
Sloane Square

CREDIT CARDS
AE, DC, MC, V

On a quiet Chelsea side street you will find the Blair House Hotel. The rooms are a bit old hat and styleless, but clean and reasonable for the area. The singles run small, but have good lighting. However, if you don't enjoy extremely close quarters, better reserve a double or twin. For shoppers, it is a little slice of heaven. Peter Jones Department Store and the trendy King's Road are only a few minutes walk from the hotel doorstep. For further shopping safaris, direct bus service to Knightsbridge, with Harrods, Harvey Nicols, etc., is only a few stops away. Culture buffs will be able to take a bus or the tube to almost any site or museum on their list of must-dos. For nighttime enjoyment, there are plenty of good restaurants and typical pubs to keep you going for at least a week.

Facilities and Services: Central heat, direct-dial phones, hair dryer, office safe, TV and radio, tea and coffeemakers, trouser presses, no lift

NUMBER OF ROOMS
17
W/BST
10
W/OBST
7
RATES
Single £45–70; double £66–80; extra bed £17; Continental breakfast included; English breakfast £4–7 extra

The Claverly
13–14 Beaufort Gardens, SW3

The Claverly is a wonderful small hotel perfect for the discerning traveler who prefers the gracious feel of a lovely private home to that of a big, impersonal chain hotel. The hotel has been awarded the British Tourist Authority's Certificate of Distinction and the coveted Spencer Trophy for the best bed-and-breakfast hotel in central and greater London. Owner Demi Antoniou is a perfectionist who has spared no effort or expense to redo each room, giving it its own style and distinctive character. Some have four-poster beds and sitting alcoves with soft sofas and arm chairs; others connect and are ideal for families. Still others are quite tailored and suitable for a businessperson in London for an extended stay. Little extras count, so pressure-pumped showers and lighted magnifying mirrors have been installed in all of the new bathrooms. To date, about ten rooms remain to be redone, so when reserving, please specify that you *do not* want a room that has not been completely redecorated.

Breakfast features fresh-squeezed orange juice, a selection of fruits, cereals, bacon, eggs, sausage, and all the trimmings, plus waffles with maple syrup, warm toast, and fresh croissants. It is served in a beamed country-style basement dining room on nice china, set at round tables. The richly paneled reading room is arranged with leather chesterfields where

TELEPHONE
071-589-8541
FAX
071-584-3410
TUBE
Knightsbridge
CREDIT CARDS
MC, V
NUMBER OF ROOMS
31
W/BST
26
W/OBST
5 (singles only)
RATES
Single £62–75; double £100–170; triple £150; English breakfast included

guests can spend a quiet moment or two browsing through current periodicals or books. While prices here may be high for many Cheap Sleepers, they are competitive for Knightsbridge and offer good value for those with more flexible purse strings.

Facilities and Services: Central heat, direct-dial phones, hair dryers in most rooms, laundry service, lift, office safe, cable TV

Magnolia Hotel
104–105 Oakley Street, SW3

TELEPHONE
071-352-0187

FAX
071-352-0187

TUBE
Sloane Square, then bus
#11 or #22

CREDIT CARDS
AE, DC, MC, V

NUMBER OF ROOMS
20

W/BST
2

W/OBST
18

RATES
Single £30–40; double £40–50;
triple £60; Continental
breakfast included

If you can forsake the chandelier and chintz scene for this basic Chelsea hotel a half block off the King's Road, you will experience a Cheap Sleep in London. Back room windows in this 150-year-old house offer little to gaze upon, but at least if berthed here you will not have any disturbing noise. The rooms are budget basic: mix-and-match furniture and fabrics. While you probably would not want to call them home for long, the rooms do provide a decent place to sleep in this tab-happy sector of London. A Continental breakfast is served in a small breakfast room with copper pots and pans set on recessed shelves. From the hotel you can walk along the King's Road where there are dozens of trendy boutiques, a staid Marks and Spencer, and numerous Cheap Eats.

Facilities and Services: Central heat, public phones in hall, no lift, office safe, TV, iron and ironing board available, desk open 7 A.M.–10 P.M.

Oakley Hotel
73 Oakley Street, SW3

TELEPHONE
071-352-5599

FAX
071-727-1190

TUBE
Sloane Square
(long walk; must then take bus
No. 11, 19, or 22)

CREDIT CARDS
None

NUMBER OF ROOMS
13

It is friendly, it is youthful, and is it ever basic! If you are blessed with an abundance of energy and don't mind a long walk or changing to a bus for the rest of the trip from the nearest tube stop, this eleven-room Cheap Sleep in London can save you significant pounds. If you are willing to share a room with three others, the rent will be a mere £10 per person per night. The laid-back management allows cooking privileges, has tea and coffee available around the clock, and offers a loaner iron for clothes that have spent too much time in transit. The rooms are predictably tatty with cast-off furniture and their fair share of garish color splashes. The shower room on the top floor and the three toilets on the floors below are adequate, but without heat. Okay, so it is not the Ritz, but for the bargain-basement price that includes a big English breakfast, would you expect more?

Facilities and Services: Electric heat, public phone downstairs, TV and video in lounge, office safe, cooking privileges, iron available, tea and coffee available 24 hours, no lift

W/BST
None

RATES
Single £20; double £35; triple £45; four £50; shared dorm rooms for women only £70 per week for the room; English breakfast included

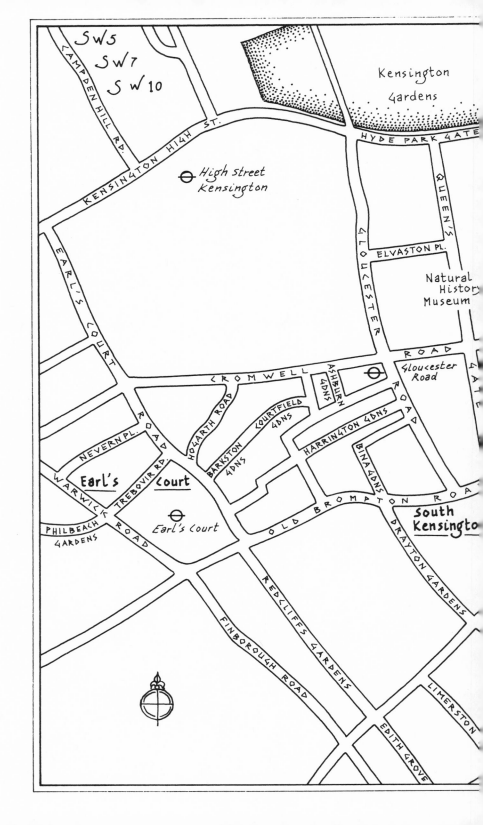

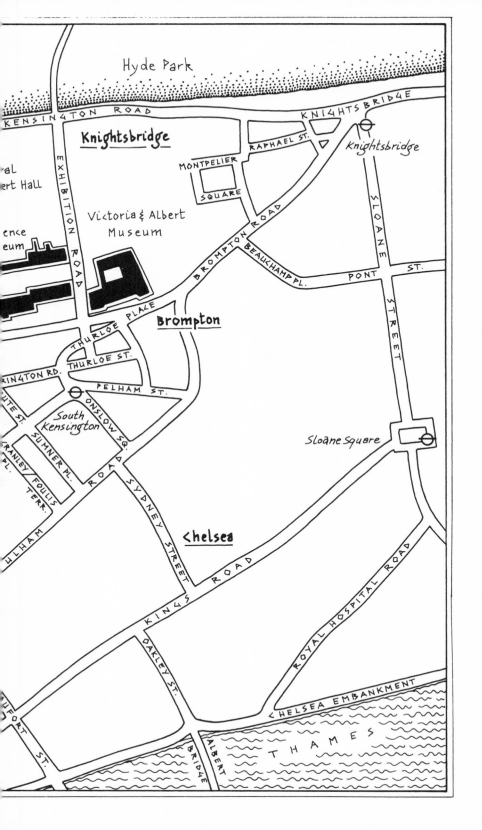

SW5 ✦ EARL'S COURT

Earl's Court is often called "Kangaroo Court" because it serves as unofficial headquarters for London's large Australian student community. It is known for its two large exhibition centers: Earl's Court and Olympia. The area is a mixed bag of hotels, ranging from charming, antiques-filled, restored town houses to chains and some of the worst London has to offer. Most accommodations are geared toward people with low budgets and an abundance of youth on their side. To go with these Cheap Sleeps are a multitude of Cheap Eats restaurants, but only a handful serve anything approaching quality food. From a tourist's point of view, the area offers very little, but transportation is good, and you can be in London central within 30 minutes.

HOTELS

Aaron House	126
The Beaver Hotel	127
The Burns Park Hotel	127
Chelsea Hotel	99
The Cranley	128
Henley House Hotel	129
Hogarth Hotel	130
Hotel 167	130
Nevern Hotel	131
Rushmore Hotel	132
Sky Star Hotel	99
Swiss House Hotel	132
York House Hotel	133

OTHER OPTIONS

Renting a Flat

Five Emperors Gate and Eight Knaresborough Place	165

Youth Hostels

Earl's Court Youth Hostel	189

TELEPHONE
071-370-3991

FAX
None

TUBE
Earl's Court

CREDIT CARDS
MC, V

Aaron House
17 Courtfield Gardens, SW5

Aaron House is among the best Cheap Sleep picks in this budget strip in Earl's Court. The hotel occupies an old town house with an original tiled entry floor and lacy scrolled staircase heading up to the 23 rooms. Several large rooms overlook a pretty Victorian Square in front where traffic and night noise should not be a problem. Some rooms have television and private baths, and all have the electric teapots the English deem so necessary, even in the most modest of accommodations. While the hotel is not long on service, decor, or cushy amenities, it is friendly, clean, and reasonably priced, and therefore should please most bargain-guided hotel shoppers.

Facilities and Services: Electric room heaters, public phones in hall, some rooms with TV, tea and coffeemakers, no lift or safe, desk open 8 A.M.–11 P.M.

NUMBER OF ROOMS
23
W/BST
10
W/OBST
13
RATES
Single £28–35; double £40–45; triple £50–55; Continental breakfast included

The Beaver Hotel
57–59 Philbeach Gardens, SW5

In this far corner of London, the Beaver Hotel delivers more for your Cheap Sleeps pound than most. Two rooms boast waterbeds; there is a car park for a small £3.50 fee per day; and tea and coffee are available whenever you want. Rooms are clean and vary from small without bath, to reasonably spacious with all facilities, and are priced accordingly, starting at £30 for a snuggle fit. The wood-paneled Austrian-style breakfast room has cushioned chairs and banquettes. The daily breakfast menu is posted on a blackboard. For socializing, you can play pool in the next room, or join the sports fans who gather around the television. The tube stop is about a 15-minute walk away, which might be a drawback for some, but the 10 percent discount for longer stays should overcome any shortcomings.

Facilities and Services: Central heat, direct-dial phones, hair dryers in rooms with private facilities, car park (£3.50 per day), office safe, TV in some rooms, 2 waterbeds, tea and coffee always available, no lift

TELEPHONE
071-373-4553
FAX
071-373-4555
TUBE
Earl's Court
CREDIT CARDS
AE, MC, V
NUMBER OF ROOMS
38
W/BST
22
W/OBST
16
RATES
Single £30–49; double £40–62; triple £75; car park £3.50 per day; English breakfast included

The Burns Park Hotel
18 Barkston Gardens, SW5

If you pay the rack rate at the Burns Park, you won't be getting a Cheap Sleep in London. If, however, you time your visit to include a weekend

TELEPHONE
071-373-3151
FAX
071-370-4090

TELEX
27885 BURNS G

TUBE
Earl's Court

CREDIT CARDS
AE, DC, MC, V

NUMBER OF ROOMS
106

W/BST
All

RATES
Single £86; double £96;
suite/apt £120; extra bed £16;
Continental breakfast £5 extra;
English breakfast £7.50 extra.
Weekend Rates
£40 per person per night,
includes English breakfast.
Holiday, Summer Saver, Two-
Night Breaks, and Special
Holiday rates that include an
English breakfast and
sometimes dinner on request.

(Thursday through Sunday) or a holiday, you will save significantly and will be getting an excellent Cheap Sleep in an exceptionally nice hotel.

As you enter the hotel, you cross a marble reception room, dramatically done in reds and blues with a stunning glass chandelier embedded in a mirrored ceiling recess. The Tulip Bar to one side offers a quiet place to relax over a drink after a busy London day. Dinner in the Park Grill, where traditional English dishes are served, is another convenient bonus. The bedrooms can be small, and in some cases, sound-proofing needs to be checked. If you have a twin-bedded room or a suite, you will not face these problems. Nonsmokers can request rooms on the back of the hotel. All rooms are furnished in unaggressive good taste using four color schemes: dark and light blue, burnt orange, and soft yellow. Everything from the wallpaper and carpeting, to the bedspreads and upholstery fabrics coordinate. The marbled baths have all the necessities, plus heated towel racks, fluffy towels, fans that really do their job, and a basket of fragrant toiletries.

Facilities and Services: Bar, central heat, direct-dial phones, hair dryer, lift, office safe, restaurant, room service, TV, tea and coffeemakers

The Cranley
10–12 Bina Gardens, SW5

TELEPHONE
071-373-0123; toll-free from
U.S. 1-800-553-2582
Mon–Fri, 8 A.M.–5 P.M.
central time

FAX
071-373-9497;
U.S. 313-995-1050;
Michigan 313-995-4400

TELEX
911503

TUBE
South Kensington

CREDIT CARDS
AE, DC, MC, V

NUMBER OF ROOMS
36

The Cranley is a textbook example of a small hotel done with great style and elegance. In 1990, owner Bonnie DeLoof from Ann Arbor, Michigan, restored three town houses in South Kensington. In the process she kept intact the high ceilings with handsome moldings, the large floor-to-ceiling windows, and several Victorian fireplaces. The stunning interior follows the English country recipe of chintz, traditional antiques, swaggered draperies, beautiful flower arrangements, and a lovely garden in back. Mrs. DeLoof has incorporated all the touches Americans love to find in a hotel, matching modern facilities with those of a large, luxury hotel. The individually decorated rooms include equipped kitchenettes hidden behind paneled doors; American mattresses; and wonderful bathrooms complete with fluffy towels, warm terry-cloth robes, assorted English toiletries, and deep bathtubs. In each room is a folder of valuable information listing interesting neighborhood walks, suggested restaurants and shops, and the best ways to get around the city. All rooms, of course, are lovely, but naturally a few stand out. Number 105, a deluxe double, has an oriental motif and its own fireplace. The fourth-floor, one-bedroom suite has a balcony and a view of the top of St. Paul's Cathedral. There are two ground-floor suites with private terraces and jacuzzis. The hospitable staff does its utmost to provide attentive personal service for each guest. A stay at The Cranley is guaranteed to be memorable for anyone who appreciates the finer things in life.

Note: See also One Cranley Place, page 144.

Facilities and Services: Bar, central heat, direct-dial phones, hair dryer, kitchenettes, lift, 1-day laundry, office safe, room service for light snacks, cable TV, business services, 2 jacuzzis

W/BST
All

RATES
Single from £104; double £104–177; garden rooms and suite £200; apt £215; special discounts available during off-season and weekends; Continental breakfast £4–9; English breakfast £12

Henley House Hotel
30 Barkston Gardens, SW5

If you are looking for a touch of luxury in Earl's Court, the newly revamped Henley House stands apart in looks, comfort, and value. With only twenty rooms, the staff has time to be helpful, and over the years, has learned how to please a demanding clientele. Red and blue colors, tie-back curtains, and pretty wallpaper with matching trim create a fresh and appealing look to the delightful rooms. The attractive breakfast room is well done in peach with terra-cotta accent pieces and pots of dried flowers. In the comfortable lobby and reception room, a shelf of books is available for guests who tire of the British telly programming.

Facilities and Services: Central heat, direct-dial phones, hair dryer available, no lift, office safe, cable TV, tea and coffeemakers, desk open 7:45 A.M.–11:30 P.M.

TELEPHONE
071-370-4111, 370-4112

FAX
071-370-0026

TUBE
Earl's Court

CREDIT CARDS
AE, MC, V

NUMBER OF ROOMS
20

W/BST
15

W/OBST
5 singles, without toilet, but with shower

RATES
Single £35–50; double £45–65; triple £55–70; Continental breakfast included; English breakfast £3 extra

Hogarth Hotel
Hogarth Road, SW5

TELEPHONE
071-370-6831; toll-free in
U.S. 1-800-528-1234

FAX
071-373-6179

TELEX
895 1994

TUBE
Earl's Court

CREDIT CARDS
AE, DC, MC, V

NUMBER OF ROOMS
85

W/BST
All

RATES
Single £70; double £85;
triple £95; four £105; special
weekend rates and lower rates
for longer stays available
through the hotel directly;
English breakfast included

Another redecoration project that installed better carpets, drapes, tiled bathrooms, and good lighting has made this Best Western hotel near the Earl's Court Exhibition Center very popular. In fact, the manager told me, "Customers have been booking very early to be assured of a room, which means we must be doing our job properly." It is true: the staff *is* doing its job well in providing a fine welcome with plenty of service in a modern hotel that offers no unpleasant surprises. The list of amenities is long and appealing for both tourists and businesspeople. Who wouldn't appreciate a bathroom drying rack for quick washes, a convenient car park, 24-hour room service, and a dining room with something for everyone from a burger and chips to a daily fixed-price menu featuring homemade desserts. There are nonsmoking rooms and a floor with extra security measures geared to women alone. If you want a full-service hotel for a reasonable tab in the Earl's Court sector of London, this is your best bet.

Note: The hotel offers weekend rates and lower rates for longer stays. To get these price breaks, you must deal with the hotel directly, not with the reservations office in the U.S.

Facilities and Services: Bar, central heat, direct-dial phones, hair dryer, same-day laundry service, lift, parking, room safe, restaurant, room service, cable TV, radio, trouser press, picnic lunches on request

Hotel 167
167 Old Brompton Road, SW5

TELEPHONE
071-373-0672,
071-373-3221, 373-3222

FAX
071-373-3360

TUBE
Earl's Court (South Kensington
exit)

CREDIT CARDS
MC, V

Number 167 Old Brompton Road is a corner Victorian house adapted into a smart bed-and-breakfast hotel where you will find savvy travelers in their twenties and thirties enjoying its upbeat, eclectic style. The livable rooms have been individually designed in a variety of color schemes and motifs. You may stay in a room that has an Art Deco or Japanese theme, or one that is modern in tone. Bathrooms are small but serviceable and some are decorated with pretty border tiles. Wooden-slat blinds let in light and at the same time assure privacy; double glazing on the windows in all rooms is insurance against the busy Brompton Road traffic noise. A Continental breakfast with fresh orange juice and croissants is served on tiny marble-topped tables in a pale-gray room dominated by an old pine sideboard and a collection of interesting contemporary paintings. The hotel is not too far from nice shops and some of Christie's auction rooms. The area is also full of very good restaurants in all categories (see *Cheap Eats in London*).

Facilities and Services: Central heat, direct-dial phones, hair dryer, mini-bar, office safe, cable TV, video, tea and coffeemakers

NUMBER OF ROOMS
19

W/BST
All

RATES
Single £58–66; double £70–80; extra bed £15; Continental breakfast included; English £6 extra

Nevern Hotel
31 Nevern Place, SW5

No matter how you look at it, the Nevern adds up to a well-run, recommended Cheap Sleep that offers the basics. My notes on the hotel read: safe Earl's Court location; clean, no mold in the bathrooms; decent wallpaper; lots of light even though some rooms have brown velvet curtains to block morning sun. The stern, Polish manager will not allow loud activities of any kind, but his prices, especially in the off-season, are great for pence-pinchers. Best rooms? I like Number 7, a back triple with big windows opening onto a green space. Number 9 is also a good choice, done in gray with a fresh coat of white paint on the walls. The lounge area is à la bus station, with a ring of chairs placed around a plain room carpeted in bright red. The pine dining room reminded me of a mountain lodge. Here is where you will be served a complimentary breakfast of tea and toast, or you can go whole hog and order the full English grease-out breakfast consisting of bacon, sausage, eggs, maybe beans or a tomato, and buttered toast. That should set you up for the rest of the day!

Facilities and Services: Central heat, direct-dial phones, hair dryer available, lift, office safe, TV, 24-hour desk

TELEPHONE
071-370-4827, 071-244-8366

FAX
071-370-1541

TUBE
Earl's Court

CREDIT CARDS
AE, MC, V

NUMBER OF ROOMS
34

W/BST
15

W/OBST
19

RATES
Single £30–45; double £45–58; triple £60–70; four £65–75; lower off-season rates; Continental breakfast included; English breakfast £4 extra

Rushmore Hotel
11 Trebovir Road, SW5

TELEPHONE
071-370-3839, 370-6505,
071-835-1431
FAX
071-370-0274
TELEX
297761 REF 193
TUBE
Earl's Court
CREDIT CARDS
AE, MC, V
NUMBER OF ROOMS
22
W/BST
All
RATES
Single £50; double £60; triple
£80; lower off-season rates on
request; Continental breakfast
included

If you are a do-it-yourself person with an artistic flair, you owe it to yourself to see this beguiling hotel. It is a great lesson in how to create something beautiful out of nothing. Using faux finishes, trompe l'oeil techniques, and draped fabrics on windows, walls, and furniture, the owners have cleverly turned a worn-out faded wreck of a hotel into a smart Earl's Court address. All 24 rooms are one of a kind. No. 7 is in dark green, with stripes painted on the walls. Its stand-out piece of furniture is a huge, canopied double bed. The floor-to-ceiling windows frame a covered window seat that overlooks the garden. The most imaginative rooms fall into the middle price range. One of the best of these is No. 5, which has soothing hues of blues and greens with ocean scenes painted on the walls. The pink and gray breakfast room with three inset murals is painted to go with the trim on the china. Because this is a turn-of-the-century building, don't look for large baths, much closet or luggage space, or an elevator.

Facilities and Services: Central heat, direct-dial phones, hair dryer available, office safe, cable TV, access to health club/gym at special rates, tea and coffeemakers, no lift, desk open 7:30 A.M.–midnight

Swiss House Hotel
171 Old Brompton Road, SW5

TELEPHONE
071-373-2769 (reservations),
071-373-9383 (guests)
FAX
071-373-4983, ext. 218
TUBE
Gloucester Road
CREDIT CARDS
MC, V; 5% surcharge on all
bills paid by credit card
NUMBER OF ROOMS
15
W/BST
11
W/OBST
4

The courteous staff, directed by owner Peter Vincenti, has the ability to make guests who walk through the door feel as though they have come home. Here, home consists of fifteen pretty rooms decorated with an abundance of flowering chintz. One of the nicest is No. 212, a top-floor triple with a fireplace and a view to the gardens beyond. Other quiet garden rooms to remember are Nos. 2, 5, 8, 12, and 17. If you are in one of the streetside rooms, better bring earplugs, because the traffic along Old Brompton Road never seems to stop. A large, self-service Continental breakfast is served in a downstairs breakfast room with blue-and-white country curtains and dried floral arrangements as accents. Room service, an almost unheard-of extra in a modest B&B of this type, delivers soup, sandwiches, omelettes, and salads from noon until 9 P.M.

Facilities and Services: Central heat, direct-dial phones, hair dryer available, office safe, room service from noon–9 P.M., cable TV, iron and ironing board available, no lift

RATES
Single £35–50; double £55–65; extra bed £10; Continental breakfast included; English breakfast £4 extra

York House Hotel
27–29 Philbeach Gardens, SW5

Winnie, the friendly receptionist, has been on the front desk for twelve years. Her warm welcome and outgoing personality mark the beginnings of a pleasant stay at this thrifty hotel. The York House is nothing fancy, but it is sensible, sturdy, and to the point when it comes to Cheap Sleeps in this corner of London. The rooms are clean and sunny, with high ceilings and no musty odors, nicks, dents, or tears. If you are a nonsmoker, they have rooms especially for you. Rates are indeed charitable compared to some of the almost obscene prices charged by some in the neighborhood. Your final bill will be even less if you stay a week or more and can take advantage of the 25 percent discount given for long stays. There is a nice television lounge stocked with an interesting selection of current periodicals. Breakfast is served in a white-washed room with red and white tablecloths. On warm days, chairs and tables are set out in the garden for guests. The good news is that the 38 rooms can house around 50 people. The bad news is they often do, so make your reservation as early as possible. Warning: Be positive about your dates because the deposit is nonrefundable, period.

Facilities and Services: Electric room heat, public phone, hair dryer available, radio, TV lounge, no lift

TELEPHONE
071-373-7519 (reservations); 071-373-7579, 071-373-1821 (guests)

FAX
None

TUBE
Earl's Court, Warwick Road exit

CREDIT CARDS
AE, MC, V

NUMBER OF ROOMS
38

W/BST
2

W/OBST
36

RATES
Single £30–42; double £40–60; triple £55–70; four £65; 25% discount for long stays; English breakfast included

SW7 ✦ SOUTH KENSINGTON

South Kensington is a treasure trove for culture seekers. It is home to the Royal Albert Hall, where concerts are held, as well as the vast museum complex that includes the Victoria and Albert, Natural History, and Geological and Science. Stately Victorian houses, Georgian mansions, and charming mews houses with picture-perfect gardens characterize this very desirable residential area. In the springtime, clusters of pink and white blooms on the ornamental cherry trees turn it into a fairyland that draws many photographers.

HOTELS

Abcone Hotel	135
Albert Hotel	135
Aster House Hotel	136
Baden-Powell House	137
Embassy House Hotel	138
Five Sumner Place Hotel	139
The Gore	140
Harrington Hall	141
Kensbridge Hotel	142
Number Sixteen	143
One Cranley Place	144
The Park International Hotel	145

OTHER OPTIONS

Renting a Flat

Ashburn Garden Apartments	161
Aston's	161
Five Emperors Gate	165
The Kensbridge Hotel Group—Flat Rentals	167
Knightsbridge Service Flats	168
Roland House	170

University Dormitory Accommodations

Imperial College	183
Linstead Hall—Imperial College of Science and Technology	176
More House	179
Queen Alexandra's House	181

Abcone Hotel
10 Ashburn Gardens, SW7

There must have been a huge sale on green paint, green carpeting, and green linens when the Abcone Hotel was redecorated some years ago. This hotel is *green,* from the lobby and dining room right on through to the halls and bedrooms. Green still dominates the public portion of the hotel, but the symphony of green is more subdued in the rooms, which are now being redecorated in universal hotel beige with red and blue accents. Marble baths add a touch of luxury, and a friendly management team personalizes this South Kensington location. The hotel is in back of the huge Forum Hotel, so taxis are always available, and with a little luck, you might be able to convince the concierge at the Forum to get you tickets for a sold-out show or concert. During Christmas and New Year's, the Abcone offers a 25 percent discount on all room rates. For the businessperson in your group, a full complement of business services is available.

Facilities and Services: Bar, central heat, direct-dial phones, hair dryer in most rooms, lift, cable TV and video, office safe, tea and coffeemakers, iron and ironing board available, laundry and dry cleaning services

TELEPHONE
071-370-3383
FAX
071-373-3082
TUBE
Gloucester Road
CREDIT CARDS
MC, V
NUMBER OF ROOMS
35
W/BST
26
W/OBST
9
RATES
Single £40–60; double £55–65; triple £70–100; four £90–110; Continental breakfast included; English breakfast £5 extra

Albert Hotel
191 Queen's Gate, SW7

When staying at the Albert, one *must* adopt a philosophical attitude about this once-grand old home that now houses about one hundred backpackers, starving students, and other desperate Cheap Sleepers in London. On arrival, everyone is issued a "bedding bag" consisting of one sheet, a comforter, and pillow. These you place on your assigned bed in a single or double room or dorm that houses up to eight individuals. Towels and soap are up to you. This is the type of place where thefts might occur if you are not vigilant, so if you are traveling with valuables, have them locked up in the office. The housekeeping staff could use a few pointers, and so

TELEPHONE
071-584-3019
FAX
071-823-8520
TUBE
Gloucester Road
CREDIT CARDS
None
NUMBER OF ROOMS
100 beds
W/BST
Singles and doubles have private facilities

RATES
Single £30; double £35;
triple £15 per person; four £15
per person; 6-bedded room £12
per person; 8-bedded room £11
per person; Continental
breakfast included

could management, on the peeling paint, stains, and nicks that seem to multiply every time I see this place. However, for £11–15 a night in a dorm room sleeping four to eight people, you can get a place to sleep and breakfast the next morning. Another boon to travelers on the cheap is the restaurant open daily 7:30 A.M.–10 P.M. With not much over £2.50 or £3, it won't qualify as a 3-star Michelin recommendation, but for that low, low price, you can fill up on burgers, meat pies, sandwiches, soup, and specials. You can also bank on socializing with a youthful international set that is well plugged into the travel scene from a low-budget viewpoint.

Facilities and Services: Central heat, public phone, restaurant, cable TV in lounge, coin laundry, no lift

Aster House Hotel
3 Sumner Place, SW7

TELEPHONE
071-581-5888
FAX
071-584-4925
TUBE
South Kensington
CREDIT CARDS
MC, V
NUMBER OF ROOMS
12
W/BST
All
RATES
Single £55; double £70–88;
suite/apt £90; rates *do not*
include 17½% VAT; 2-night
minimum stay, no refund
14 days or less before arrival;
payment in full for length of
stay on arrival; no refund for
earlier than scheduled
departures; buffet breakfast
included

In recent years, the Aster House Hotel has been the recipient of many awards, including the Spencer Trophy for the best B&B in London, and it is a three-time winner of London in Bloom, an award given for the best hotel floral displays.

There is no outside sign to indicate this is a hotel. When you arrive, look for No. 3 Sumner Place and ring the bell. You will walk across a pink marble floor to the reception desk, where you will be given your own key to the front door.

It is almost impossible to select a favorite room, because each of the twelve bedrooms has been individually decorated with silk wall treatments and exceptional furniture. Nice bathrooms and room fans in the summer add even more. The garden suite with its own patio is a romantic choice, and so would be any of the rooms with four-poster, half-canopied beds. The owners, Rachel and Peter Carapiet, ask that you do not smoke in the bedrooms, or any place else in the hotel. The most stunning feature of the hotel is the recent addition of a glassed-in garden conservatory dining room called L'Orangerie. The usual heavy fried English breakfast has been replaced with lighter alternatives of poached or scrambled eggs, homemade yogurt, whole-grain bakery products, cereals, fresh fruit, and cheese. All food must be consumed here and not taken to your room to snack on later.

Note: A word of caution on reservations. To discourage no-shows and early unannounced departures, a two-night minimum stay is required and payment for the length of stay must be paid on arrival. If you cancel, you must do so 14 days prior to arrival to get a refund. If you shorten your stay after arrival, there are no refunds.

Facilities and Services: Central heat, direct-dial phones, hair dryer available, mini-bar, room safe, TV, room fans, no smoking, no lift

Baden-Powell House
Queen's Gate at Cromwell Road, SW7

Opened in 1961, the Baden-Powell House fulfills the dream of the founder of the Boy Scouts, Lord Baden-Powell, that there would be a permanent place where the Boy Scouts and Girl Guides of the world might meet or stay when they come to London. The wonderful part is that the facilities of this remarkable hotel are open not only to members of the Scouts and Guides, but to their families as well, whether or not the member is present. Even if your child or grandchild is a first-year Cub Scout or Brownie, you are eligible to take advantage of this sensational Cheap Sleep deal.

The hotel is situated in the heart of London's museum district. The Natural History Museum is across the street and the Science, Geological, and Victoria and Albert museums are minutes away. Also within easy reach are the Royal Albert Hall and Kensington Palace. Other sites such as the Tower of London and Westminster Abbey are a quick tube or bus ride away. The rooms, from singles to a ten-bedded dorm, are simple—think summer camp—with showers and toilets on each floor. The TV is in the lounge, a coin-operated laundry is always open, the staff is happy to help with sightseeing plans, and a

TELEPHONE
071-584-7031

FAX
071-581-9953

TUBE
Gloucester Road

CREDIT CARDS
MC, V

NUMBER OF ROOMS
45

W/BST
3, but all dorm rooms have a sink

W/OBST
42

RATES
Single £26–28 ; double £22–25 per person; family rate, adult £16, child £14; multi rate (over 16 years) £16, 3 bedded room or larger; dorm rate (under 16 years) £11; towels *not* included; English breakfast included, £4.50 to general public

MISCELLANEOUS
The hotel is closed for two weeks between Christmas and New Year's Day.

BOOKING POLICIES
Groups, British A nonrefundable deposit of £2.50 per person is required as confirmation. The balance of

no less than 50 percent of the full payment will be required eight weeks prior to arrival. *Groups, Other* A nonrefundable deposit of £5.50 per person per night and 50 percent of full payment required eight weeks prior to arrival. *Family and Individuals* A nonrefundable deposit of £7 per person for each booking. *Cancellation* If a booking is cancelled in whole or in part less than 60 days before arrival, or in the event of nonarrival, the full price for the room(s) will be charged unless they are relet. *Payment* Full payment required upon arrival unless other arrangements made. Payment can be in cash, traveler's checks, or by credit card.

notice board keeps everyone up to the minute on theater and concert performances. Breakfast is included in the nominal rate, and for very little more, two- and three-course lunches and dinners are served daily in the cafeteria. If you are going on a day trip via British Rail, consider having the kitchen pack you a box lunch to avoid subjecting yourself to the poor quality of food offered on trains.

Every time I go back to the Baden-Powell House I cannot believe how much value is offered for such a modest price. For serious budgeteers with a Scout in the family, you cannot afford not to take advantage of this unequalled Cheap Sleep in London.

Facilities and Services: Central heat, public phones, garage (£5 for 24 hours—and that is as CHEAP as you will ever see in London), restaurant—also open to the public for 3 meals a day, TV lounge, gift shop, coin laundry, lift

Embassy House Hotel
31–33 Queen's Gate, SW7

TELEPHONE
071-584-7222; toll-free in U.S.
1-800-247-3643

FAX
071-589-8193;
U.S. 919-881-0571

TELEX
914893

TUBE
Gloucester Road

CREDIT CARDS
AE, DC, MC, V

NUMBER OF ROOMS
70

W/BST
All

RATES
Single £90–100; double £100–115; triple £115; four £130; Continental breakfast included; English breakfast £6 extra. Inquire directly with hotel for Bargain Break rates and special holiday and summer rates.

A well-conceived refurbishing turned this downcast hotel into a recommendable location close to Hyde Park and Kensington Gardens. The Royal Albert Hall is around the corner and three of London's most famous museums, including the Victoria and Albert, are down the road. During the remodeling, every effort was made to preserve the tone of this nineteenth-century historic site. You can still see the stuccoed facade, the elaborate ceilings, the York stone staircase, and the mirrored doors of the original private residence. The spacious rooms have luggage racks, good bathroom space, and neutral decor. If you are a light sleeper, avoid those facing the street . . . the noise lasts 24 hours a day. This is a full-service hotel with all conveniences available to the guest. You can have a drink at the bar, eat dinner, book a show or rental car, have your pants pressed, or send a fax telling the boss you will be back a week late. The hotel is part of Jarvis Hotels, and rates tend to be high for most Cheap Sleepers, but if you take advantage of their Bargain Breaks or other special rates, you can enjoy a very nice hotel for a price that is affordable.

Facilities and Services: Air-conditioning in suites, bar, central heat, direct-dial phones, hair dryer, same-day laundry service, lift, office safe, restaurant, room service, TV and radio, porter, tea and coffeemakers, trouser presses, secretarial services, bookings for shows

Five Sumner Place Hotel
5 Sumner Place, SW7

Many small, select London hotels have turned genteel coziness into an art form. Five Sumner Place is no exception. To show you how far ahead of the competition it is, it was recently voted the best B&B in London by the British Tourist Association. When you consider the number of hotels in the running, this is quite an achievement. The hotel's many devotees certainly agree it receives top marks for its lovely tone and decor, pleasing service, and appealing residential location along a beautiful row of white Victorian town houses built in 1848. When you arrive, you will recognize an air of a well-run country home with understated luxury. Comfortable furniture in fine, traditional-English style graces each smart guest room and bath, which come equipped with everything you will need for a relaxed stay. A stunning glass conservatory breakfast room with hanging plants overlooks a pretty side garden. What a wonderful place to begin your London day, enjoying a buffet breakfast while glancing through a stack of complimentary daily newspapers. The hotel is ideally placed for visiting the sights of London by bus, tube, or taxi. The South Kensington tube, with a direct link to Heathrow Airport, is less than five minutes away on foot, and major museums and a score of restaurants in all price ranges are within an easy stroll (see *Cheap Eats in London*).

Facilities and Services: Central heat, direct-dial phones, hair dryer, mini-bar in most, lift, office safe, TV, 24-hour desk, complimentary afternoon tea

TELEPHONE
071-584-7586
FAX
071-823-9962
TUBE
South Kensington
CREDIT CARDS
AE, MC, V
NUMBER OF ROOMS
13
W/BST
All
RATES
Single £60–75; double £85–100; extra bed £20; buffet breakfast included; rates do not include 17½% VAT

The Gore
189 Queen's Gate, SW7

TELEPHONE
071-584-6601; toll-free in the
U.S. 1-800-528-1234

FAX
071-589-8127

TELEX
296244

TUBE
Gloucester Road

CREDIT CARDS
AE, DC, MC, V

NUMBER OF ROOMS
54

W/BST
All

RATES
Single £110–120;
double £150–165; suite/apt
£210; Continental breakfast
£6.50 extra

A stay at The Gore provides guests something out of the ordinary that will add considerably to the pleasures of a London visit. Privately owned and managed by Brian and Aminge Dale-Thomas, this impressive town house once belonged to the Marquess of Queensberry's family. It was made into a hotel in 1908. As you enter, beautiful oil paintings line the reception area leading to an emerald-green sitting room filled with large, comfortable sofas and chairs. A roaring winter fire adds a cheery touch. For a stylish and delicious meal, reserve a table at Antony Worall-Thompson's Bistrot 190, the current rage in London dining (see *Cheap Eats in London*). For a more formal experience, the downstairs dining room serves traditional food in elegant and expensive surroundings.

There are regular single and double rooms with all the nice furnishings and appointments one expects to find in a small hotel of this caliber. The Gore is well known for its magnificent collection of four-thousand vintage English prints hung throughout the hotel and in each room. However, the *real* fun of staying here begins when you reserve one of their special suites. Probably the best known and most popular is the Tudor Room, where a dark-wood paneled entrance leads to a massive Gothic room with Oriental rugs scattered on its wooden plank floors. Further touches include a huge wood-burning fireplace, leaded stained-glass windows, and carved beamed ceilings with gargoyles. To one side, a ladder takes you to the "minstrel's gallery," a perfect sleeping loft for children. Downstairs, Mom and Dad can share the four-poster canopy bed. For another unusual experience in hotel living, check into Venus, No. 211, and sleep in a gilded bed that once belonged to Judy Garland. A four-by-six-foot nude graces the wall over the sofa, and in the marbled bathroom, a hand-painted Zeus driving a chariot looms over the bathtub. Another suite of note is the Tiger Room, with a real tiger rug with amber eyes that seem to follow you everywhere. Rates are higher at The Gore, but for its many followers, it is well worth the extra for its unique atmosphere and cordial service.

Facilities and Services: Bar, central heat, direct-dial phones, hair dryer, mini-bar, laundry service, lift to 4 floors, room safe, restaurant, room service, TV, radio

Harrington Hall
5–25 Harrington Gardens, SW7

Harrington Hall used to be a block of dilapidated, has-been flats. Not anymore! The complete restoration of the buildings left only the architecturally beautiful facade and totally gutted the rest of the building. The result is a magnificent new hotel with every possible comfort and convenience, and more important, at affordable prices if you go on a weekend or in the off-season. The marbled lobby and reception area sets the elegant tone for the rest of the hotel. The bar, with its own fireplace, combines warmth and elegance with comfortable, traditional furniture in complementary colors. The rooms and suites offer stylish accommodations for guests who appreciate all the little extras. In addition to air-conditioning and rooms exclusively reserved for non-smokers, you will find cable television, a mini-bar, and a telephone answering machine. Bathrooms are stocked with a variety of toiletries and absorbent towels, and offer good light and plenty of mirrors. The business center, for the exclusive use of guests, offers secretarial services, including word processing, photocopying, and telex and fax services. Conference and banquet facilities for several hundred are beautifully arranged. In addition to all this, guests can work out in the hotel gym, listen to quiet piano music while sipping afternoon tea, or spend a relaxing evening dining in the restaurant, followed by a night-cap at the night club. The concierge will secure tickets for any West End production, and uniformed porters will see to it that you never lift anything heavier than your purse. The lower off-season and

TELEPHONE
071-396-9696; toll-free in U.S. 1-800-44-UTELL

FAX
071-396-9090; from U.S. 402-398-5484 (Utell offices)

TELEX
London: 290603; U.S.: 4972677

TUBE
Gloucester Road

CREDIT CARDS
AE, DC, MC, V

NUMBER OF ROOMS
200

W/BST
All

RATES
Single £110; double £110; suite £160; Continental breakfast £7 extra; English breakfast £10 extra

weekend rates, which are available from the hotel directly, make this fine hotel even more alluring.

Facilities and Services: Air-conditioning, bar and night club, central heat, direct-dial phone and answering machine in each room, hair dryer, mini-bar, same-day laundry and dry cleaning, lift, office safe, restaurant, 24-hour room service, cable TV, radio, tea and coffeemaker, trouser press, gym, concierge, 24-hour desk

Kensbridge Hotel
31 Elvaston Place, SW7

TELEPHONE
071-589-6265

FAX
None

TUBE
Gloucester Road

CREDIT CARDS
None

NUMBER OF ROOMS
25

W/BST
10

W/OBST
15

RATES
Single £30–40; double £40–55; triple £70; suite/apt for 4 £80–96; Continental breakfast included in rooms without kitchens

MISCELLANEOUS
Hotel open to anyone from late spring to end of December.

For Cheap Sleepers seeking a few extras not generally found in budget B&Bs, the Kensbridge is one answer. During the school year, the hotel is under contract to provide student accommodations. From late spring until the end of December, it is open to anyone. The hotel is managed year-round by a delightful woman, Ms. Murphy, who will charm you with her lovely red hair and decidedly Irish accent. The rooms are far from luxurious or eyecatching. For my money, the best ones are on the top floor. For budgeting families, one of the three flats with a fitted kitchen makes sound money-saving sense. There is a lift to all floors, a plus if climbing stairs with heavy luggage and shopping treasures is not for you. From here you can walk to museums, the Royal Albert Hall, or hop on the Gloucester Road Underground and be in Piccadilly Circus in less than 20 minutes.

Warning: Ms. Murphy is on duty *only* from Monday through Friday. If you arrive, or try to call for information or reservations on the weekend, you will be out of luck. Students seem to man the phones and desk and have no authority whatever to deal with questions or guest situations. Best to time arrivals and calling during the week when Ms. Murphy can take care of you.

Facilities and Services: Central heat, public phones downstairs, mini-bars, lift, office safe, TV, tea and coffeemakers, irons available, 3 flats with fitted kitchens

Number Sixteen
16 Sumner Place, SW7

On a cold day, when I am sitting in a comfortable chair sipping a cup of tea in front of the fire in the blue and yellow sitting room at Number Sixteen, it is hard for me to remember I am in a London hotel and not a friend's living room. This is the effect the hotel has on its guests; everyone feels right at home and is always eager to return.

Four Victorian town houses were linked together to create this wonderful hotel. As each house was added, the gardens were expanded in back, and the result is one of the loveliest expanses of flowers and greenery in South Kensington, especially in the spring when the tulips are a riot of color. The recent addition of a glass conservatory overlooking this garden makes its enjoyment a year-round pleasure.

The beautiful bedrooms are all handsomely fitted with a combination of antiques and traditional furniture that represents the best in English taste and charm. Four special ground-floor rooms have their own terraces that overlook the gardens and many have balconies. All of the well-appointed rooms include remote-controlled television sets, stocked minibars, and bathrooms with terry-cloth robes and baskets of English soaps and creams. In the morning, a Continental breakfast that includes cold cereal, an egg, and juice is brought to your room whenever you order it.

If you are planning to be in London several times in one year, consider becoming a member of Club Sixteen, a package that offers the use of all the facilities within the hotel as well as the following extras: priority booking; members' preferential room rate and room upgrades when possible; free newspapers; free laundry and dry cleaning; telephone charges at 10p a unit; fax and telex charges at 10p a unit; small conference facilities.

Personal membership is £35; corporate membership is £150 per company.

TELEPHONE
071-589-5232

FAX
071-584-8615

TELEX
266638 SXTEEN

TUBE
South Kensington

CREDIT CARDS
AE, DC, MC, V

NUMBER OF ROOMS
36

W/BST
30

W/OBST
6

RATES
Single £60–95; double £110–140; triple £160–170; Continental breakfast included

Facilities and Services: Honor bar, room fans, central heat, direct-dial phones, hair dryer, mini-bar, laundry & cleaning service, lift to first 2 floors, room safe, TV, radio, clock, porters, desk open 6:45 A.M.– 11 P.M., health and fitness club facilities available from £5 up for pool, sauna, steam room, and gym

One Cranley Place
1 Cranley Place , SW7

TELEPHONE
071-373-0123, 071-598-7704; toll-free in U.S. 1-800-553-2582 Mon–Fri, 8 A.M.–5 P.M., central time

FAX
U.K. 071-373-9497; U.S. 313-995-1050; Michigan 313-995-4400

TUBE
South Kensington

CREDIT CARDS
AE, DC, MC, V

NUMBER OF ROOMS
10

W/BST
All

RATES
Single £65; double £85; suite £105; Continental breakfast £7 extra; English breakfast £10 extra

If you are willing to spend a little more for a hotel that has great charm and overall appeal, I suggest One Cranley Place, owned by Bonnie DeLoof, who also owns The Cranley (see page 128). The hotel is hidden on a quiet residential street in a South Kensington neighborhood of white Regency mews houses with bay windows, iron railings, and colorful window boxes. The hotel was lavishly redone in 1993, and the moment you step through the front door, you realize you are someplace special. Antiques from Christie's and elsewhere are placed throughout the hotel, from the reception area with its glowing fire to the exquisitely decorated rooms. Green and white predominate in the sunny garden dining room with its extensive collection of hand-painted china displayed in an antique breakfront. Pots of seasonal flowers add bright notes to tables set with pretty china. Each comfortable room has its own character and is decorated impeccably. Fireplaces, writing desks, Oriental rugs, and doors opening onto private balconies lend further luxurious touches. The marvelous bathrooms have Italian tile, sculpted basins, long tubs, terry-cloth robes, and stacks of big towels. For a stay of any length, I am always happy to call One Cranley Place my London home.

Facilities and Services: Central heat; direct-dial phones; hair dryer available; TV and radio; list of useful addresses and telephone numbers for doctors and dentists, restaurants, health club, etc.; office safe; no lift

The Park International Hotel
117–125 Cromwell Road, SW7

The Park International has everything you would expect in a large, metropolitan hotel. From here you can send a fax, watch cable TV, work out in a nearby gym, or have dinner in the dignified restaurant. The decor is coordinated down to the last tie-back curtain, reflecting comfort and pleasing color schemes. Double-bedded rooms run small, so if it is space you are after, book a twin. The location on Cromwell Road is noisy, so ask for something on the back if uninterrupted sleep is a priority. Rack rates are high for Cheap Sleeping enthusiasts, but the weekend breaks, which include a room plus dinner and a full English breakfast the next morning, are great bargains. Just be sure to time your stay to include a Saturday night and your tab for both sleeping and eating in gracious surroundings will be low.

Facilities and Services: Bar, central heat, direct-dial phones, double-glazed windows in front rooms, hair dryer, laundry service, lift, office safe, restaurant for breakfast and dinner, room service, business services, cable TV, health club privileges available, tea and coffeemakers, trouser press

TELEPHONE
071-370-5711

FAX
071-244-9211

TELEX
296822 RAB KEN

TUBE
Gloucester Road

CREDIT CARDS
AE, DC, MC, V

NUMBER OF ROOMS
117

W/BST
All

RATES
Single £95; double £105; suite £140; weekend breaks £40 per person, includes room, dinner, and English breakfast; Continental breakfast £6 extra; English breakfast £8.50 extra

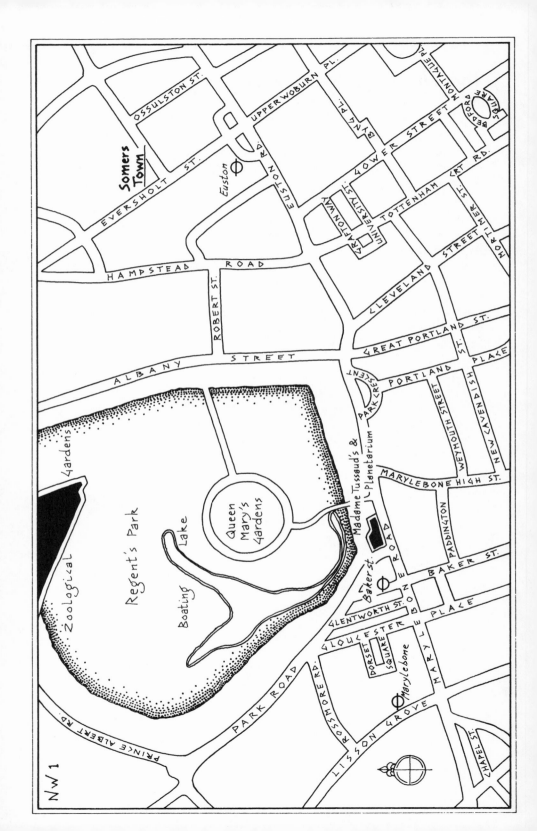

NW1 ✦ REGENT'S PARK

Originally the private hunting ground for Henry VIII, this huge 400-acre park is famous for its zoo, concerts, summer open-air theater, puppet shows, and live bandstand. There is a pond with boats, acres of gardens and lawns, and the Regent's Canal, where you can take a leisurely boat ride on a lazy Sunday afternoon and contemplate moving to London for good.

HOTELS

Dorset Square Hotel   147
Regent's Park Hotel   148

Dorset Square Hotel
39–40 Dorset Square, NW1

For whatever reason you can think of—a birthday, an anniversary, or just to celebrate being in London with someone special—the Dorset Square Hotel receives my highest recommendation and praise. I must warn you, however, that once you stay here, all other hotels will pale by comparison.

The hotel overlooks two acres of gardens that were the site of Thomas Lord's (the famous English cricket player) first cricket ground. Everything about this wonderful hotel is individual and beautiful, from the exclusive interiors to the lovely dining room with its cricket theme and the vintage Bentley Continental automobile available for guests to hire. Like all rooms in the hotel, the sitting room is furnished with lovely pieces owner Kit Kemp would select for her own home. A nineteenth-century rolltop desk with a telephone from an old hotel in Southampton sits along one wall. Displayed on the mirrored mantel are candelabras made from pieces of a chandelier and small vases originally used as whiskey measures. Staffordshire bowls of potpourri, artistic faux finishes, the finest wall coverings, silk draperies, and massive floral arrangements complete the serene room. The 37 bedrooms and suites are each a pure joy to occupy. Everything you can imagine has been done to create a luxurious, yet livable, atmosphere, where antiques,

TELEPHONE
071-723-7874; toll-free from the U.S. 1-800-543-4138; toll-free from Australia 0014-800-127787

FAX
071-724-3328

TELEX
263964 DORSET

TUBE
Baker Street

CREDIT CARDS
AE, MC, V

NUMBER OF ROOMS
37

W/BST
All

RATES
Single from £90; double from £120, luxury double from £145; suite/apt from £165; Continental breakfast £8 extra; English breakfast £12 extra

bold colors, flowers, laces, and collectables are mixed with lavish abandon. The marble and mahogany bathrooms have scales; baskets of the best soaps, creams, and shampoos; terry-cloth robes; huge towels; big mirrors; and even a tissue box covered in a fabric that coordinates with those used in the adjoining bedroom. A collection of English carving platters hangs in the Country Manners Restaurant, which also showcases a mural of early cricket matches, a whimsical collection of cricket hats, and a large silver tea and coffee service sitting on an oval footed tray.

To uphold its extremely high standards of service and maintenance, the hotel has someone permanently on the staff just to care for its collection of decorative antique laces. Another person makes sure the floral displays never fade or wilt, and a full complement of maids, porters, and valets is always on hand to see to a guest's every need. The hotel might be considered by some to be a bit off the beaten track, but the Baker Street tube stop is nearby, and don't forget that chauffeur-driven Bentley you can use for elegant trips to the theater or for a day trip to Windsor Castle or Hampton Court.

Facilities and Services: Air-conditioning in most rooms, honor bar, central heat, direct-dial phones, hair dryer, laundry and cleaning services, office safe, restaurant, room service, lift to first 3 floors—steps to 4th, TV and radio, secretarial services, Bentley car hire

Regent's Park Hotel
156 Gloucester Place, NW1

TELEPHONE
071-258-1911
FAX
071-258-0288
TUBE
Baker Street
CREDIT CARDS
AE, DC, MC, V
NUMBER OF ROOMS
30; 10 apartments, all with BST

Regent's Park Hotel has made a comeback from its badly tarnished and rundown other life as an el-cheapo no one would consider. The refurbished standard issue rooms are predictable in that they are small, all done alike in pastel hues of pink and blue, with blond wood. Now, half have private facilities and there are ten fully fitted apartments for those staying longer or wanting more space. If you need a sunny outlook each day, don't reserve a back room or flat because they face walls. The Singapore Garden restaurant is part of the hotel and offers at least 100 dishes for both lunch and dinner. The hotel is minutes away from the Baker tube stop and within walking distance to Mme. Tussaud's, the Sherlock Holmes Museum, and Regent's Park. While it is not a temple of luxury and soft-footed service, it is a practical address if you like this area of London.

Facilities and Services: Central heat, direct-dial phones, hair dryer, no lift, office safe, restaurant, room service, TV, 24-hour desk, tea and coffee-makers, iron available

W/BST
15

W/OBST
15

RATES
Single £40–48; double £60–70; triple £85; studio apt £300 per week; two-room apt £500 per week; maisonette £850 per week; Continental breakfast included

OTHER OPTIONS

Other than traditional hotel rooms, visitors to London have a wide variety of available options that make sound Cheap Sleeps sense. With several of the private bed-and-breakfast lodgings and flat rentals, you will be required to pay for your stay in cash. With all, you will be asked for a hefty deposit in advance of arrival. Both private B&Bs and flat rentals usually demand that the balance of your stay be paid on arrival. Refund policies for both are, frankly speaking, merciless. To avoid costly headaches if you have to cancel or cut short your trip, *please* be sure to invest in trip-cancellation insurance. These policies are available through various state automobile associations or your travel agent. I cannot overstress the importance of this insurance, which I hope you will never need, but if you do, could save you thousands of dollars in forfeited money.

Bed and Breakfast in a Private Home	151
Camping	156
Renting a London Flat	159
Strictly for Students	172
Staying in a University Dormitory	174
Ys	184
Youth Hostels	188

BED AND BREAKFAST IN A PRIVATE HOME

London is full of small establishments advertising themselves as bed-and-breakfast hotels. This usually means they are mum-and-pop operations with fewer than 20 rooms, few private bathrooms, no lift, homey decor, and breakfast served in a cozy basement dining room.

But if you want to gain a greater insight into life in London, go for the *real* thing: a bed-and-breakfast stay in a private London home. Facilities and prices vary widely, depending on each residence and what it has to offer you. Think about it carefully before you reserve because you are, in effect, a guest in someone's home and thus do not have hotel privileges and services as part of the package. To avoid disappointment, *be sure* to lay out all your needs and expectations in advance. Specify such things as whether a nonsmoking household is a must and whether you are allergic to dogs, cats, children, or noise, or if you need a private bathroom or have specific dietary requirements for breakfast, etc. You may also want to know whether liquor is allowed in the room and if entertaining in the host's living room is permitted.

The Bulldog Club	151
London Homes	153
Stayaway Abroad	154
Traveller's B&B in the U.K.	154
Uptown Reservations	155

The Bulldog Club
35 The Chase, London SW4 ONP
North American office: Beverly Boyle, 6 Kittredge Court, Richmond Hill, Ontario, Canada L4C 7XC

We look forward to extending our special welcome to you as a member of The Bulldog Club and to sharing London and the countryside as it has always been for those who stay with friends.

—The Bulldog Club

With an energy and spirit matched by few, Amanda St. George has taken the frumpy image of the typical English bed-and-breakfast accommodation and turned it upside down. With her last child off to boarding school and nothing to do while she

TELEPHONE
071-622-6935; from the U.S. 1-416-737-2798

FAX
071-720-2748; from the U.S. 1-416-737-3179 (Direct U.S. phone and fax inquires to Beverly Boyle)

CREDIT CARDS
AE, MC, V paid to the Club, not to your host. *Only* open to members of the Bulldog Club; membership £25 per person, £250 corporate membership

RATES
Single £60 for any Bulldog Club residence; double £75 per couple for any Bulldog Club residence; English breakfast included; dinner available if arranged in advance at most Bulldog Country homes for £20 per person, 3 courses and wine

and her husband rattled around in their large home, she began to take in paying guests who were friends of friends. This was such an unqualified success that she convinced pals in Kensington, Chelsea, and other parts of London to do the same thing. Thus was born the Bulldog Club, named for her bulldog Emily.

By paying a £25 membership fee (£250 for corporate membership) you can become a member of the club and stay in some of London's grand homes at rates considerably less than those of a moderate hotel. All twenty 5-star properties are magnificent down to the last detail and offer the guest personal and exclusive attention from the moment of inquiry until departure. Many businesspeople now think of their favorite Bulldog home as "their own" and would never consider the impersonal Hilton or Sheraton again. Each room in a Bulldog Club home is equipped with a private bath complete with hair dryer and a basket of the best English toiletries, a color television, and tea and coffeemaking facilities. In keeping with the times, many offer faxing privileges. Fresh flowers and fruit are always in each room, and a bottle of Perrier or English Malvern water is by the bedside. A full English breakfast is served in the guest's private dining area, and a copy of the *London Times* is beside the tea or coffee cup. For relaxing during the day, the guest has the use of a private sitting room.

New! Bulldog goes country! There are now twenty Bulldog houses throughout the English, Welsh, and Scottish countrysides, as well as in Edinburgh, Oxford, and Salisbury. These historic private castles, mansions, and manor homes are set in exquisite gardens and parklands and cost the same as any Bulldog home in London. Dinner, with three courses and wine, can be booked in advance for a mere £20 per person. All of these beautiful locations are selected and monitored by Amanda herself, and must meet the same exacting standards she requires of her twenty London properties. It is important to note that every Bulldog home is exclusive; no one else can rent them to you. This keeps the quality control even higher.

It is all very British, terribly upper crust, and "really a must for every civilized person visiting London or the countryside," as one delighted guest put it. I think he is 100 percent correct and give The Bulldog Club my highest recommendation and endorsement.

Facilities and Services: All locations include central heat, private sitting and dining rooms, TV, mineral water, hair dryer. London: chauffeur-driven limousine, guided tours, shopping consultant, full business services (offices, secretarial, faxes), private entertaining facilities, all to be booked and quoted in advance. Countryside: many have tennis courts, swimming pools, and provide dinner if booked in advance.

Country locations in or near; Bath, Edinburgh, Oxford, Salisbury, Stonehenge, Stratford, York, Cotswolds, Gloucestershire, Hampshire, Leicestershire, New Forest, Northumberland, Suffolk, Wiltshire, Scotland, Wales.

London Homes
6 Hyde Park Mansions, Flat G, Cabbell Street, NW1

Competently run by Heather Kassell and her daughter Denise Hurst, London Homes has been in business for twenty-seven years, providing friendly accommodations in private London homes at reasonable rates. There are several categories to choose from, depending on location and facilities. If you want to stay in the thick of things and have your own toilet and shower, you will pay more than if you are willing to commute from Kew or Richmond and share the family bathroom. All homes are personally checked once a year so you will not wind up in a spot that is dirty or full of noisy children or pets. Also available is a small selection of flats and houses in the greater London area that are let for a minimum stay of two weeks.

Facilities and Services: Depends on home

TELEPHONE
071-262-0900
FAX
071-706-1061
TUBE
Edgware Road
CREDIT CARDS
None
RATES
Single from £20; double from £18 per person; Continental breakfast included; English breakfast £3 extra
AREA
Depends on home

Stayaway Abroad
71 Fellows Road, NW3

TELEPHONE
071-586-2768

FAX
071-586-6567

CREDIT CARDS
MC, V

RATES
A Category from £25 per person, per night; B Category from £20 per person, per night; C Category from £17 per person, per night; English or Continental breakfast included

AREA
Depends on home

In this day of impersonal hotel service dictated by computers, fax machines, voice mail, and all the other electronic wonders of our time, people are becoming nostalgic for the personal touch accompanied by a genuinely friendly smile and open-armed hospitality. If that appeals to you, too, consider staying in a private home on your trip to London. There are many agencies devoted to securing bed-and-breakfast accommodations throughout London. One of the best I found, and certainly the most competent, is Stayaway Abroad, run by the dynamic Julia Stebbing. Julia personally oversees all of her listings and told me that none of her hosts have what she termed, "heaving bosoms," which she translated to "have problems that would affect a guest in any way." That is reassuring. Her homes offer quality guest rooms in select London homes in good neighborhoods and convenient locations. Each home and host is different, but whether you stay in a large home toward outer London, a tastefully done flat in Victoria, or a lovely row house with a prize-winning garden overlooking the River Thames, you will be warmly received by the host family. Prices quoted are per person and include breakfast. Many of the homes are nonsmoking, so be sure to state if that is a priority for you. The homes are offered in three price categories, based on location and whether they have private facilities.

Facilities and Services: Depends on home

Traveller's B&B in the U.K.
149 Richmond Park Road, Bournemouth, Dorset, BH8 8UA, England (Write to this address for a detailed listing and brochure, stating your needs in your letter of inquiry.)

TELEPHONE
020-253-8036

FAX
020-251-4986

This company is beautifully run by two sisters-in-law, Jenny Long and Thea Druce, and has a long list of happy and satisfied customers from around the world. Many of their London addresses are in the suburbs and require train, tube, and bus transport to reach London central. While that can be appealing to some, it would not be to those who want the bright lights and late-night options at their fingertips. If you do not want to spend valuable time and energy commuting (remember, you're on vacation!), request an accommodation within the Circle Line of the London Underground. Besides London listings, Traveller's has a wide network of places throughout England, Scotland, and Wales. Their choices range from a farmhouse owned by Prince Charles and once the home of the infamous Captain Bligh, to a manor house in the Yorkshire Dales, and a tiny bungalow in Aberdeen. All reservations are confirmed with travel directions and descriptions of places of interest in the area.

Facilities and Services: Depends on location

CREDIT CARDS
MC, V for reservation deposit, but you must pay host in pounds Sterling

RATES
All rates are per person, per night: London £16 (outskirts)– 26 (more central); countryside (England, Scotland, and Wales) £15–25; individual homes, rates on request; London, Continental breakfast included, English breakfast £2.50 extra; countryside, English breakfast included

AREA
London and the countryside of England, Scotland, and Wales

Uptown Reservations
50 Christchurch Street, SW3

After years of being a hostess to friends and family, Monica Barrington decided in 1991 to turn "professional" and widened her circle of available rooms. The result was Uptown Reservations, offering exclusive B&B accommodations in the posh districts of Knightsbridge, Sloane Square, Chelsea, Mayfair, St. James's, and Kensington. The homes are selected personally by Monica, and she monitors them on a regular basis to be certain they are keeping pace with her standards. All rooms have private bathrooms. Efforts are made to match guests with the hosts who come from a variety of backgrounds and professions. Be sure to state your needs when booking, and remember, you are a guest in a private home, so everything will not be "hotel perfect." However, with Monica at the helm, I can assure you it will come very close. If you need a flat for a longer time, or are traveling beyond London and want similar B&B accommodations, Uptown Reservations will be able to help you.

Facilities and Services: Depends on home

TELEPHONE
071-351-3445

FAX
071-351-9383

CREDIT CARDS
None

RATES
Single £40; double £68 per couple; triple £75; Continental breakfast included

AREA
Depends on home

CAMPING

You are not going to get a much Cheaper Sleep in London than you will sleeping under the stars in your own tent or camper in a campground on the edges of London. Naturally, these sites are far removed from the center of the city, so be prepared for long commutes of one or two hours *each* way, using a combination of foot, train, bus, and tube to get to your final London destination. If you have your own transportation, consider the heavy traffic, confusing one-way London streets, and steep parking fees before you decide to drive yourself.

Abbey Woods Co-op Camping & Caravaning Site	156
Caravan Harbour	157
Hackney Camping	157
Lee Valley Park	158
Tent City	158

Abbey Woods Co-op Camping & Caravaning Site
Federation Road, Abbey Wood, London SE2

TEL: 081-310-2233

FAX: None

TRAIN STOP: Abbey Wood Station, 10-minute walk

CREDIT CARDS: MC, V

RATES: Adults (17 and older), £4 per person per night; caravans, motor homes, trailer tents, £3.50 per night (members), £5.50 per night (nonmembers); tents with cars, £5 per night; tents with motorcycles, bicycles, or hikers, £4 per night; electrical hookup from £1–1.50 per night.

AREA: Abbey Wood, outside London

FACILITIES AND SERVICES: Electrical hookups; grocery/convenience shop; public phones for outgoing calls *only*, no incoming calls; laundry room with iron; children's play area; showers and toilets

Advance reservations necessary for Easter, spring holidays, and July and August. If you are in a motor home or have a car trailer, you can make advance reservations. Send £5 deposit and a self-addressed envelope (with International Postal Coupon) for confirmation. No advance reservations are made for tents, bicycles, or hikers. If you belong to a trailer or caravan club, bring your card for a discount. Open all year.

Caravan Harbour
Crystal Palace Parade, London, SE19

TEL: 081-778-7155

FAX: None

TRAIN STOP: Crystal Palace stop on British Rail. 20-minute walk to the campground, uphill all the way. Trains go directly to Victoria Station. Buses are a 5–10 minute walk from the campground to the train station.

CREDIT CARDS: MC, V

RATES: 2 persons in motor home, £10 (members), £12 (nonmembers); 2 persons in tent with car, £11; 2 persons on motorcycle with tent, £10; 1 extra person ages 5–16, £1.50 extra per night; child under 5, free; electrical hookups, £1–1.50 per night; maximum stay 7 nights in summer, 2 weeks in winter; open year round.

AREA: Crystal Palace, outside London

FACILITIES AND SERVICES: Laundry; toilets; showers, small convenience store selling milk, juice, and eggs

Advance booking for motor vans and trailers: send £5 to secure a spot. This will be deducted from total charge when you arrive. Tent space on first-come, first-served basis.

Hackney Camping
Millfields Road, Hackney Marshes, E5

TEL: 081-985-7656

FAX: None

BUS STOP: Take bus #38 from Victoria or Piccadilly Circus to Clapton Park and walk down Millfields Road, or bus #22a from Liverpool Station to Mandeville Street and cross bridge to Hackney Marshes

CREDIT CARDS: None

RATES: £6 per person per night

FACILITIES AND SERVICES: Showers; snack bar; baggage storage; no caravans; open June–August; office open daily 8 A.M.–11:45 P.M.

AREA: Hackney Marshes, outside London

Lee Valley Park
Picketts Lock Centre, Picketts Lock Lane, London, N9

TEL: 081-803-4757, 081-345-6666

FAX: 081-884-4975

TRAIN STOP: From Liverpool Station in London take British Rail to Edmonton Green, then bus W8 to Picketts Lock. Stops by campground. Trip takes 30 minutes each way.

CREDIT CARDS: None

RATES: Adults 15 years and up, £5 per night; children under 15, £2 per night; electrical hookups, £2.50 per night

FACILITIES AND SERVICES: Laundry; swimming; golf course; gym; sauna; shop; toilets and showers; public phone for outgoing calls only, no incoming

AREA: Picketts Lock, outside London

Tent City
Old Oak Common, East Acton, W3

TEL: 081-743-5708

FAX: None

TUBE: East Acton

CREDIT CARDS: None

RATES: £6 per person in dormitory-style tents

FACILITIES AND SERVICES: Only tent living in dormitory tents that are already set up; showers; snack bar; baggage storage; open June–September

AREA: East Acton

RENTING A LONDON FLAT

There is no place like home, so on your next trip to London, why not consider renting a flat? A stay in a flat gives you more space than a hotel, for less money. Almost as important, it allows you to get to know a neighborhood of London that you will soon think of as your own. If you are staying longer than a few days, a flat makes sense because discounts can often be negotiated based on the time of year and length of stay. If you are traveling with children, the kitchen can be a money-saving lifesaver, even if you only fix breakfast and a few snacks a day.

When researching the London flat scene, I can promise you I ran across some real bomb sites that were not only ugly, rundown, and depressing, but dirty and operated by unfriendly people who would never darken the door of your flat if you faced any sort of problem. Just as with all of the hotels and shops listed in *Cheap Sleeps in London,* I have personally inspected all of the apartments I recommend to you.

Even though I mention it as the number one tip on apartment rentals, it is so important it bears repeating here: If you plan on staying in a flat, be sure you clearly understand the payment and refund policies. It is beyond the scope of this book to detail the various policies you will encounter, but they are usually draconian and hit hardest when the chips are down and you must change your plans. If you accept only one piece of advice from me on apartment rentals, let it be this: *Buy cancellation insurance.* This small investment will pay off handsomely if you have to change plans about going, or must suddenly cut short your stay.

CHEAP SLEEPING TIPS ON RENTING A LONDON FLAT

1. Most important: Know the cancellation policy and buy cancellation insurance.

2. State your needs clearly: size of flat needed; number of people occupying it and types of beds required; stall shower vs. hand-held shower nozzle in tub; etc.

3. Is there a phone and how do you pay for the calls? Is an answering machine available?

4. Who pays for utilities? Chances are you do via a hefty deposit most of which you will never see again.

5. How far is the nearest market, laundry and dry cleaner, tube stop, pharmacy, pub, restaurant?

6. How far is the flat from *your* center of interest in London? Ask for a city map with the flat marked on it.

7. Is maid service included, and if not, is it available?

8. Who is responsible for laundering sheets and towels? If you are, you will probably want a washer and dryer in the unit, or at least in the building.

9. Is the apartment suitable for children? Is a park or playground nearby?

10. Is there a lift to your flat? While that 5th-floor penthouse has a million dollar view, do you really want to lug suitcases up and down, as well as bags of groceries and shopping finds? Think about this one carefully . . . stairs get old, *fast*.

London Flats

Ashburn Garden Apartments	161
Aston's	161
Books for Cooks Flat	162
Dolphin Square	163
E & E Apartments	164
Five Emperors Gate and Eight Knaresborough Place	165
The Independent Traveller	166
The Kensbridge Hotel Group—Flat Rentals	167
Knightsbridge Service Flats	168
Nell Gwynn House Apartments	168
London Homes	153
Roland House	170
Two Hyde Park Square	170
Uptown Reservations	155

Hotels with Flats to Let

Hotel Concorde	36
Elizabeth Hotel & Apartments	103
Kensbridge Hotel	142
Morgan Hotel	85
One Cranley Place	144
Regent's Park Hotel	148
Searcy's Roof Garden Bedrooms	111
Winchester Hotel	116

Flats in University Dormitories

London School of Economics and Political Science	177

Butler's Wharf Residence   177
Fitzroy and Maple Street Flats   178
Northhampton Hall—City University   180

Ashburn Gardens Apartments
3–4 Ashburn Gardens, SW7

I never would have found these wonderful flats had I not been up the street checking on some that turned out to be absolutely out of the question. I consider these flats exceptional, but I am not alone, thanks in no small part to the on-site managers, Susan and James Convey, whose warmth and cheerful hospitality has endeared them to scores of regulars. After just one or two nights here, you will feel like family in your home away from home. James serves as porter and handyman and is full of great tips about what to see and do in London. Susan supervises the excellent housekeeping staff and looks after all her guests with the same care and dedicated enthusiasm as she gives her own family. The spacious flats are a little short on the latest style but are spotless and always in perfect order. I like those on the higher floors because the bedrooms are on the quiet side of the building and there is more light. If you have children, you can ask for babysitting, a cot, or highchair. There is a launderette close by and the biggest and best supermarket in London, Sainsbury's, is one block away. Public transportation is a snap and less than five minutes on foot. For an economical, pleasing stay in a friendly flat, Ashburn Gardens is *the* one.

Facilities and Services: Central heat, direct-dial phones with private number, lift, office safe, TV, fitted kitchens, maid service Mon–Fri

TELEPHONE
071-370-2663

FAX
071-370-6743

TELEX
94016318 APTSG

TUBE
Gloucester Road

CREDIT CARDS
None

NUMBER OF ROOMS
25 flats

W/BST
All

RATES
One-bedroom for 1–2 persons £80 daily, £440 weekly; two-bedroom for 4 persons £110 daily, £770 weekly; lower rates November–March; additional beds/cots £18 daily, £80 weekly

AREA
South Kensington

Aston's
39 Rosary Gardens, SW7

Aston's has built a well-deserved reputation for providing top London accommodations in several price categories. Tucked away on a quiet side street off Brompton Road are the three stately Victorian homes that make up Aston's.

TELEPHONE
071-370-0737, 071-730-1100

FAX
071-835-1419, 071-730-2382

TUBE
South Kensington

CREDIT CARDS
None

NUMBER OF ROOMS
53 Budget Studios, no private bathrooms; 15 Designer Studios, all with private bathrooms; 10 Luxury Apartments, all with private bathrooms

RATES
Budget from £35 per day for one to £90 for four; designer from £85–100 per day for one or two persons; one-bedroom luxury apartment from £800 per week; rates vary with high and low season

AREA
South Kensington

Aston's Budget Studios These studios are simply the best budget offerings in London. They combine authentic period architecture with coordinated bright colors and simple modern accessories. Behind double doors is a compact, equipped kitchenette with refrigerator, sink, and hotplate. There are no private toilets or baths in these studios, so guests must share those in the hall. Maid service is provided once a week when linens are changed.

Aston's Designer Studios For those who want private facilities, more space, and truly lovely surroundings, these designer studios are great choices. Each is done in a contemporary color scheme with comfortable furniture. They have everything from air-conditioning and answering machines to welcome provisions in the kitchen and daily maid service.

Aston's Luxury Apartments For a real increase in elegance and space, upgrade to one of these apartments, where grace and old-world charm go hand in hand. They have everything the designer studios do, but the general feel is one of luxury.

For a stay of a week or a year, Aston's is on top of my A list of London recommendations, not only for the price and overall appeal, but for the competent and friendly management provided by owner Shelagh King and her competent staff.

Facilities and Services: Budget Studios: Space heating, public phone, TV, linens, weekly maid service, kitchen, no private bathrooms, no lift. Designer Studios: Air-conditioning, direct-dial phones, answering machine, marble baths with gold fittings, hair dryer, robe, TV and video, kitchen with welcome provisions, maid service, no lift. Luxury Apartments: Same as Designer Studios, also with laundry facilities.

Books for Cooks Flat
4 Blenheim Crescent, W11

TELEPHONE
071-221-1992

FAX
071-568-3886

TUBE
Notting Hill Gate

When I discovered the Ristorante in back of the Books for Cooks shop (see *Cheap Eats in London*) I knew I had hit a jackpot. When I learned that the private flat above the shop was available for short- or long-term stays, I knew I had hit not one jackpot, but two. It would not take much to convince me to move immediately into this stylish flat and call it home for a long time. The country-style rooms are attractively turned out, with coordinated provincial fabrics, nicely polished pines and other natural woods, and an interesting collection of accessories, books, and prints. The flat is on three levels (and there are stairs to climb) consisting of two bedrooms, a full bath with a liberal supply of large towels and a mirrored closet, an exhibition kitchen that doubles as a demonstration kitchen for visiting chefs, a large lounge with a wall of good books to read, a tiny sitting room opening onto a rooftop garden, and a full security system. Hotel guests are invited to eat at the Ristorante downstairs (open for lunch only), or they can wander in almost any direction and find other good restaurants. Of course, guests are encouraged to browse through the cookbooks downstairs and be inspired to shop at the outdoor street market only a block away to pick up all the fixings for their own gourmet meals.

This very special accommodation is not advertised, but good news travels fast. If you think you would enjoy this type of stay in London, make your arrangements as soon as possible.

Facilities and Services: Central heat, direct-dial phone, kitchen, TV, no lift, no safe, no daily maid service

CREDIT CARDS
AE, DC, MC, V

NUMBER OF ROOMS
1 flat

W/BST
yes

RATES
Double £55; triple £80; four £90; breakfast not included

AREA
Portobello Road

Dolphin Square
Dolphin Square, SW1

Dolphin Square, the 7½-acre riverside block of flats which in the past housed Christine Keeler, the prostitute at the center of the Profumo scandal; Sir Oswald Mosley, the World War II leader of British Fascists; and John Vassall, the Admiralty spy, is soon to be the home to a rather more illustrious couple, Princess Anne and her new husband, Commander Timothy Laurence. It is the first time a member of the Royal Family has lived in a private apartment in the capital. Don't think they are giving up all royal trappings, because they will still retain the use of the Princess's apartment at Buckingham Palace, and

TELEPHONE
071-834-3800

FAX
071-798-8735

TUBE
Pimlico

CREDIT CARDS
AE, DC, MC, V

NUMBER OF ROOMS
152

W/BST
All

Gatcombe Park in Gloucestershire will still be their main home.

If you enjoy the services offered by a deluxe hotel, plus sports facilities, shops, and a place to park your car, join the royal couple and book an apartment at Dolphin Square. The flats range from studios to three-bedroom accommodations with fireplaces, above-average kitchens, large baths, and loads of actual living space. Prices are based on the size of the flats, not the number of people occupying them. Aside from just staying in nice surroundings, there is much more to enjoy. Guests are extended membership in the Health Club, with a 60-foot, heated indoor swimming pool, sauna, and steam room. A staff is on hand to provide massages and beauty treatments. The energetic can book a tennis court or join a squash game on one of eight courts. Two restaurants and room service take care of those not in the mood to cook. For those who are, shopping in the arcade is a cinch with everything you will need right there: a greengrocer, supermarket, deli, wine shop, travel and theater booking agent, chemist, newsstand, dry cleaner, and hairdresser.

Facilities and Services: Two bars, central heat, conference facilities, direct-dial phones, hair dryer in premier flats, laundry and cleaning shop on premises, lift, parking, office safe, restaurants and room service, cable TV, radio, video (£10 per day), trouser press in some flats

E & E Apartments
90 Wilton Road, SW1

Elaine Charton and Edwina Noland operate E & E Apartments, which offer sixty rentals in Pimlico and three in South Kensington. These one-, two-, and three-bedroom flats are individually owned and decorated, and offer guests all the comforts and conveniences of a well-furnished abode. You will find nothing tacky, plastic, or unsightly in any of these units. Everyone knows South Kensington is a tony address. Pimlico, on the other hand, is thought by some to be rather passé. On closer inspection, I found it has a good deal more to offer than first glances suggest. There is a daily outdoor market, several very good Cheap Eats (see *Cheap Eats in London,* SW1) and a quiet, neighborly atmosphere you will never find in Mayfair.

Customer satisfaction with your apartment is guaranteed. If you don't like the apartment you are given, ask to be moved and everything possible will be done to accommodate you. To avoid this, be sure to clearly state your special needs: double bed, stall shower, lift, close to tube stop and grocery shopping, laundry facilities, etc. There is a three-night minimum stay and reduced rates begin after the fourth week. Deposits are necessary, full payment is required before arrival, and cancellation penalties apply. Be sure to read all the fine print.

Facilities and Services: Depends on flat

Five Emperors Gate and Eight Knaresborough Place
5 Emperors Gate, SW7
8 Knaresborough Place, SW5

Five Emperors Gate and Eight Knaresborough Place are owned and managed by Robert Arnold and his two sisters, Michelle and Susan. Robert is in charge of the business end while the sisters handle interior decorating and day-to-day running of their two blocks of serviced flats. Judging from the many repeat guests, especially Americans, this is a winning team. I prefer the block of twelve flats at Knaresborough Place because they are newer, better located, have good security, and offer the added convenience of a laundry room with a Maytag washer and dryer. The interiors here are very smart and up to the minute, and several flats have private patio gardens or balconies with chairs and tables for sunny days.

There is always someone at the desk from 7 A.M.– 11 P.M. at Knaresborough Place, whereas at Emperors Gate, there is no on-site manager at any time. At both locations, the Arnolds pride themselves on keeping exceptionally high standards of housekeeping and providing personal service. The maids clean the flats,

RATES
Studio Flatlet (one bedroom, kitchen, bathroom) from £290 weekly; large 3 bedroom (lounge, kitchen, bathroom) for 6 £750 weekly; superior apartments (one bedroom) £390–560 weekly; type 1 penthouse for 4–6 £1050 weekly; type 2 penthouse for up to 9 £1375 weekly; lower off season rates from November 1–March 31
AREA
Pimlico and South Kensington

TELEPHONE
071-244-8409, 071-373-0323
FAX
071-373-6455
TELEX
295441
TUBE
Gloucester Road
CREDIT CARDS
AE, MC, V
NUMBER OF ROOMS
20 in both
W/BST
All
RATES
From £90–155 per night for up to 4 people; minimum stay 2 nights; breakfast not included
AREA
Five Emperors Gate—South Kensington; Eight Knaresborough Place—edge of South Kensington and Earl's Court

change the linens, and do the dishes seven days a week. Complimentary newspapers are delivered to your door, and a green plant adds a welcome and colorful touch to your quarters.

Facilities and Services: Central heat, daily maid service, direct-dial phones, hair dryer available, laundry facilities, TV, complimentary daily newspapers, no lift or safe

The Independent Traveller
Thorverton, Exeter EX5 5NT

The Independent Traveller was established in 1980 for those who enjoy traveling on their own. Headed by Mary Spivey, this family-run business lists London apartments in central and suburban London, country cottages from Cornwall to Inverness, and small hotels, inns, and B&Bs throughout Britain. They stress that their London suburban addresses will not only save you money over a more central location, but will give you more living space. What you save in money and gain in space should be weighed carefully against what you will spend in time commuting back and forth into London, if that is going to be the focus of your trip. If it isn't, then the fringes should be fine.

All properties are inspected regularly and there is an excellent group of owners, many of whom have been with this organization for over ten years. More than half their clientele is repeat business and that is a very strong recommendation. High- and low-season rates are offered and so is cancellation insurance. While you can't always take advantage of the lower seasonal rates, you should definitely take out cancellation insurance.

Facilities and Services: Varies with accommodation

TELEPHONE
039-286-0807
FAX
039-286-0552
CREDIT CARDS
MC, V
RATES
£100–950 per week, depending on type and location; lower rates for longer stays; high- (April 1–October 31) and low-season (November 1–March 31) rates
AREA
Varies with accommodation

The Kensbridge Hotel Group—Flat Rentals

For reservations contact the main office at Kensgate House, 38 Emperor's Gate, SW7

These flats managed by Walter Harris are not sophisticated by any stretch of the imagination. If you need someplace for a long-term London stay and can live in a no-frills, no-charm spot with fifties veneer, dated colors, and user-friendly furniture, you will no doubt be just fine, and certainly pleased with the money you will save. If you are willing to share a bathroom with another flat, the bargain gets even better. Some of the singles are mighty small and the kitchen (of sorts) does not always have a sink . . . you might have to use the one in the bathroom. But, never mind . . . they are clean and, again, think of the money you are saving that you can spend on the theater or a nice dinner out. The locations are close to bus and tube transport, and household shopping needs can easily be met in nearby supermarkets and neighborhood shops.

Facilities and Services: Varies with each location

TELEPHONE
071-589-2923

FAX
071-373-6183

TUBE
For office only: Gloucester Road

CREDIT CARDS
None

RATES
Singles start at £100 per week plus 17½% VAT; doubles start at £175 per week plus 17½% VAT

AREA
Kensington and Victoria

Kensington
Harrington Gardens House
34 Harrington Gardens, SW7
Office: 071-373-2673; guests: 071-373-2838
Tube: Gloucester Road

Kensgate House
38 Emperor's Gate, SW7
Office: 071-370-1040; guests: 071-370-6624
Tube: Gloucester Road

Elvaston Lodge
12 Elvaston Place, SW7
Office: 071-589-9412; guests: 071-584-0873
Tube: Gloucester Road

Victoria
Eccleston House
64 Eccleston Square, SW1

Office: 071-834-0985; guests: 071-834-8253
Tube: Victoria

Riverside Court
121 St. George's Square, SW1
Office: 071-821-8219; guests: 071-821-8121
Tube: Pimlico

Knightsbridge Service Flats
45 Ennismore Gardens, SW7

TELEPHONE
071-584-4123
FAX
071-584-9058
TUBE
Knightsbridge
CREDIT CARDS
MC, V
NUMBER OF ROOMS
12 flats
W/BST
All
RATES
Single £50 per night; double £65 per night; reservations guaranteed on receipt of one week's rent in advance. All rent payable weekly in advance.
AREA
Knightsbridge

If you are expecting to entertain dignitaries or want high-roller surroundings, these flats are not for you, despite the celebrity-studded neighborhood. Ava Gardner lived across the street for twenty years, and her flat (that rumor has it was paid for by Frank Sinatra) is now for sale. For the ultimate in London shopping, you can take a shortcut through "the hole-in-the-wall" and be at Harrods door in minutes.

The flats are furnished in a mixture of furniture from the forties and fifties. Some have been redone in bland beige, others are still in off greens and pungent oranges. Most have beds in the sitting room and too many chairs. On the plus side, the bathrooms are very good and the kitchens have everything you will need for boiling water for a cup of tea to roasting your Christmas goose. The top-floor flats are the best because they have better views and more light. There is a basement "garden" flat that opens onto a patio. Alongside this is a sun room with a sofa and two chairs. There is an eat-in kitchen and spacious bathroom. Because the flats are so practical and clean, and so reasonably priced, I recommend them as an excellent Cheap Sleep flat choice.

Facilities and Services: Central heat, direct-dial phones, lift, TV

Nell Gwynn House Apartments
Sloane Avenue, SW3

Nell Gwynn House Apartments stand in the heart of Chelsea, one of the most exclusive residential districts in London. The 130 luxury studios and one- and two-bedroom apartments are individually furnished to provide complete comfort and convenience.

Each has good closet space with plenty of shelves, hanging space, and luggage storage. There is an equipped kitchen, a color television, an iron and ironing board, a large bathroom with a huge tub, central heat, direct-dial phones, and answering machines available for a small weekly charge. Maid service is included Monday to Friday, linens are changed twice a week, and mail is delivered direct to your flat. For fitness fans, there is a full-service health club with indoor pool, sauna, fully equipped gym, and a long list of services including a beauty salon and massage therapists. The entire staff, from the upstairs maids to the friendly porters and the office personnel, goes out of its way to make guests feel welcome and is available to make your stay pleasant.

Across the street is a row of shops including a dry cleaner, convenience grocery, liquor and wine shop, and pharmacy. For long-term housekeeping and cooking needs, King's Road with two excellent supermarkets is just five minutes walk away. Walton Street, a wonderful street full of tempting boutiques, is only a block away. Elystan Place, an aristocratic square, is a block away. Here you can have tea in a pretty combination tearoom and bakery, get your hair done, do your laundry, or drop it off at the cleaners and let them do it. You can buy fresh fish, meat, cheese, flowers, and the finest produce in London. There are also several restaurants (see *Cheap Eats in London*), a pub, antiques shops, and a hardware store. If you can't find it here, chances are you don't really need it. Taxis take only three or four minutes to flag down, even in rush hour; two tube stops and the best bus routes in London are less than a few blocks away.

Over the years I have inspected many, many London flats, but when I am in London, I always stay at Nell Gwynn. For its price, top location, facilities, and overall services, it is simply unbeatable.

Facilities and Services: Central heat, direct-dial phones (own private number), answering machines on request, lift, parking, office safe, TV, 24-hour porter, concierge, health club with pool, sauna, gym, massage and facials available, beauty salon

TELEPHONE
071-589-1105

FAX
071-589-9433

TUBE
Sloane Square or South Kensington

CREDIT CARDS
AE, MC, V

NUMBER OF ROOMS
130 flats

W/BST
All

RATES
Studio £240–380 weekly; larger apartments £460–660 weekly. A refundable deposit of £200–300 is required to reserve and against cancellation, the use of the telephone, and damages. The balance of the deposit is refunded after the monthly phone bill has been received and paid. Four weeks' cancellation notice required. Payment for the first 22 days (or portion if staying less) is due upon arrival.

AREA
Chelsea

Roland House
121 Old Brompton Road, SW7

TELEPHONE
071-370-6221
FAX
071-370-4293
TUBE
South Kensington, Gloucester Road
CREDIT CARDS
AE, DC, MC, V
NUMBER OF ROOMS
80 flats
W/BST
All
RATES
Studio £60 daily, £475 weekly; larger studio £70 daily, £475 weekly; one bedroom £85–90 daily, £575–600 weekly; two bedroom £100 daily, £685 weekly; corporate and group discounts; 10 percent discount after one month; longer stays negotiable
AREA
South Kensington

Roland House has all the zip and pizzazz of a pair of sturdy English oxfords. That doesn't mean, however, that it is not likable, comfortable, or recommendable. It is all of these things and more: it is well priced and very clean. After a month, there is a 10-percent reduction, and beyond that, price is negotiable. Your functional apartment will come with six-day-a-week maid service, linen change, cable television, lift, fitted kitchens with microwaves, ample closet space, and good bathrooms. The decor is simply done in mauves and blues with white-washed oak furniture. The smallest studios are elfin in size with no sofa and only a single bed, small table, and one upholstered chair. However, if traveling alone and not planning on cooking up a storm, they will do. The location is a bit far for an easy walk to the supermarket, but restaurants are close. Tube and bus service from the South Kensington station is excellent, and only a five- or ten-minute walk away.

Facilities and Services: Central heat, direct-dial phones, equipped kitchens, lift, office safe, cable TV, 24-hour desk, maid service, laundry and cleaning service, secretarial services, fax, photocopying

Two Hyde Park Square
2 Hyde Park Square, W2

TELEPHONE
071-262-8271
FAX
071-262-7628
TUBE
Paddington, Lancaster Gate, Marble Arch
CREDIT CARDS
MC, V
NUMBER OF ROOMS
74
W/BST
All

Two Hyde Park Square is "positioned with perfection," just as its brochure states. This part of London boasts some of the most expensive real estate turf in the city, and these 74 luxury studios and apartments keep pace, but surprisingly enough, *not* in price. A redone studio goes for less than $100 a night, and when you consider the high quality and comfort displayed in all the units, this is a first-class bargain. When I visited, some of the units had not been redone. When you reserve, insist on a rejuvenated unit or you might be disappointed. Many of the apartments overlook leafy Hyde Park Square, where it is hard to believe you are actually centrally located in London. A variety of shops and restaurants make wining and dining a pleasure either in your own flat or out. Business guests will find fax, copying, and secretarial services available. Motorists will have a secure car park for a nominal daily fee. All guests will be very well positioned to strike out for all of London's major attractions. As a final bonus for all, there are *free* laundry facilities.

Facilities and Services: Central heat, direct-dial phones, free washing machine, lift, maid service Mon–Fri, car park £6 per day, business services, TV

RATES
Studio £350 per week; one-bedroom apt £400–480 per week

AREA
Hyde Park

STRICTLY FOR STUDENTS

There are places in London that deal only with students, offering them cheap places to sleep. Basically, they are the pits . . . run-down hotels with absolutely no regard for cleanliness, safety, or eye appeal. There are, however, exceptions and I've listed two here.

International Students House   172
Lee Abbey International Students' Club   173

International Students House
229 Great Portland Street, W1

TELEPHONE
071-631-3223

FAX
071-636-5565

TUBE
Great Portland Street

CREDIT CARDS
MC, V

NUMBER OF ROOMS
200 in 3 locations

W/BST
4

W/OBST
196

RATES
Short-term (up to 6 weeks): Single £20–25; double £19–22; triple £15–18; four £11–14. Prices are per night, per bed and include breakfast and club membership. *Long-term:* Single first 4 weeks £95, longer £85; double first 4 weeks £75, longer £67; triple first 4 weeks £48, longer £45. Dorm first 4 weeks £35, longer £30. Prices are per week, no breakfast or club membership. Nonrefundable £20 booking fee

AREA
Marylebone, Regent's Park

MISCELLANEOUS
International Students House is also a club open to all full-time students, professional trainees, student nurses, and au pairs. Half price membership fees for student nurses and au pairs. Membership rates on request.

For my money, the International Students House is one of the best of its kind in London. Most important for Cheap Sleepers, it is open throughout the year to students who are staying only temporarily. For sheer number of services offered, it is unequaled. Even if you are not staying here, but are a full-time student, you can pay a membership fee on a weekly, monthly, quarterly, or yearly basis and participate in their wide range of planned activities. You are also eligible to buy discounted tickets for the theater or concerts; take day trips; play on one of their sports teams; take aerobics, ballroom dancing, or karate lessons; or play snooker, tennis, bridge, or chess. Anyone staying here can have the bargain meals served in the coffee shop or cafeteria; watch full-length films; check the bulletin board for jobs, rides, or lonely hearts; change money; buy a stamp; borrow a hair dryer or iron; or shop in the gift store. If you think you will become a member, be sure to bring three passport-sized photos and proof that you are engaged in full-time study.

Facilities and Services: Bar, central heat, hall phones, hair dryer available, laundry room, lift in 1 building, garage £12 overnight, office safe, coffee shop and cafeteria, TV, video, gym, vast array of services and activities, gift shop, conference facilities

Lee Abbey International Students' Club

57–67 Lexham Gardens, W8

If you want a cut above the usual student digs, check into this Christian-run students' club, founded in 1964 by the Lee Abbey Council, headed by The Right Reverend The Lord Coggan, former Archbishop of Canterbury. Here you will find way-above-average clean and pleasing single or shared rooms offered to people of all faiths and nationalities. It is staffed by a group of young men and women who live on site and work together as a Christian community. Breakfast and dinner are served; lectures, debates, and films are arranged throughout the year; there is a chapel, large garden, study facility, photocopying service, and laundry. Short-term stays are open to any young person, but if you plan on more than three months, you must be a valid, card-carrying student.

Facilities and Services: Central heat, public hall phones, coin-operated laundry, lift, office safe, restaurant, TV and video lounge, pool and ping-pong tables, backyard barbecue

TELEPHONE
071-373-7242

FAX
None

TUBE
High Street Kensington, Gloucester Road

CREDIT CARDS
None

NUMBER OF ROOMS
100

W/BST
20

W/OBST
80

RATES
Short-term (first 28 days charged at higher rate): Single daily £20–25; weekly £140–160; double daily £17–21; weekly £110–130; triple daily £15–18; weekly £95–115; Continental breakfast included; deposit for any short-term stay £20.
Long-term: First 28 days, single daily £16–25, weekly £100–145; double daily £15–18, weekly £100–115; triple daily £14–16, weekly £89–96. After 28 days, single daily £16–20, weekly £100–125; double daily £15–16, weekly £95–110; triple daily £12–14, weekly £81–87; all require £200 deposit. Charges include English breakfast, evening meal, lunch on Saturday and Sunday, and afternoon tea from Mon–Sat.

AREA
Kensington

STAYING IN A UNIVERSITY DORMITORY

Some of the Cheapest Sleeps in London are in university dormitories. During the school term, these facilities operate for students only. In the summer months, and often at Christmas and Easter when the students are home on vacation, these utilitarian sites are open to the public. Most are well located, many offer inexpensive cafeteria-style lunches and dinners, but few have private bathrooms or much style. Some of the dormitories have rooms that can sleep four to six persons who are not necessarily traveling together. Lockers are provided, but theft is common. To protect your belongings, it is wise to invest in the best padlock you can *before* leaving home. Since most of the bathing facilities are communal, it is a good idea to bring along shower shoes and soap. Towels are usually provided, or can be had for minimal cost, which beats dragging wet towels away in your duffel bag when you leave. Each residence hall has its own payment and cancellation policies. Generally, cash is king and plastic credit is out. A dim view is taken of cancellations, and penalties are usually at least 10 percent of the entire stay, and in some cases as high as 50 percent. No-shows rarely get one cent refunded. Cancellation insurance is strongly recommended.

University Dormitories
Allen Hall   175
Centre Français de Londres   176
Linstead Hall—Imperial College of Science and
    Technology   176
London School of Economics and Political
    Science   177
    Butler's Wharf Residence   177
    Carr Saunders Hall & Fitzroy and Maple
        Street Flats   178
    Rosebery Avenue Hall   179
More House   179
Northampton Hall—City University   180
Queen Alexandra's House   181
Ramsay Hall—University College London   181

Intercollegiate Halls
Canterbury Hall   182
Commonwealth Hall   182
Connaught Hall   182

Hughes Parry Hall	182
International Hall	182
Nutford House	182

College Residences
Ifor Evans Hall	182
Imperial College	183
King's College Halls	183
Ingram Court	183
Lightfoot Hall	183
Queen Elizabeth Hall	183
Wellington Hall	183
Middlesex Hospital Medical School	183
University College, Campbell Hall	183

Other Residences
| London House for Overseas Graduates | 183 |

Allen Hall

28 Beaufort Street, SW3

Allen Hall is a seminary where men train for the priesthood ten months of the year. During July and August it is open to groups, families, or individuals looking for a Cheap Sleep in London. The building was built on the site of the home of St. Thomas More and his family, which makes it historically interesting. The location in Chelsea is close to King's Road and all the boutiques and restaurants it has to offer. The rooms are all dormitory-style and reminiscent of military comfort and decorating levels. Those really watching their pounds can prepare light snacks in the kitchen, or help themselves to a cup of tea or coffee any time. There is a nonrefundable deposit of £10, and payment for the entire stay must be paid in British pounds upon arrival.

Facilities and Services: Central heat, public phone downstairs, kitchen privileges, tea and coffee always available, no lift

TELEPHONE
071-351-1296

FAX
071-351-4486

TUBE
Sloane Square, then bus No. 11, 19, or 22

CREDIT CARDS
None, cash upon arrival

NUMBER OF ROOMS
45

W/BST
None

RATES
Single £20; double £34; English breakfast included

AREA
Chelsea

Centre Français de Londres
61–69 Chepstow Place, W2

TELEPHONE
071-221-8134

FAX
071-221-0642

TELEX
895 0959 C Franc

TUBE
Notting Hill Gate

CREDIT CARDS
MC, V

NUMBER OF ROOMS
47

W/BST
None

RATES
Short-term: Single £23.75 per night, £140 per week; double £19 per night per person, £115 per week per person; triple £17 per night per person, £100 per week; dorm (8-12 per room) £14 per night, £81 per week. For short-term, no deposit required, but must pay in advance upon arrival. *Long-term:* Single £120 per week; twin £95 per week; triple £85 per week. Deposit required and cancellation penalties; Continental breakfast included

AREA
Notting Hill Gate

If you want to brush up on your French-speaking skills, a stay at this youth-oriented budget bet will probably do the trick. A bilingual (French-English) staff welcomes guests the year round. Despite the run-down lounge and ratty carpeting, the dorm rooms are above average with lockers, white bunks, and wall murals. The residential location in Notting Hill Gate is close to Kensington Palace and the Portobello Road Market (see Shopping, page 196). Three tube lines and several bus routes will have you in the center of London in less than thirty minutes. Special language package deals can be arranged for groups and individuals.

Facilities and Services: Bar, central heat, hall phones, office safe for groups only, restaurant (groups only), TV and video in lounge, must bring own towels, 24-hour desk, no lift

Linstead Hall—Imperial College of Science and Technology
15 Prince's Gardens, Exhibition Road (entrance off Watts Way), SW7

TELEPHONE
071-225-6192, 071-225-8684

FAX
071-225-8697

TUBE
South Kensington

CREDIT CARDS
MC, V

NUMBER OF ROOMS
550

W/BST
None

Trying to find the reception office in a maze of institutional brick buildings can be very discouraging. The entrance is off Watts Way, not, as the address suggests, Prince's Gardens. To keep your frustration level to a minimum when you arrive, be sure to ask that a map of the facility be sent to you when you make your reservations. A few twin-bedded rooms are available, but most are singles. Children under 10 are not allowed, and the building is unsuitable for the disabled. The rooms, of the usual dorm variety, are cleaned each day, and the maid also changes the sheets every three days and will make your bed every day if you want. The hall toilets and showers are shared by only four rooms. In addition to a bar, dining room, and small grocery store, there is a bookshop, a new sports center, and a bank. The hall is located in a nice residential area on the boundary of Kensington and Chelsea, not far from museums and the Royal Albert Hall.

Facilities and Services: Bar, central heat, public phones in hall, laundry, restaurant, grocery store, book shop, bank, sports center, TV in lounge, lift in one building, kitchen facilities, soap, bath gel and hand lotion provided, faxing and photocopying facilities

RATES
Single £20–25; double £37–39; stays of 7 nights or more cost less. Ten-percent deposit is required on confirmation of reservations; a 40% payment of total charge to be paid *3 months* prior to arrival. Rates can be revised upward before a stay. If you cancel less than 3 months ahead, 50% will be forfeited. If you are a no-show, there is no refund. English breakfast included

AREA
South Kensington

London School of Economics and Political Science

The London School of Economics and Political Science offers comfortable, low-cost accommodations to the public when the school term is not in session. You can stay in one of the residence halls during Easter or in summer, and rent a flat for two to six people during the summer. With residence halls run like a B&B, and flats in the heart of London, plus a new complex of flats near the Tower Bridge, the LSE's facilities are an excellent choice for the budget traveler who can time a visit when its facilities are available. Individual rooms have wash basins, central heat, decent beds, welcome children under 12 for half price, and include a full English breakfast. Towels and linens are provided. Everything but breakfast is included in fully equipped flats. To arrange accommodation, contact the individual residence halls or apartments directly. A brief description of each follows.

Butler's Wharf Residence
11 Gainsford Street, SE1

Butler's Wharf is the newest LSE complex offering rooms and flats close to the Tower Bridge. It is opposite the St. Katharine Docks and close to the

TELEPHONE
071-403-8533, 071-407-7164

FAX
None

TUBE
Tower Hill, London Bridge

CREDIT CARDS
None

NUMBER OF ROOMS
250

W/BST
Flats all, rooms none

RATES
Rooms £25 per person; flats
£20 per person; English
breakfast included with rooms,
not with flats

AREA
Hays Wharf

Design Museum, Hays Wharf, and across the river from The Tower of London, the Barbican, Covent Garden, and the West End. All rooms are centrally heated and all linens are provided. The flats sleep up to seven in private bedrooms that share a communal living room, kitchen, and bathroom.

Facilities and Services: Rooms and flats: Bar, central heat, lift, linens, laundry facilities. Rooms: TV lounge, disabled access. Flats: garage

Carr Saunders Hall & Fitzroy and Maple Street Flats
18–24 Fitzroy Street, W1

TELEPHONE
071-580-6338, 071-323-9712

FAX
071-580-4718

TUBE
Warren Street

CREDIT CARDS
None

NUMBER OF ROOMS
157

W/BST
3

W/OBST
154

NUMBER OF FLATS
79

RATES
Rooms £23 per person,
children under 12 half price;
flats £20 per person per day.
Rooms are open to the public
during Easter and Christmas,
and July, August, and
September. Flats available only
July–September. English
breakfast included with rooms,
not with flats

AREA
Bloomsbury

This residence hall and block of flats are located between Regent's Park and Oxford Street and within easy reach of the West End's shopping and theaters. The flats are available during July, August, and September. Each apartment is fully self-contained, comfortably furnished, and equipped with cooking facilities and bed linens.

Facilities and Services: Rooms: Bar, central heat, lift, laundry facilities, limited garage space, kitchen on each floor with lockers for food. Flats: fully equipped with linens and towels, weekly maid service, lift, garage, bar, laundry facilities. Cafeteria open to all guests.

Rosebery Avenue Hall
90 Rosebery Avenue, EC1

From some of the rooms you will have a view of the famed Sadler's Wells Theater; from others you will see St. James's Church, built in 1792. As in all dormitory rooms, you can expect only the basics: hot and cold water, a bed, desk, chair, and small closet. Toilets and showers are on each floor. The tube stop here is Angel, which to many may seem like the edge of nowhere, but actually it isn't. The area is called Clerkenwell, and it was here that Oliver Twist was taught to pick pockets by the Artful Dodger. You are close to the Barbican Center, St. Paul's Cathedral, and the City of London. For a more contemporary side, you are in exploring distance from the Camden Passage Antiques Market, fringe theater events, and a traditional London street market in Chapel Street.

Facilities and Services: Bar, central heat, limited disabled access, TV lounge, laundry facilities, cafeterias, kitchen on each floor, no lift

TELEPHONE
071-278-3251

FAX
071-278-2068

TUBE
Angel

CREDIT CARDS
None

NUMBER OF ROOMS
193

W/BST
None

RATES
Single £21; double £29–42; triple £38; English breakfast included

AREA
Clerkenwell

MISCELLANEOUS
Open Easter, mid June–end of September

More House
53 Cromwell Road, SW7

More House is named for Sir Thomas More, a famous saint of the English Reformation who was Lord Chancellor under King Henry VIII and lived in nearby Chelsea. The house is run by the Sisters of St. Augustine, and during the school term is used as a dorm for students attending London University Colleges. In July and August, More House offers bed-and-breakfast accommodations at prices reminiscent of bygone days. Those planning to stay a week or more will have a 10 percent discount. If you are only staying one night, you will pay a £5 supplement. Groups receive favorable rates, and children under 6 stay free if they share their parents' room. Each sparse room has hot and cold running water and dormitory furnishings. Baths, showers, and toilets are on each floor and so are tea and coffeemakers, a microwave, refrigerator, and telephone to receive incoming calls. If you want to place a call, you have to dial it from a pay phone downstairs. A full English breakfast, with

TELEPHONE
071-584-2040

FAX
None

TUBE
South Kensington, Gloucester Road

CREDIT CARDS
None

NUMBER OF ROOMS
60

W/BST
None

RATES
Single £21–24; double £30–38; triple £41–45; dorm £12 per person; English breakfast included

AREA
South Kensington

MISCELLANEOUS
Accommodation inquiries: The Warden, More House, 53 Cromwell Road, London, SW7 2EH

juice, bacon, sausage, eggs, beans or tomatoes, cereal, rolls, toast, tea, and coffee, is served in the cafeteria. The South Kensington location is good, right across from the Natural History Museum. A nonrefundable £10 reservation deposit is required and this is deductible from the total bill. All payment must be in Sterling. If you are interested in this popular Cheap Sleep, get your reservation in ASAP because the word is out on this one.

Facilities and Services: Individual room heaters, public hall phones, microwave, refrigerator, tea and coffeemakers on each floor, TV in lounge, lift

Northampton Hall—City University
Bunhill Row, EC1

Northampton Hall is a 19-story highrise located in an office neighborhood on the edge of Islington and The City of London. The area is a wasteland at night and on weekends, but it close to St. Paul's Cathedral and the Barbican Center. The 9 x 11 rooms are available year round, which is an advantage. Each floor has shower facilities (coed), a small kitchen, and public telephone. There is a coin-operated laundry facility in the building. For a few pounds more, and a great increase in amenities, consider one of the seven private bedrooms in the Chancellor Suite on the top floor. These bedrooms share a living room, kitchen, and bathroom. There is a balcony and view, better furniture, and decent carpeting. The supplement runs around £15 per night.

Facilities and Services: Bar, central heat, phones in hall, laundry facilities, lift, office safe, restaurant, TV and video lounge, kitchens on the floor. Open year round (13 rooms); otherwise, July to October, Christmas, and a month at Easter

TELEPHONE
071-638-2953

FAX
None

TUBE
Angel

CREDIT CARDS
None

NUMBER OF ROOMS
Year round, 13 rooms, including 7 in the Chancellor Suite; otherwise, 486 rooms

W/BST
Some

W/OBST
Most

RATES
Single £19; double £28 (twin beds only); Chancellor Suite add £15; English breakfast included

MISCELLANEOUS
For information about other City University accommodations, contact The Accommodation and Conference Service, City University, Northampton Square, London EC1 VOHB (071-477-8037)

Queen Alexandra's House
Bremner Road, behind Royal Albert Hall, SW7

From July to mid-August, women students of all ages can check into Queen Alexandra's House. It is definitely not sumptuous, but it is a safe and well-located spot next to the Royal Albert Hall. One advantage is that most of the rooms are singles, so you won't have to bunk with strangers. It is popular, and advance reservations are strongly recommended because drop-ins rarely can be housed. To save more money, you can prepare meals in the small kitchen located on each floor. Coin-operated laundries and ironing facilities make it even more appealing to many.

Facilities and Services: Central heat, public phone in hall, iron, coin-operated laundry, kitchen on each floor, office safe, TV, restaurant, lift

TELEPHONE
071-589-3635

FAX
071-589-3177

TUBE
South Kensington

CREDIT CARDS
None

NUMBER OF ROOMS
100

W/BST
None

RATES
£24 per person in single or double room; Continental breakfast included

AREA
Kensington

Ramsay Hall—University College London

Ramsay Hall provides inexpensive, mainly single rooms during the Christmas and Easter holidays and from July 1 until September 30. The basic rooms come with hot and cold running water, and the rates include a cooked breakfast each morning. The kitchen will prepare packed lunches, but no other noon meal is served. Dinner, with two meat dishes and one vegetarian selection, is available. There are ground-floor rooms suitable for anyone in a wheelchair, and a shower and toilet for the disabled. From here the walk to Regent's Park and the British Museum is easy, and the public transportation for farther jaunts is very good.

Facilities and Services: Central heat, public phones in hall, coin-operated laundry facilities, lift, safe for passports only, TV and video in lounge, restaurant, 24-hour desk

TELEPHONE
071-387-4537

FAX
071-383-0843

TUBE
Great Portland Street or Goodge Street

CREDIT CARDS
None

NUMBER OF ROOMS
400

W/BST
None

RATES
£21 per person for all rooms; evening meal £7 per person; English breakfast included

AREA
Camden

MISCELLANEOUS
Inquiries: The Site Manager, Ramsay Hall, 20 Maple Street, London W1P 5GB

OTHER COLLEGE AND UNIVERSITY ACCOMMODATIONS

This list includes those residences most likely to have accommodations available during university vacations at Easter and in the summer. Full details of charges and facilities may be obtained by writing or telephoning the warden of the specific hall you choose. Your reservation will have to be secured with a deposit in pounds, and up to 50 percent of the charge for your stay will probably have to be sent three months in advance. Accommodations are spare . . . much like boot camp.

Intercollegiate Halls
Canterbury Hall
3 Cartwright Gardens, London WC1
Tel: 071-387-5526
Open: Easter and summer

Commonwealth Hall
Cartwright Gardens, London WC1
Tel: 071-387-0311
Open: Easter and from July 9–August 23

Connaught Hall
41 Tavistock Square, London WC1
Tel: 071-387-6181

Hughes Parry Hall
Cartwright Gardens, London WC1
Tel: 071-837-1477
Open: Easter and from July 5–August 3

International Hall
Brunswick Square, London WC1
Tel: 071-837-0746
Open: Easter and summer

Nutford House
Brown Street off George Street, London W1
Tel: 071-723-5020

College Residences
Ifor Evans Hall
Whitcher Place, Rochester Road, London NW1
Tel: 071-485-9377
Open: Easter and summer

Imperial College
South Side, Prince's Gardens, London SW7
Tel: 071-589-5111

King's College Halls
Ingram Court, 552 King's Road, London SW10
Lightfoot Hall, Manresa Road, London SW3
Queen Elizabeth Hall, Campden Hill Road, London
    W8
Wellington Hall, 71 Vincent Square, London SW1
Tel: 071-351-6011 for all King's College Halls
To reserve:
King's College Vacation Bureau
King's College London
552 King's Road, London SW10

Middlesex Hospital Medical School
Astor College, Charlotte Street, London W1
Tel: 071-580-7262
Open: Easter and summer

University College
Campbell Hall, 5–10 Taviton Street, London WC1
Tel: 071-387-7050, 071-388-0060
Open: Summer

Other Residences
London House for Overseas Graduates
Mecklenburgh Square, London WC1
Tel: 071-837-8888
Open: All year

Ys

For reliable, safe accommodations at great Cheap Sleeping prices, consider staying at one of the Ys in London. For the price, you will get bed, breakfast, and in some cases, dinner, too. If you have to pay for your own dinner in the Y restaurant, it will definitely be a Cheap Eat you will not be able to better. All Ys encourage long-term stays with reduced rates. Some are not very well located, but those included here are. If you want a list of all the Ys in London, call the National Council of YMCAs in London at 081-520-5599.

Barbican YMCA	184
Elizabeth House	184
Indian Student YMCA	185
Lancaster Hall Hotel (German YMCA)	186
London City YMCA	186
YMCA Central Club	187

Barbican YMCA

TELEPHONE
071-628-0697

FAX
071-638-2420

TUBE
Barbican

CREDIT CARDS
MC, V

NUMBER OF ROOMS
196

W/BST
None

RATES
Single £22 per day, £126 per week, includes English breakfast and dinner; double £20 per day per person, £110 per week per person, includes English breakfast and dinner

AREA
Barbican

2 Fann Street, EC2

One hundred and ninety-six rooms on sixteen floors make this one of the biggest Ys in London. It is new and popular, making reservations two months in advance almost a necessity. Rates include breakfast and dinner as well as use of the health and fitness center.

Facilities and Services: Central heat, public phones in hall, hair dryer available, lift, office safe, restaurant, TV in lounge, 24-hour desk

Elizabeth House

TELEPHONE
071-630-0741

FAX
None

118 Warwick Way, SW1

Pimlico, south of Victoria Station, is sprinkled with B&B hotels, most of which I find unacceptable. One stands out, however, and that is Elizabeth

House, a YWCA hotel providing beds in clean and safe surroundings to Cheap Sleepers of all ages. There are singles, doubles (some with private facilities, no less), and dorm rooms at remarkably low prices. The rooms are not spacious, but at least they are color-coordinated, even if the colors are orange and lime green. There are two television lounges, one for non-smokers, and a garden and patio used in warm weather. A filling Continental breakfast is included. Pound for pound, you may sleep cheaper, but you won't get as much value for your money as you do at Elizabeth House.

Facilities and Services: Central heat, direct-dial phones, iron available, office safe, no lift

TUBE
Victoria or Pimlico

CREDIT CARDS
None

NUMBER OF ROOMS
27

W/BST
10

W/OBST
17

RATES
Single nightly £25, weekly £145; double nightly £45, weekly £265; twin-bed room nightly £45-50, weekly £275-300; dorm room sleeps 3 or 4 nightly £17, weekly £115; nonrefundable deposit of £12 required to secure reservations; membership in the YWCA is 10p per week; Continental breakfast included

AREA
Pimlico

Indian Student YMCA
41 Fitzroy Street, WC1

After having breakfast at the Indian YMCA cafeteria (see *Cheap Eats in London*), I asked to see the student accommodations. Quite honestly, I did not expect to be very impressed. When I saw how clean and modern the facilities were, compared to many other student digs in London, I knew I had to tell Cheap Sleepers in London about this special bargain. The sunny rooms have light-colored wooden built-in furniture, three-drawer desks with shelves above, comfortable chairs, and acceptable beds. Sheets and towels are changed every three days and the maid comes in to dust once a week. The beauty of this particular student lodging is that, subject to availability, it is open for short-term stays year round to any person, with no age limit. Traditionally for Indian male guests, it does have a limited number of spaces for women. The price includes breakfast and dinner—Indian style—and there is *no* reduction if you don't eat here. If you like Indian food, this is a deal you will never beat. Even if you skip dinner

TELEPHONE
071-387-0411

FAX
071-383-7651

TUBE
Warren Street

CREDIT CARDS
None

NUMBER OF ROOMS
120

W/BST
None

RATES
Single £30; double £40; must pay membership fee of £1 if not YMCA member; buffet breakfast and dinner included Mon–Fri; breakfast, lunch, and dinner weekends

AREA
Bloomsbury

altogether, it is a Cheap Sleep you will have to go a long way to equal.

Facilities and Services: Central heat, lift (often out of order), cafeteria, TV in lounge, game room, study room, library

Lancaster Hall Hotel (German YMCA)
35 Craven Terrace, W2

TELEPHONE
071-723-9276

FAX
071-706-2870

TUBE
Lancaster Gate

CREDIT CARDS
MC, V

NUMBER OF ROOMS
100

W/BST
80

W/OBST
20 (student and group annex)

RATES
Single £52; double £68; group rates on request for parties of 20 or more. Annex (for persons under 26 or groups): Single £22; double £35; triple £45; four £55; Continental breakfast included in hotel and annex

AREA
Lancaster Gate

As we all know, searching for an accommodation in London that is comfortable, inexpensive, and well-located can be a frustrating experience. I am happy to tell you the search has narrowed, once you have found the Lancaster Hall Hotel, which is owned and operated by the German YMCA in London. German efficiency and sparseness are reflected from the main lobby to the 20-room student annex. An army of uniformed maids, pushing heavy-duty vacuum cleaners, swoops through the hotel each day making sure everything is absolutely shipshape. The basic rooms have matching curtains and bedspreads, laminated-pine furniture, closets with shelf space, and bathrooms with medicine chests and absorbent towels. The annex is geared for groups and students under 26, and none of the rooms have private baths. But with these unheard-of low prices, especially for groups, who cares?

The ground-floor lounge adjoins the Palatine Restaurant, a sedate fifties-style room with about as much personality as a physician's waiting room. Dinner is served at prices one usually dreams about: a three-course dinner including service goes for about £12.

For an all-around budget hotel, this is a top Cheap Sleep in London if there ever was one.

Facilities and Services: Bar after 6 P.M., central heat, direct-dial phones in hotel, office safe, TV, radio, restaurant, tea and coffeemakers in hotel rooms, lift in hotel

London City YMCA
8 Errol Street, EC1

TELEPHONE
071-628-8832

FAX
071-628-4080

Only single rooms are available at this Y, which is near the Barbican. During the year it is full of students, so getting space can be a problem. In the summer, you will have a better chance. Even though none of the rooms has private facilities, only two rooms share a toilet and shower so it really isn't too bad. Each room has its own TV, a bonus for some. Fitness nuts can sign up for aerobics, held four times a week in the evening.

Facilities and Services: Central heat, no phones, lift, TV in room, office safe, desk open 8:30 A.M.–10 P.M.

TUBE
Barbican or Moorgate

CREDIT CARDS
MC, V

NUMBER OF ROOMS
111

W/BST
None

RATES
Single rooms only, £24 per night, £126 per week; includes English breakfast and dinner

AREA
Barbican

YMCA Central Club
16–22 Great Russell Street, WC1

The YMCA Central Club, in the heart of Bloomsbury, provides a good, low-cost choice. It is located in the Lutyens House, a listed building named for the architect who designed it, Sir Edwin Lutyens.

While I would not nominate the 127 utilitarian rooms for any international decorating prizes, they are clean, fresh, light, spacious, and a safe bet, especially for single travelers looking for a central launching pad in London. All rooms have hotel amenities such as televisions, direct-dial phones, and central heat. Guests can use the swimming pool, laundry facilities, hairdressing salon, gym, and solarium. A cafeteria is handy for those who prefer to eat in. The food is basic English, with dishes like toad-in-the-hole, roast beef, and bread and butter pudding heading the lineup. If you loaded your tray to overflowing, you would have trouble spending more than £5 for a filling dinner.

Facilities and Services: Central heat, direct-dial phones, lift, office safe, cafeteria, TV and radio, tea and coffeemakers, coin laundry, hairdresser, swimming pool, gym, solarium

TELEPHONE
071-636-7512

FAX
071-636-5278

TUBE
Tottenham Court Road

CREDIT CARDS
MC, V

NUMBER OF ROOMS
127

W/BST
None

RATES
Single £32 per night, £200 per week, £680 per month; double £58 per night, £368 per week, £1250 per month; triple £20 per person; four £20 per person; five £18 per person; suite/apt £40 per person; breakfast not included

AREA
Bloomsbury

YOUTH HOSTELS

London youth hostels offer excellent value for anyone over the age of 5 wanting to eat and sleep cheaply on vacation. In order to stay at a hostel, you must be a member of either the American Youth Hostels or the International Youth Hostel Federation (if you are a resident of the U.K.). Either membership allows you access to 6,000 hostels in 70 countries, including 200 locations in the U.S. There are a number of hostels in London, some better located than others. I like the Earl's Court Youth Hostel because it is friendly, and the Rotherhithe and Carter Lane locations because they are new. If the youth hostel way of traveling appeals to you, write for information as far ahead as possible. Reservations can be made six months in advance, using either MasterCard or Visa. Hostels in popular destinations fill up quickly, and you don't want to be left out in the cold.

Reserve your space (booking fee of $2) by visiting reservation centers in the following cities: Boston, Los Angeles (Santa Monica), Miami Beach, Montreal, New York City, Ottawa, San Francisco, Seattle, Toronto, and Washington, D.C. You can also call, write, or fax Hosteling International/American Youth Hostels, 733 15th Street NW, Washington, D.C. 20005 (telephone and fax: 202-783-6161). To book London directly, call 071-248-6547, or fax 071-236-7681.

Prices are quoted per person. The uniform price for breakfast (if not included), is £3; lunch pack £2.50; dinner from £4.

Facilities at all London hostels include money changing at bank rates, locking rooms, personal storage lockers (bring your own locks), laundry, onward bookings, discount tickets to major attractions, and theater reservations. Sheets and sleeping bags can be rented at each site. The City of London Hostel restaurant is open to nonresidents 7 days a week for meals, snacks, tea, and coffee. This is important to know, especially on weekends when almost everything in the area is closed.

The City of London Youth Hostel	189
Earl's Court Youth Hostel	189
Hampstead Heath Youth Hostel	189
Highgate Village Youth Hostel	190
Holland House, King George VI Memorial Youth Hostel	190
Oxford Street Youth Hostel	191
Rotherhithe Youth Hostel	191

The City of London Youth Hostel
36 Carter Lane, EC4

TEL: 071-236-4965
FAX: 071-236-7681
TUBE: St. Paul's, Blackfriars, Cannon Street
CREDIT CARDS: MC, V
NUMBER OF ROOMS: Dormitory only
W/BST: None
RATES: £20 per person; Continental breakfast included
FACILITIES AND SERVICES: Central heat, public phones, TV in lounge, restaurant, money changing, theater booking, laundry
AREA: The City
MISCELLANEOUS: Reopened in February 1992, this Victorian building is adjacent to St. Paul's Cathedral and was, until 1968, the school for St. Paul's Choir boys. It is not suitable for groups because of inadequate parking.

Earl's Court Youth Hostel
38 Bolton Gardens, SW5

TEL: 071-373-7083
FAX: 071-835-2034
TUBE: Earl's Court
CREDIT CARDS: MC, V
NUMBER OF ROOMS: Dormitory only
W/BST: None
RATES: £18; Continental breakfast included
FACILITIES AND SERVICES: Central heat, restaurant, coin laundry, kitchen privileges, money changing, public phones, TV lounge, theater booking, dorms only
AREA: Earl's Court
MISCELLANEOUS: An old town house offers accommodation in an area popular with budget travelers. Many of London's museums are within 15 minutes and the exhibition halls at Olympia and Earl's Court are nearby.

Hampstead Heath Youth Hostel
4 Wellgarth Road, London NW11 7HR

TEL: 081-458-9054, 458-7196

FAX: 081-209-0546
TUBE: Golder's Green
CREDIT CARDS: MC, V
NUMBER OF ROOMS: Dormitory only
W/BST: None
RATES: £15; breakfast not included
FACILITIES AND SERVICES: Central heat, public phones, TV lounge, money changing, theater booking, laundry, restaurant, parking on site
AREA: Outside London, adjacent to Hampstead Heath
MISCELLANEOUS: Located in a quiet suburb away from Central London. You can reach the city in 30 minutes on the train.

Highgate Village Youth Hostel
84 Highgate West Hill, London N6 6LU
TEL: 081-340-1831
FAX: 081-341-0376
TUBE: Archway, Highgate
CREDIT CARDS: MC, V
NUMBER OF ROOMS: Dormitory only
W/BST: None
RATES: £14; breakfast not included
FACILITIES AND SERVICES: Central heat, public phones, TV lounge, theater booking, meal service for breakfast only, kitchen privileges, parking on site. Hostel closes 10 A.M.–5 P.M. and midnight–7 A.M.
AREA: Highgate, near Hampstead Heath
MISCELLANEOUS: Hostel is 30-minute trip from London central.

Holland House, King George VI Memorial Youth Hostel
Holland Walk, Kensington, W8
TEL: 071-937-0748
FAX: 071-376-0667
TUBE: High Street Kensington
CREDIT CARDS: MC, V
NUMBER OF ROOMS: Dormitory only
W/BST: None
RATES: £19; Continental breakfast included

FACILITIES AND SERVICES: Central heat, public phones, restaurant, kitchen privileges, TV lounge, money changing, laundry, theater booking

AREA: Kensington

MISCELLANEOUS: Part of a Jacobean mansion built in 1607, this hostel is set in a park. It has been refurbished.

Oxford Street Youth Hostel
14–18 Noel Street, W1

TEL: 071-734-1618

FAX: 071-734-1657

TUBE: Tottenham Court Road, Oxford Circus

CREDIT CARDS: MC, V

NUMBER OF ROOMS: 2, 3, and 4 to a room

W/BST: None

RATES: £19; breakfast not included

FACILITIES AND SERVICES: Central heat, public phones, lift, TV lounge, money changing, theater booking

AREA: Oxford Street/Soho

MISCELLANEOUS: Right in the heart of Soho and Oxford Street, this hostel is the best location for short-term London stays.

Rotherhithe Youth Hostel
Island Yard, Salter Road, Rotherhithe, London SE16 1LY

TEL: 071-232-2114

FAX: 071-237-2919

TUBE: Whitechapel and change to East London Line to Rotherhithe Station

CREDIT CARDS: MC, V

NUMBER OF ROOMS: 2, 3, and 4-bedded rooms

W/BST: None

RATES: £19; breakfast not included

FACILITIES AND SERVICES: Central heat, public phones, money changing, TV lounge, theater booking, laundry, restaurant, easy parking

AREA: One mile east of Tower of London, on South Bank of the Thames

MISCELLANEOUS: New hostel on the edge of London.

QUICK REFERENCE

BIG SPLURGES

The following hotels fall into the Big Splurge category. They are higher priced due to amenities, ambiance, service, and overall appeal. These are hotels to consider if your budget is more flexible, or if you are going to London with someone special.

HOTEL	POSTAL CODE	PAGE
Academy Hotel	WC1	75
Bonnington	WC1	77
Bryanston Court Hotel	W1	35
The Burns Park Hotel	SW5	127
The Byron Hotel	W2	50
The Claverly	SW3	121
The Cranley	SW5	128
The Delemere Hotel	W2	52
Diplomat Hotel	SW1	101
Dorset Square Hotel	NW1	147
Embassy House Hotel	SW7	138
The Fielding Hotel	WC2	91
Five Sumner Place Hotel	SW7	139
The Gore	SW7	140
Harrington Hall	SW7	141
Hazlitt's	W1	41
Number Sixteen	SW7	143
The Park International Hotel	SW7	145
The Pastoria	WC2	93
Pembridge Court Hotel	W2	58
The Portland Bloomsbury	WC1	86
The Portobello Hotel	W11	68
Royal Trafalgar Thistle Hotel	WC2	94
Searcy's Roof Garden Bedrooms	SW1	111
Tophams Ebury Court	SW1	112

GLOSSARY

America and Britain are two great nations divided by a common language.
—George Bernard Shaw

The following words could cause confusion or misinterpretation on the other side of the Atlantic.

ENGLISH	AMERICAN
A	
all-in	all inclusive
anorak	hooded jacket (parka)
B	
bank holiday	legal holiday
bath room	a room for baths
bed-sit or bedsitter	studio or one-room apartment
bespoke	custom-made clothing
bill	check (restaurant)
bobby	police officer
bonnet (car)	car hood
book *(v.)*	reserve
boot	car trunk
braces	suspenders
briefs	jockey shorts
brolly or bumbershoot	umbrella
C	
caravan	trailer, mobile home
car park	parking lot
chemist	pharmacist
chemist shop	drugstore, pharmacy
coach	tour bus
cot crib	baby crib
cotton	thread
cotton wool	absorbent cotton
cupboard	closet
D	
directory enquiries	telephone information/directory assistance
double	hotel room with double bed
E	
eiderdown	comforter
en suite	hotel room with private toilet, shower and/or bathtub

F

face flannel	wash cloth
first floor	second floor
flat	apartment
flex	electric cord
fortnight	two weeks

G

ground floor	first floor

H

hair grip	bobby pin
hair slide	barrette
high street	main street
hire *(v.)*	rent (as in rent a car)

I

ironmonger	hardware store

J

jumper	sweater, pullover

K

knickers	underpants

L

let *(v.)*	lease, rent
lift	elevator
loo	toilet
lorry	truck

M

mackintosh	raincoat

N

nappy	diaper
net curtains	sheer curtains
nought	zero

O

off-licence/wine merchant	retail liquor store
off the peg	ready-made

P

pants	shorts (men's underwear)
personal call	person-to-person telephone call
petrol	gasoline
phone box or call box	telephone booth
point, power point	outlet, socket
post	mail
postal code	zip code
push chair	stroller

Q

queue	waiting line

R

reception (hotel)	front desk
return ticket	round-trip ticket

S

self-catering	accommodation with kitchen
self-drive	car rental
service flats	apartment hotel
single ticket	one-way ticket
subway	underground passageway
suspender belt	garter belt
suspenders	garters

T

telly	television
tights	panty hose
torch	flashlight
treble (room)	triple hotel room with one double bed and one single
triple (room)	hotel room with three single beds
trousers	slacks, never called pants
trunk call	long distance
tube (Underground)	subway
turn-ups (trousers)	cuffs on trousers
twin (room)	hotel room with two beds

V

VAT (value-added tax)	sales tax
vest	man's undershirt

W

waistcoat	vest
wardrobe	closet
water closet (WC)	toilet

Z

zebra crossing	pedestrian crossing
zed (letter)	z

SHOPPING: CHEAP CHIC

If ever there was a world-class city for shopping, London is it. Whatever you need or want, there is a shop in London where you can buy it, order it, or have it especially made for you.

According to the British Tourist Authority, shopping is the most popular tourist activity in London, outstripping visits to the Tower of London, Madame Tussaud's, the theater, the Changing of the Guard, and the Elgin Marbles. There are shops catering to everyone from the Queen and the English gentry to East End Cockneys and those on the wild side of today's fashion.

With the sinking value of the U.S. dollar and inflation in double digits, you probably won't come home with the bargain of a lifetime, but that's not the point. The great sport of London shopping lies in exploring different places, finding unusual things, and enjoying them once you are home. There are values to be found in china, woolens, and stylish clothes created by young, undiscovered designers.

Discount shopping as we know and love it, I am sorry to report, is not a strong shopping alternative here. Sales are held in January and July, and these events attract buyers from around the globe. People wait all year for these few weeks, when prices are slashed up to 50 percent on most goods. Some shopping lunatics camp out overnight before Harrods opens on the first day of its January sale. The less devoted will still snag lots of terrific bargains if they can withstand the crowds who seem to lose their usual sense of British decorum during the hunt.

Cheap Chic shoppers should pay close attention to second-hand couture shops. These are not smelly, little used-clothing shops hidden on dreary back streets; they are really some of the smartest shopping addresses in town. Here customers are able to sell their designer clothes and pick up others, as well as end-of-season stock and work by up-and-coming new faces on the fashion scene.

As Bette Midler said, "When it is 3 o'clock in New York, it is still 1938 in London." Shopping hours are behind the times from an American merchandising viewpoint. The British still stay home on Sunday and lock their shop doors before supper time. From Monday through Saturday, they are open from 9 or 9:30 in the morning until 5:30 or 6 in the evening. Shops in Knightsbridge and Chelsea stay open until about 8 P.M. on Wednesdays, and those around Oxford Street and Kensington High Street are open until 8 P.M. on Thursdays. Except for some shops around Covent Garden, and many second-hand book shops along Charing Cross Road, London stores are locked tight on Sundays and bank holidays.

Besides its myriad shops and department stores, London is famous for street markets. Don't go to one of these huge outdoor circuses expecting to find hidden and valuable treasures for only a few pence. Go instead for the overall experience and the fun of just being there. These open-air bazaars are good places to pick up little gifts and mementos to take home, but don't get taken in by a glib dealer who will try to sell you the moon. If it smells like vinyl, it is not a rare leather product out of the Amazon jungle, no matter what the stall dealer claims. If you remember there are no bargains, just lucky purchases, you will do fine.

It is beyond the scope of *Cheap Sleeps in London* to detail the vast London shopping scene. To get you started, however, I have outlined the major shopping areas, listed major department stores, indoor and outdoor markets, museum stores, and a sampling of interesting shops. This information about the shops and markets was correct at press time, but details do change. Some places will have closed, changed hands, or altered their hours. If you are making a special trip, I urge you to call ahead and check the facts so you will not waste time on a false hope.

CHEAP CHIC SHOPPING TIPS

1. Know your prices at home so you will be able to spot a good buy when you see it in London.

2. If you want it, can get it home, and can afford it, then buy it when you see it. If you wait until later, it probably won't be there when you go back, or you will see it someplace else for twice the price.

3. Bring color swatches of anything you are trying to match. There are no returns once you get it home and find it does not quite go.

4. Pack an empty, soft folding suitcase in your luggage so you can transport your treasures home with you without the extra hassle and expense of mailing. An extra suitcase over the airline limit of two, plus a carry-on, will cost you around $100, which is payable at check-in time. This is cheap when you consider mailing and insurance costs, and the worry that the box may not arrive, or be damaged en route.

5. Take time to fill out the paperwork for the VAT, and remember to turn it in at the customs office at the airport *before* you relinquish your luggage or go through customs and passport

control. (For further details on the ins and outs of the VAT refund, see page 200.)

6. If you are a committed shopaholic, consider a trip to London during the twice-yearly sales in January and July. Check with the airlines and some of the higher-priced hotel chains in London. Many offer four- and five-day package deals around these sale times with prices too cheap to ignore. The January sale at Harrods is legendary. More than 300,000 shoppers surge through the store on the first day, and 2,000 temporary clerks are added to take care of them. The bargains are good in all departments, but be careful of the bin merchandise which has been brought in specifically for the sale and is of lesser quality than Harrods' regular goods.

7. Unless you are a big-time antiques dealer, buy for the pleasure an object will give you, not for long-term investment qualities the dealer will extoll. After all, if you like it, you won't want to part with it.

8. When buying from a street market or antiques dealer, don't forget to haggle. It is expected. Everything is negotiable, and usually the higher the price, the more you can deal. Always buy the best you can afford and do not settle for something cracked, chipped, or otherwise damaged . . . even if the dealer insists it won't matter. Good phrases to remember are: "What is the best price on that?" or "What is the trade on that?" which implies you are in the antiques business.

9. *Never* change money in a shop or at a money-changing booth at a flea market. Large department stores like Harrods and Selfridges have their own banks and the rates are competitive, but in the small shops, the exchange rate will *never* be in your favor. In department stores, use plastic. When shopping street markets, bring cash to strike the best deal.

10. Each person returning from abroad is allowed to bring back $400 worth of duty-free items. You must have these items with you, or have sent them in duty-free packages not exceeding a value of $50 per package. This duty-free allowance is per person, so if you are traveling with others, you can use their $400 allowance, but you will have to claim it under their name. If you ship purchases back to the States, anything worth $50 or less can be shipped as an unsolicited gift and is duty free. If the value is more than $50, it will be subject to duty.

WHAT SIZE IS THAT IN AMERICAN?

British sizing can be very confusing if you don't have a head start on how to deal with it. Most manufacturers have their own cuts, and some even put smaller sizes in larger items to flatter those with a "fuller figure." The key to success is to try on everything you can. This isn't always possible, so be sure to bring measurements for those not with you and carry a tape measure with both inches and centimeters. (England recently converted to the metric system.) Watch out on men's shirts. The sleeve length is not mentioned, so you will have to measure them. Table and bed sizes are also different from ours, so be careful.

WOMEN'S COATS AND DRESSES

U.S.	4	6	8	10	12	14	16	18
U.K.	28	30	32	34	36	38	40	42
Continental	34	36	38	40	42	44	46	48

WOMEN'S BLOUSES AND SWEATERS

U.S.	4	6	8	10	12	14	16
U.K.	30	32	34	36	38	40	42
Continental	36	38	40	42	44	46	48

MEN'S SUITS, COATS, SWEATERS

U.S. & U.K.	34	36	38	40	42	46
Continental	44	46	48	50	52	54

MEN'S SHIRTS

U.S. & U.K.	14	14½	15	15½	16	16½
Continental	36	37	38	39	40	41

WOMEN'S SHOES

U.S.	6	6½	7	7½	8	8½	9	9½
U.K.	4½	5	5½	6	6½	7	7½	8
Continental	36	37	37½	38	38½	39	40	41

MEN'S SHOES

U.S.	8	9	10	11
U.K.	7½	8½	9½	10½
Continental	41	43	44	45

CHILDREN'S CLOTHING

U.S.	3	4	5	6	6x
U.K.	18	20	22	24	26
Continental	98	104	110	116	122

CHILDREN'S SHOES

U.S.	8	9	10	11	12	13	1	2	3
U.K.	7	8	9	10	11	12	13	1	2
Continental	24	25	27	28	29	30	32	33	34

VAT REFUND (VALUE-ADDED TAX REFUND)

You *must* ask for the VAT refund; no one will volunteer it.

WHAT IS IT?

Value-added taxes (VAT) are taxes added to the price of most goods, including hotel rooms, cars, books, jewelry, and clothing. You cannot get a rebate for the hotel VAT, but you can for your shopping purchases, unless you are buying from a flea market vendor.

HOW DOES IT WORK?

Visitors to Britain planning to leave within six months of arrival may claim back the VAT they spent on shopping purchases. When you are in a store, ask what their minimum expenditure is for you to claim the VAT refund. The amount varies, but all stores have a minimum-purchase requirement, usually around £100, and some (Marks & Spencer) will insist it be made in one branch, not in a combination of several. You do not have to buy everything all at once, but you must save your receipts and total them when you know you have finished shopping at that store. Most major department stores have VAT departments where they will help you with the paperwork, but if not, don't worry, the paperwork is really a snap, and well worth the few extra minutes it takes. *Important:* You *must* show your passport at the store granting the VAT. Without it you won't get to first base. The store will ask you if you want the refund credited to your credit card, mailed to you in a pounds Sterling check, or in rare instances, refunded to you in a check for U.S. dollars. The best bet is to have it credited to your credit card. It is not only much faster than waiting for the check to arrive, but the credit will be in U.S. dollars, not pounds Sterling, which will cost you to convert at your bank. If you have the refund put on your credit card, you will also save any service charges the store may impose for "handling" the check, i.e., mailing it.

Before you leave England, you *must* have the forms completely filled out. When you arrive at the airport, go directly to the customs official who deals with the VAT. There will be a sign, or ask if you don't see it. You have to do this *before* you send off your luggage or clear customs. The officer will stamp your papers and there will be a mailbox by the desk where you deposit the envelopes. That is all there is to it. Then you go home and wait from eight to twelve weeks for the refund to arrive. Considering that the VAT can run up to 17½ percent, it is worth the extra time and effort involved.

SHOPPING AREAS

Most shopping is concentrated along certain streets and in specific areas, making London an easy city in which to plan a shopping expedition. Each area is different, with its own character and atmosphere. Traditional men's clothing is always found on Savile Row; both Old and New Bond streets are known for their fashionable boutiques, art galleries, and auction houses; while King's Road and Kensington are the places for the last word in new wave fashions. Book-lovers will head for Foyles at 113–119 Charing Cross Road, and one-stop power shoppers will find everything they need at Harrods, the famous Knightsbridge department store that covers over 20 acres of retail selling space.

THE WEST END (W1)

The West End is the heart of London and one of the most important shopping areas of the city. The big shopping streets are here: Oxford and Regent streets, Savile Row, Jermyn Street, Old and New Bond streets, and Piccadilly. Also here is the beautiful and expensive Burlington Arcade, Aquascutum, Hamley's toy store, Liberty, and much more. If you only have time to window shop for an hour or so, you will not forget your time spent on New and Old Bond streets. The shops are magnificent; so are the prices.

KNIGHTSBRIDGE (SW3)

After the West End, Knightsbridge has the largest concentration of shops. The most important streets to remember are Brompton Road (Harrods is here), Sloane Street (Harvey Nichols and designer show boutiques), and Beauchamp Place (pronounced "beech-um"). This is a block-long strip of exclusive shops where Princess Diana's favorite designer, Bruce Oldfield, has his shop. Another of her favorites along here is Janet Reger, a specialist in luxurious lingerie. This is the place to pick up a little silk nighty for £800, or a pair of silk briefs for £300.

Bargain hunters will want to browse through the three Reject China shops, all on Beauchamp Place.

KENSINGTON (W8)

When you get off at the High Street Kensington tube stop, you will be right in the middle of this wonderful shopping area concentrated along Kensington High Street and Kensington Church Street. If you love far-out fashions, do not miss Hyper-Hyper or the Kensington Market, both on Kensington High Street, for the last word in fashions from the fringe. For the more traditionally minded, there is a Marks & Spencer, House of Fraser, a branch of the British Home Stores, Laura Ashley, and Jigsaw. Antiques lovers will enjoy strolling along Kensington Church Street, where both sides of the street are lined with jewel-like shops featuring museum-quality antiques and collectables.

CHELSEA (SW3, SW10)

Saturday is the best day to experience Chelsea. Take the tube to Sloane Square and start with a quick look through Peter Jones Department Store and then work your way down both sides of King's Road. The shops along here come and go, but they all display what the well-to-do under-40 set is wearing. Once the home of punkers wearing skin-tight leather and spiked purple hair, things have calmed down a bit because most of these fashion victims have moved on to Kensington High Street. You will probably see more Sloane Rangers (British yuppies) in their Ralph Lauren and Laura Ashley clothes, behind the wheel of a British Range Rover, than you will freaky dressers, but the farther you go along the King's Road toward Fulham, the crazier things get. Antiques buffs will want to save time for the Chenil Galleries or Antiquarious, both good spots for affordable collectables to tuck into your suitcase.

COVENT GARDEN (WC2)

The old flower and vegetable market has been turned into a complex of snazzy shops and boutiques that seem to come and go faster than you can say "Rex Harrison and Julie Andrews in *My Fair Lady*." It is an upbeat part of London, jammed with clothing shops, arts and crafts booths, restaurants, and cafes. Outside, a carnival atmosphere prevails, with a constant show put on by sidewalk mimes, jugglers, magicians, and musicians. All around the market itself are shops, pubs, and more restaurants. It is a great area, alive and fun, day or night. You shouldn't leave London without at least walking through it.

STORE LISTINGS

SHOPS IN W1

The Body Shop   203
Boots   204
Brown's—Labels for Less   204
The Button Queen   205
The China Ware House Company   205
Classic Jewelry   206
The Countryside Bookshop   206
Culpeper   206
James Smith & Sons (Umbrellas) Ltd.   207
Liberty Clearance Shop   207
Metropolis   208
Paco Life in Colour   208
Reject China Shop   209
South Molton Drug Store   209

DEPARTMENT STORES IN W1

Debenhams   224
D. H. Evans   224
Dickens & Jones   224
Fortnum & Mason   224
Liberty   225
Lilywhite   226
Marks & Spencer   226
Selfridges   226

MARKETS IN W1

Grey's Antique Markets   228

MUSEUM SHOPS IN W1

Royal Academy Shop   232

The Body Shop
32–34 Great Marlborough Street, W1
TELEPHONE: 071-435-5137
TUBE: Piccadilly Circus
CREDIT CARDS: AE, DC, MC, V
TYPE: Natural cosmetics and skin care products
HOURS: Mon–Wed, Sat 9:30 A.M.–6 P.M.; Thurs until 7:30 P.M.; Fri until 7 P.M.

The Body Shop is Britain's largest skin- and hair-care retailer specializing in natural products. All products are as pure as possible and *never* tested on animals. Some of their unusual ingredients include cucumber, aloe, carrot, elderflower, seaweed, and grape. All shops are self-serve, and each product has an explanation of what it can do for you. Several sizes are available, making it easy to experiment before investing great sums. The small sizes are great to tuck into a travel bag or to take home as little gifts. Prices are very reasonable. For instance, in the cosmetics section, eyeliners, blushers, lipstick, and powders are mostly priced under £4.

The Body Shop has branches throughout London. A few of the more central include 54 King's Road, SW3; 203 Kensington High Street, W8; 13 The Market, Covent Garden, WC2; 15 Brompton Road, Knightsbridge, SW3; The London Pavillion, Piccadilly Circus, W1; 66 Oxford Street, W1.

Boots
182 Regent Street, W1
TELEPHONE: 071-734-4934
TUBE: Oxford Circus, Piccadilly Circus
CREDIT CARDS: AE, MC, V
TYPE: Drugstore with everything
HOURS: Mon–Sat 9 A.M.–5:30 P.M.; Wed or Thurs until 6:30 p.m depending on location

Boots is one of England's best-known chemists (drugstores) with more than 90 locations in London and 40 in the West End. Actually, most branches are more like mini-department stores, with sections devoted to home decorating, stationery, food, household items, and gardening supplies as well as a full array of cosmetics and health-care products. The prices are competitive and the supply good. They stock my favorite French makeup brand, Bourjois (the prototype for Chanel), and Cyclax, Jacqueline Onassis's pet brand. They also sell their own cosmetic line. The Boots on Regent Street is listed here because it is the biggest store, but almost every neighborhood has a Boots.

Brown's—Labels for Less
50 South Molton Street, W1
TELEPHONE: 071-491-7833; 071-493-1230, ext 252; fax: 071-408-1281
TUBE: Bond Street
CREDIT CARDS: AE, DC, MC, V
TYPE: Discounted designer labels
HOURS: Mon–Sat 10:30 A.M.–6 P.M.

Along South Molton Street are several Brown's boutiques, all but one beyond the pocketbooks of most Cheap Chic shoppers. The one you want is at 50 South Molton Street. Here you will find men's and women's designer clothing that did not sell in any of the other Browns shops. The labels vary, but should include some of the following: Chloe, DKNY, Montana, Moschino, Byblos, and Comme des Garçons.

The Button Queen
19 Marylebone Lane, W1
TELEPHONE: 071-935-1505
TUBE: Bond Street
CREDIT CARDS: MC, V
TYPE: Buttons of every description
HOURS: Mon–Fri 10 A.M.–6 P.M.; Sat 10 A.M.–1:30 P.M.; closed all holidays and last 2 weeks in August

Button, button, who has the button? The Button Queen does, at 19 Marylebone Lane. For the definitive word in buttons, this is the place. Owners Toni and Martyn Frith have an enormous supply of buttons in pearl, wood, glass, silver, and porcelain, as well as buttons for collectors, dress designers, military buffs, or anyone else wanting something different. If you go around lunchtime, stop by Paul Rothe & Son at 35 Marylebone Lane for a great corned beef sandwich on rye (see *Cheap Eats in London*).

The China Ware House Company
14–16 Ganton Street (corner of Carnaby Street), W1
TELEPHONE: 071-734-2174; fax: 071-287-5977
TUBE: Oxford Circus
CREDIT CARDS: AE, DC, MC, V
TYPE: Discount china
HOURS: Daily 10 A.M.–7 P.M.

All bargain shoppers worth their salt know about London's Reject China Shops (see page 209). Frankly, I think the China Ware House Company is just as good, and in some cases a little cheaper. This is a single small shop, overloaded with merchandise with little space for maneuvering, but the selection is good. And if you don't see exactly what you are looking for, chances are it can be ordered and shipped directly to your home. Here you will find first quality English china, miniature cottages by David Winter and Lilliput Lane, Portmeirion china and linens, and pretty dolls with sweet bone china faces and hands. As with all discounters, the stock varies; some days the store may be a goldmine and on others you may find nothing at all.

Classic Jewelry
44 Berwick Street, W1
TELEPHONE: 071-287-4746
TUBE: Oxford Circus
CREDIT CARDS: None
TYPE: Costume jewelry, hats, belts, handbags
HOURS: Sat noon– 5 P.M.

Everyone is "darling" to Ali, the burly owner of this corner jewelry store where everything is outrageously fake and ridiculously cheap. This tiny wholesale shop is open to the public only on Saturday afternoon from noon until 5 P.M. It is just the place to pick up the right necklace, bracelet, or pair of earrings to complete any outfit. Also available are hats, belts, handbags, and a selection of funky watches. Pick up a basket by the front door to gather loot as you browse. Bring cash; Ali doesn't bother with credit cards.

The Countryside Bookshop
39 Goodge Street, W1
TELEPHONE: 071-636-3156; fax: 071-323-6879
TUBE: Goodge Street
CREDIT CARDS: MC, V
TYPE: Books on gardening, flowers, crafts, interiors; maps and guides to the British Isles; cookbooks; second-hand books on these subjects; wide selection of greeting cards
HOURS: Mon–Fri 9:30 A.M.–6:30 P.M.; Thurs 9:30 A.M.–7:30 P.M.; Sat 11 A.M.–6 P.M.

The Countryside Bookshop should be a required stop for everyone heading out into the hills and dales of the English countryside, or who is interested in English gardens or interiors. This shop stocks hundreds of detailed maps and guides covering every aspect of the British Isles. There is a second-hand section downstairs, a children's section, and a fine selection of greeting cards. A knowledgeable staff offers sound advice on whatever your interest might be. They will ship your order and charge only postage, without a handling fee.

Culpeper
21 Bruton Street, Berkley Square, W1
TELEPHONE: 071-629-4559
TUBE: Bond Street, Green Park
CREDIT CARDS: AE, MC, V
TYPE: Products made from fresh herbs and spices
HOURS: Mon–Fri 9:30 A.M.–6 P.M.; Sat 10 A.M.–5 P.M.

The emphasis at Culpeper is on natural ingredients. All products are as pure as possible and none have been tested on animals. The two shops stock soaps, lotions, remedies, essential oils, and a wide range of herbs, spices, honeys, and herbal jellies. You can also buy more than 75 varieties of herb and wildflower seeds, herb mustards, herb-filled home fragrances, curries, and postcards and books on herbs. No artificial colors, preservatives, or enhancers are added to Culpeper's food products. They also grow many of their own herbs for use in their cosmetics, foods, and potpourri blends. Culpeper products have a reputation for quality, simple yet attractive packaging, and excellent value.

Note: There is a branch at 8 The Market, Covent Garden, WC2, TELEPHONE: 071-379-6698. HOURS: Mon–Sat 10:00 A.M.–8 P.M.

James Smith & Sons (Umbrellas) Ltd.
Hazelwood House, 53 New Oxford Street, W1
TELEPHONE: 071-836-4731
TUBE: Tottenham Court Road
CREDIT CARDS: MC, V
TYPE: Umbrellas, walking sticks, and seat sticks
HOURS: Mon–Fri 9:30 A.M.–5:30 P.M.; Sat 10 A.M.–5:30 P.M.

An umbrella, walking stick, or seat stick purchased from James Smith & Sons will not be cheap, but it will last your lifetime, and probably that of your heirs. Even if you are not in the market for a fine umbrella, please take a few minutes just to look at this fascinating shop, which is the oldest and biggest umbrella shop in Europe. Almost unaltered in a century of doing business in the same spot, the storefront is a perfect example of Victorian shop front design. Before Smith and Sons occupied it, the building housed a dairy. When you go inside, if you look closely, you can still see some of the original dairy floor tiles. While you may think custom umbrellas may have a limited appeal, think again: over 500 are sold and 2,000 repaired every month at this shop.

Liberty Clearance Shop
11 Foubert's Place, off Regent Street, W1
TELEPHONE: 071-734-5004
TUBE: Oxford Circus
CREDIT CARDS: AE, DC, MC, V
TYPE: Liberty of London items remaining unsold in the famous department store
HOURS: Mon–Sat 9:45 A.M.–5:30 P.M.

Have I got a deal for you! If you love Liberty prints, but do not love paying the sky-high prices most of their items command, then run, do not walk, to the Liberty Clearance Shop. You will find silk and cotton neckties, ready-to-sew skirts, blouses, picture frames, coin purses, and much more, all in the famous Liberty prints. Be prepared to see last season's styles and fabrics and some color mixes you probably will not want, especially in the men's neckties. But, with some careful looking, you will be able to pick up several nuggets to take back for yourself or to give as lovely gifts.

Metropolis
3 D'Arblay Street, W1
TELEPHONE: 071-494-2531
TUBE: Oxford Circus
CREDIT CARDS: AE, MC, V
TYPE: Collectables from the 1930s to present
HOURS: Mon–Fri 10 A.M.–6:30 P.M.; Sat 11:30 A.M.–5 P.M.

Nostalgia buffs won't want to miss Metropolis, a two-level shop displaying styles and designs from the thirties and forties to the present. Look for old and new jewelry, some especially designed for this shop. Also for sale are vintage teapots, coffeemakers, lamps, china and old glass, lighters, old and new pens, and reconditioned European telephones and radios. Pages from magazines of the forties and fifties make easy-to-carry gifts and so do many of the smaller kitsch items. More difficult to take home or ship are some of the larger pieces of furniture, but they are fun to look at, anyway.

Paco Life in Colour
Unit 7, Trocadero Centre, W1
TELEPHONE: 071-434-1836
TUBE: Piccadilly Circus
CREDIT CARDS: AE, DC, MC, V
TYPE: Sweaters, leisure wear
HOURS: Daily 10 A.M.–10 P.M.

Paco began in 1985 selling beautiful sweaters at fairs. Its first store opened in Cork, Ireland, shortly after and now there are over 40 sites throughout the U.K. The colors are bold and bright, the designs new and different, and the prices affordable. Besides more sweaters than you can imagine, they carry sweats, leisure wear, knits, and jeans. It is mainly for the youthful and slim set, but if you are young in spirit, be sure to take a look. Other locations in London are 122 King's Road,

071-823-7626, and Whiteleys Shopping Center, Queensway, 071-792-2496.

Reject China Shop
134 Regent Street, W1
TELEPHONE: 071-434-2502
TUBE: Piccadilly Circus
CREDIT CARDS: AE, DC, MC, V
TYPE: Discount china, crystal, silver, pottery, and gifts
HOURS: Mon–Sat 9 A.M.–6 P.M.; Sun 10 A.M.–6 P.M.

Although it began as a reject shop years ago, the stock offered today is the same quality you will find at Harrods. The best part is you will pay less for it here. For example, if you buy six place settings of first quality, you will save 10 percent. Seconds, when available, sell at 30–60 percent below retail. If you want your order shipped, you will save the VAT, but will pay for the shipping and insurance. If you are taking your goods with you, save your receipts and when they add up to £100, you can apply for the VAT refund, but the store will deduct a £6 administration charge. The sales in January and August make shopping here even more of a good deal. Some of the staff tend to be bored with it all, but if you persevere, you can get what you want. Expect to find all the top English names in bone china, pottery, crystal, figurines, and gift items. Other branches: 183 Brompton Road, 33–35 Beauchamp Place, 56–57 Beauchamp Place. These three are in SW1 and their tube stop is Knightsbridge.

South Molton Drug Store
64 South Molton Street, W1
TELEPHONE: 071-493-4156
TUBE: Bond Street
CREDIT CARDS: MC, V
TYPE: Discounted and discontinued cosmetic products
HOURS: Mon–Fri 9 A.M.–6 P.M.; Sat 9 A.M.–5 P.M.

If you can stand the terrible music and lethal lunchtime crowds of shop girls who swarm through, you will probably find a treasure or two. The South Molton Drug Store carries discontinued lines of Elizabeth Arden, Revlon, Mary Quant, and Max Factor, all at low prices. Not all brands are always available, and as with all discount places, quality and quantity can be very spotty. The shop also has its own budget line of cosmetics with giveaway prices starting at £1.50. The turnover is enormous, so if at first you don't succeed, try again.

SHOPS IN W2
Bayswater Road Art Exhibition   210
Whiteleys of Bayswater Shopping Center   210

Bayswater Road Art Exhibition
Clarendon Place until Queensway, W2
TELEPHONE: None
TUBE: Queensway, Lancaster Gate
CREDIT CARDS: Depends on artist, but most will take MasterCard or Visa
TYPE: Original art and crafts
HOURS: Sun 8 A.M.–5 P.M.

Where do bargain hunters go on Sunday in London? To the Bayswater Road Art Exhibition. Smart shoppers arrive around 10 A.M. when the selection is best. The exhibition runs along the north side of Hyde Park and Kensington Gardens on Bayswater Road. More than 280 artists display their works at extraordinary prices. You can select from modern to romantic, watercolor or oil, pen and ink, or hand-made crafts. Most of the artists are present, so you can meet them and discuss price. Most take plastic and many will arrange shipping. If you don't want to ship and insure your new artwork (and that will cost more than the piece you have just purchased), walk up the street to the luggage shop and buy a suitcase for carting home your purchases. It will arrive when you do and cost a fraction of having it sent.

Whiteleys of Bayswater Shopping Center
Queensway, W2
TELEPHONE: 071-229-8844
TUBE: Queensway
CREDIT CARDS: Depends on shop
TYPE: Multi-level shopping complex
HOURS: Mon–Sat 10 A.M.–8 P.M. (stores); 10 A.M.–10 P.M. daily (restaurants); also daily (cinemas)

This indoor shopping complex has four floors of shops, restaurants, and cinemas, with Marks & Spencer, NEXT, the Body Shop, and much more. It is a good place to go with family because there is something for everyone to do while Mom or Dad shops.

SHOPS IN W8

Davies Antiques	211
Jigsaw	211
NEXT	211
Portmeirion Gift Shop	212

MARKETS IN W8

Hyper-Hyper	212
Kensington Market	213

Davies Antiques
40A Kensington Church Street, W8
TELEPHONE: 071-937-3379, 937-9216
TUBE: High Street Kensington
CREDIT CARDS: AE, DC, MC, V
TYPE: Antiquarian maps and prints
HOURS: Mon–Fri 9:30 A.M.–5:30 P.M.; Sat 9:30 A.M.–3 P.M.

If you appreciate antiquarian maps and prints, especially botanicals, a trip to Davies is definitely worthwhile. Try to go early in your stay in case you want something rematted or framed, both of which can be expertly and reasonably done here. The prices are exceptionally good for the area, which is considered to be one of the premier antiques hunting grounds in London. Loads of antiques shops line Kensington Church Street, with prices not geared for amateurs. Just remember this: it doesn't cost a penny to look and dream.

Jigsaw
65 Kensington High Street, W8
TELEPHONE: 071-937-3572
TUBE: High Street Kensington
CREDIT CARDS: MC, V
TYPE: Youthful fashions
HOURS: Mon–Wed, Fri 10 A.M.–7 P.M.; Thurs 10 A.M.–7:30 P.M.; Sat 10 A.M.–6 P.M.

If you are short in the cash department, but long on the latest styles, a trip to Jigsaw is worthwhile. Quality is not tops, but then neither are the prices. There are several branches in London.

NEXT
54–60 Kensington High Street, W8
TELEPHONE: 071-938-4211
TUBE: High Street Kensington

CREDIT CARDS: MC, V

TYPE: Conservative, traditional clothing for men, women, and children

HOURS: Mon–Sat 10 A.M.–6 P.M.; Thurs 10 A.M.–8 P.M.

NEXT shops are all over London, or as someone aptly put it, "Next to almost everything." These shops are very popular and quite the "in" places to shop for traditional yet stylish clothing and accessories. Prices are not cheap, but if you look hard, and check the seasonal sale racks, chances are you will pick up something you will wear and enjoy for years. I like their coordinated outfits that have pants, skirts, blazers, and blouses you can mix and match to create several looks.

Portmeirion Gift Shop

4 Holland Street, W8

TELEPHONE: 071-938-1891

TUBE: High Street Kensington

CREDIT CARDS: MC, V

TYPE: Nothing but Portmeirion pottery

HOURS: Mon–Sat 10 A.M.–5:30 P.M.

Of course, everything is cheaper at their shop in Stoke-on-Trent (see Do China in a Day, page 223), but for Portmeirion collectors limited to London, this gift shop offers the best selection of their goods. You can order any piece they make and have your purchases shipped worldwide.

Hyper-Hyper

26–40 Kensington High Street, W8

TELEPHONE: 071-937-6964

TUBE: High Street Kensington

CREDIT CARDS: Depends on designer

TYPE: Far-out fashions for men and women

HOURS: Mon–Sat 10 A.M.–6 P.M.; Thur 10 A.M.–7 P.M.

Take your teenagers and your camera to Hyper-Hyper, the testing ground for avant-garde fashion designers in London. Wet, No Such Soul, Sub-Couture, Divided by Three, and Abrasive Aorta are just a few of the names of the hopefully up-and-coming young British designers who display their talents in this supermarket of fashion on the far, far side. The designers may come and go, but they are all creating tomorrow's new-wave fashions for those not afraid to dress on the wild side today.

In addition to the incredible fashion togs, there is a ticket agency, restaurant, hairdresser, money changer, and lots of loud music.

Kensington Market
Kensington High Street, W8
TELEPHONE: None
TUBE: High Street Kensington
CREDIT CARDS: Depends on the stall
TYPE: Strange fashions considered by some to be *de rigueur*
HOURS: Mon–Sat 10 A.M.–4 P.M.

If you are into fringe, lots of leather, skin-tight jeans, bright pink spiked hair (for men), metal studs, and the latest in weirdo-wear, then you should see this series of stalls where all of this and more will be yours for a price. You *must* be tuned in to appreciate them. In other words, if you like NEXT fashions, you won't like these.

SHOPS IN W11

Portobello China & Woollens, Ltd.   213

MARKETS IN W11
Portobello Road   230

Portobello China & Woollens, Ltd.
89 Portobello Road, W11
TELEPHONE: 071-727-3857
TUBE: Notting Hill Gate
CREDIT CARDS: AE, MC, V
TYPE: Discounted china and woolens
HOURS: Mon–Sat 10 A.M.–5 P.M.

For the best prices on sweaters in London, look no further: this is *the* place. Sweaters, scarves, robes, shawls, hats, and gloves in cashmere, lambswool, and blends are stacked in bins, boxes, and on shelves in this cluttered citadel of woolen bargains. Some are seconds; some have tiny discrepancies; and some are big names like Jaeger, Peter Scott, and Robertson. A few have the labels removed. Look carefully and I assure you that you will leave with a great bargain. The shop also stocks first- and second-quality china: Christmas Tree Spode, Johnston Brothers, Wedgwood, and more are always discounted. This place is an absolute zoo on Saturday mornings when the Portobello Market is in full swing. For best choice and ease of purchase, go during the week when you can have the store and the clerk to yourself.

SHOPS IN WC1

The Discount Designer Clothes Store—Gloria
    Rachelle   214
Westaway & Westaway   214

MUSEUM SHOPS IN WC1

British Museum Shop   231
National Gallery Shop   232

The Discount Designer Clothes Store—Gloria Rachelle

14 Procter Street, WC1
TELEPHONE: 071-404-4049
TUBE: Holborn
CREDIT CARDS: MC, V
TYPE: Discount designer clothes for women
HOURS: Mon–Fri 9 A.M.–6 P.M.

New stock arrives weekly and prices are about half the usual retail. Supplies come from samples, cancelled orders, and slightly imperfect goods from famous designers most of us from the U.S. have never heard of. Not for the Hyper-Hyper crowd (see page 212), but certainly worth a stop if you are over thirty and dress conservatively.

Westaway & Westaway

62–65 Great Russell Street & 92–93 Great Russell Street, WC1
TELEPHONE: 071-636-1718; toll-free in the U.S.: 1-800-345-3219
TUBE: Holborn, Tottenham Court Road
CREDIT CARDS: AE, DC, MC, V
TYPE: Scottish knitwear specialists
HOURS: Mon–Sat 9 A.M.–5:30 P.M. Sun 11 A.M.–6 P.M.

Westaway & Westaway offers a vast selection of sweaters, kilts, and other woolen goods from Scotland. While prices are not in the bargain-basement category, they are some of the best you will find. They can make a kilt from over 400 tartans, sell you a cashmere or lambswool sweater in a variety of colors and shades, outfit your children, and mail to your home address. Be sure to look downstairs and in the back rooms for sale-priced merchandise, factory overruns, seconds, and discontinued colors. To receive a catalog or place an order, call the toll-free number.

SHOPS IN WC2

Best of British Craft Shop   215
Culpeper   206
Half-Price Ticket Booth at Leicester Square   215
The Museum Store   216
Naturally British   216
Neal's Yard Wholefood Warehouse   217
The Silver Vaults   217

MARKETS IN WC2

Covent Garden & Jubilee Market   230

MUSEUM SHOPS IN WC2

Courtland Institute Shop   231

Best of British Craft Shop
27 Shorts Gardens, WC2
TELEPHONE: 071-379-4097
TUBE: Covent Garden
CREDIT CARDS: AE, DC, MC, V
TYPE: Crafts from the British Isles
HOURS: Mon–Sat 10:30 A.M.–7 P.M.; Sun from October–December, 1–5 P.M.

A small but select choice of crafts and goods from England, Scotland, Ireland, and Wales. Many small craftspeople are represented. Worth a look for that perfect gift.

Half-Price Ticket Booth at Leicester Square, Student and Senior Citizen Discount Tickets
Southwest corner of Leicester Square, WC2
TELEPHONE: 071-836-0971
TUBE: Leicester Square
CREDIT CARDS: None, cash only
TYPE: Discount tickets for theater and concerts sold on day of performance
HOURS: Mon–Sat noon–2:30 P.M. for that day's matinees; 2:30–6:30 P.M. for that day's evening performances. Tickets for Sunday sold after 2:30 P.M. on Saturday.

Half-price tickets for that day plus a service charge (£1.50 per ticket) are sold here. What a deal you think. All the top London shows and concerts for half price. *Wrong!* Yes, you can buy tickets for some shows and concerts, but none on the top-ten hit parade. These you can book before leaving home through Keith Prowse, 234 West 44th Street, New York, NY 10036; tel. 212-398-1430 in New York or 1-800-669-8687 outside New York. Or, you can wait until you arrive in London and try your luck at the theater box office (and save all service charges) or go to a theater booking agency, or deal with the concierge in your hotel. Be forewarned, however, that agencies and concierges take a service charge, sometimes as high as 25 percent on *each* ticket, depending on the popularity of the show. If you are willing to see a less-popular production, then by all means swing by the half-price booth and see what is available that day, and decide if you really want to queue for an hour or more. Warning: be wary of ticket touts who try to sell you front-row seats to Andrew Lloyd Webber's latest hit. Often these are bogus. If you have an International Student ID Card, you are eligible to buy tickets to top shows at greatly reduced prices. Not all theaters participate in this, so call first. Those that do offer student tickets on a stand-by basis one half hour before performances. Free West End theater guides are distributed by tourist offices, ticket agencies, and most hotels. If you aren't a student, but are a senior citizen, check with the theaters to see if discount tickets are being sold, and bring along your passport for proof of age.

The Museum Store
37 The Market (Covent Garden), WC2
TELEPHONE: 071-240-5760
TUBE: Covent Garden
CREDIT CARDS: MC, V
TYPE: Selection of items sold in various museums
HOURS: Mon–Sat 10:30 A.M.–6:30 P.M.; Sun 11 A.M.–5 P.M.

If you can't get to the Metropolitan Museum of Art in New York, stop in here and see what they have from their shop. Museum stores worldwide are represented here and the stock is fascinating—everything from inexpensive posters to jewelry and gifts.

Naturally British
13 New Row, WC2
TELEPHONE: 071-240-0551
TUBE: Leicester Square
CREDIT CARDS: AE, DC, MC, V
TYPE: Handmade gifts from the British Isles
HOURS: Mon–Sat 11 A.M.–6:30 P.M.; summer noon–5 P.M.

Naturally British is a one-stop shopping source for beautiful British-made crafts and clothing. These items make wonderful take-home gifts.

Prices are not in the giveaway category, but the quality is exceptionally high and the designs unique.

Neal's Yard Wholefood Warehouse
21–23 Shorts Gardens, WC2
TELEPHONE: 071-836-5151
TUBE: Covent Garden
CREDIT CARDS: MC, V
TYPE: Wholesome food
HOURS: Varies with each shop, but generally Mon–Sat 10 A.M.–6 P.M.

At Neal's Yard Wholefood Warehouse you can buy seeds, nuts, fruit, vitamins, snacks, crackers, grains and rice, fabulous honey and natural jams, peanut butter, natural cosmetics, gingerbread, banana cake . . . all made from natural ingredients. A refrigerator is filled with fruit juices, yogurts, and cheeses perfect for assembling into a nutritious picnic. Around the Wholefood Warehouse are shops selling bakery products, organic produce and cheeses, and natural remedies. There is also a very good restaurant (see *Cheap Eats in London*).

The Silver Vaults
53–64 Chancery Lane, WC2
TELEPHONE: 071-242-3844
TUBE: Chancery Lane
CREDIT CARDS: Depends on dealer
TYPE: Silver
HOURS: Mon–Fri 9 A.M.–5:30 P.M.; Sat 9 A.M.–12:30 P.M.

No serious lover or collector of silver should miss the Silver Vaults. In the late 1800s the rich stored their valuables in private underground vaults in central London. These same vaults have been turned into more than 40 shops for dealers of modern and antique silver. If it is silver, it is here, and in all price ranges.

SHOPS IN SW1

National Trust Gift Shop and
    Information Center   218
One Night Stand   218

DEPARTMENT STORES IN SW1

Harrods   225
Harvey Nichols   225
Peter Jones   226

National Trust Gift Shop and Information Center
23 Caxton Street, off Victoria, SW1
TELEPHONE: 071-222-2877
TUBE: St. James's Park
CREDIT CARDS: AE, MC, V
TYPE: Gifts, many exclusive to the National Trust
HOURS: Mon–Fri 10 A.M.–5:30 P.M.

The National Trust is a charity founded to protect Britain's fine homes and beautiful countryside. This gift shop, located in historic Blewcoat School, has china, glassware, pottery, kitchenware, books and stationery, spices, preserves, crafts and knitwear, most of which are exclusive to the National Trust. By shopping here, you are helping the National Trust's work of conserving and protecting over 560,000 acres of countryside, 200 houses and castles, 114 gardens, 59 villages, country parks, churches, and ancient monuments. As a charity, the National Trust is not run by the government, and depends on the support and generosity of the public to continue its work.

Note: Blewcoat School was built for the education of poor children, and named for the color of the tunic worn by its pupils. It is now part of the National Trust.

One Night Stand
44 Pimlico Road, SW1
TELEPHONE: 071-730-8708
TUBE: Sloane Square
CREDIT CARDS: AE, DC, MC, V
TYPE: Fancy-dress rental
HOURS: Mon–Fri 9:30 A.M.–6:30 P.M.; Sat 10 A.M.–5 P.M.

If you have been invited to a fancy-dress ball or to the cocktail party of the season and didn't pack a thing to wear, don't despair; call One Night Stand. This fancy-dress agency will come to your rescue with a fabulous selection of party dresses for hire (Britspeak for "rent"). You can hire your gown and all the accessories for up to four days. The dresses, cleaned after wearing, are from top American and British fashion designers. If you fall in love with your outfit, you will have to be in town in February or August, the only times during the year they sell their stock. Appointments are preferred over walk-ins. Dress rental prices range from £50–120. A security deposit of £200 is refundable. Optional damage insurance is £7. Sizes: U.S. 6–14.

STORES IN SW3

Designer Sale Studio	219
La Scala	219
Levy & Friend	220
Monsoon	220
Past Times	221
The Reject Shop	221

MARKETS IN SW3

Antiquarius	227
Chelsea Antiques Market	227
Chenil Galleries	227

Designer Sale Studio
241 King's Road, SW3
TELEPHONE: 071-351-4171
TUBE: Sloane Square, then bus #19 or a long walk
CREDIT CARDS: AE, DC, MC, V
TYPE: Designer discount clothing for men and women
HOURS: Mon–Fri 10 A.M.–7 P.M.; Sat 10 A.M.–6 P.M.; Sun noon–6 P.M.

The Discount Sale Studio regularly sells last season's collections at up to 50 percent off and on sale items at a whopping 70 percent. You can expect to find clothes by Kritzia, Gianni Versace, and Lacroix; factory-direct shipments; and some things with labels cut out. They also have bags, belts, and scarves to complete your outfit. The dressing rooms are ample, the staff helpful, and if you spend £100, remember to get your VAT form for a refund.

La Scala
39 Elystan Street, SW3
TELEPHONE: 071-589-2784
TUBE: South Kensington
CREDIT CARDS: None
TYPE: New and nearly new designer clothing for women
HOURS: Mon–Sat 10 A.M.–5:30 P.M.

If you love glamorous clothes, but hate paying full price, shop at La Scala, where you can dress for less and still look like a million. I first noticed the shop when I returned to check the restaurant Au Bon Accueil, a few doors away (see *Cheap Eats in London*). Since the shop was located only a few minutes from my London flat, I passed it often, but I was sure I could never afford any of the beautiful and expensive clothes displayed in the window. Finally, I could not resist going in and just looking. Once inside, I learned that these lovely garments were either there on consignment, or were new, but last season's designs. Owner Sandy Reid has a wonderful eye for fashion, and she knows that few women today can afford the prices of most designer clothing. So, she decided to rely on her fashion sense and opened this resale shop. She stocks an excellent selection of accessories, suits and dresses, cocktail and ball gowns, coats, shoes, and handbags. Name designers are well represented, and there is even a bargain rack downstairs.

Levy & Friend
236 Brompton Road, SW3
TELEPHONE: 071-589-9741
TUBE: South Kensington
CREDIT CARDS: MC, V
TYPE: Consigned designer clothing for women
HOURS: Tues–Sat 10 A.M.–6 P.M.

Previously owned designer dresses, belts, costume jewelry, handbags, and shoes from such designers as Valentino, Armani, Bruce Oldfield, Yves St. Laurent, and more are in this shop run by Carole Levy and Linda Friend. The consigned articles are in good condition and the overall selection is above average. When I was there I was told that they might have to move, due to a dramatic increase in their rent. So, before venturing forth, be sure to call to see if they have a new address.

Monsoon
33D King's Road, SW3
TELEPHONE: 071-730-7552
TUBE: Sloane Square
CREDIT CARDS: AE, DC, MC, V
TYPE: Fashions for the young at heart
HOURS: Mon–Sat 10 A.M.–6 P.M.; Wed 10 A.M.–7 P.M.

Monsoon is an English chain with brightly colored clothing designed in England and made up in India, Thailand, and Hong Kong. The styles are young, with strong colors and bright prints color coordinated for mixing and matching. Prices are affordable, and when they have a sale, very low. The price on the garment reflects the quality of the sewing, so check them over carefully before buying. Locations throughout London.

Past Times
146 Brompton Road opposite Beauchamp Place, SW3
TELEPHONE: 071-581-7616
TUBE: Knightsbridge
CREDIT CARDS: AE, DC, MC, V
TYPE: Replicas, crafts, books, and cards covering Britain's history
HOURS: Mon–Sat 9:30 A.M.–5:30 P.M.

Past Times showcases a collection of authentic replicas of crafts, toys, stationery, and jewelry that cover 4,000 years of Britain's history. These pleasing and practical items from every age of Britain's past make lovely gifts for yourself or friends. Prices start at 50p and there are many possibilities under £10. They also have a mail order catalog and organized tours (called Heritage Weekends) to interesting old homes, castles, and manors throughout England.

The Reject Shop
245 Brompton Road, SW3
TELEPHONE: Not available
TUBE: Knightsbridge
CREDIT CARDS: MC, V
TYPE: Variety of discounted merchandise
HOURS: Mon–Sat 10 A.M.–6 P.M.

Not to be confused with the Reject China Shop, The Reject Shop stocks a variety on two floors of everything from Christmas tree ornaments (in season) to party goods for your toddler's next birthday bash. There is no "regular" stock; it is mostly overruns, odd lots, and things that haven't sold elsewhere. In other words, you never know what treasures you will see. Some of the bargains are too big to tote home, but plenty are not. There is a branch at 234 King's Road, SW3, TUBE: Sloane Square.

STORES IN SW7
Pandora   222

STORES IN SW10
Ganesha   222
The Packing Shop   222

MUSEUM SHOPS IN SW7
Natural History Museum Shop   232
Science Museum Shop   232
Victoria & Albert Museum Shop & Crafts
  Council Shop   233

Pandora
16–22 Cheval Place, SW7
TELEPHONE: 071-589-5289
TUBE: Knightsbridge
CREDIT CARDS: AE, MC, V
TYPE: Consignment clothing
HOURS: Mon–Sat 10 A.M.–5 P.M.

Since 1947, fashion savvy women have brought their own designer clothing to sell, and bought replacements from Pandora, the biggest and one of the best consignment resale shops in London. The turnover is large and rapid, and the savings add up to at least 40–50 percent of retail. All garments are arranged according to size, ranging from U.S. 6–16. They also have belts, bags, jewelry, hats, and shoes. Pandora is across Brompton Road from Harrods, between Montpelier Street and the corner of Montpelier Walk and Cheval Place.

Ganesha
6 Park Walk, SW10
TELEPHONE: 071-352-8972
TUBE: South Kensington
CREDIT CARDS: AE, MC, V
TYPE: Gifts from the Orient
HOURS: Daily noon–7 P.M.

It is not worth a special trip from the West End, but if you are around Fulham Road, take a quick detour on Park Walk and browse through this upscale, jam-packed Asian-style dime store that stocks something for every pocketbook. The tiny ground-level room is stuffed with trinkets and treasures from all over Asia and India. It is a good place to pick up clever and cheap gifts. The downstairs room is devoted to large items—tables, chests, etc.—at reasonable prices. Don't expect much from the aloof owner, who positions herself behind the front counter and chain-smokes.

The Packing Shop
535 King's Road, SW10
TELEPHONE: 071-352-2021
TUBE: Sloane Square (long walk)
CREDIT CARDS: AE, DC, MC, V
TYPE: Packing and sending parcels worldwide
HOURS: Mon–Fri 9 A.M.–6 P.M.; Sat 10 A.M.–1 P.M.

What to do with all your shopping loot now that it is time to go home and your suitcases cannot take one more thing without splitting? There are two options. You can buy another suitcase (because the empty one you brought is already full) and pay the airline excess baggage fee of approximately $100. This will most likely be cheaper than insuring and mailing a large box, and it will arrive (we hope) when you do. Or, you can call The Packing Shop, and they will pick up, wrap, insure, and send your treasures to any destination worldwide. There is a minimum pick-up, packing, and sending charge that depends on the size and destination of your items. Insurance costs are built in, and, in the case of antiques, The Packing Shop can arrange with the seller to show that the goods have left the U.K., allowing you to avoid VAT charges. This company deals with customs red tape, promises same-day delivery anyplace in Britain, and only 24 hours delivery time to Europe and the States. They have sent everything from Ming vases and fine antiques to Hard Rock T-shirts and live rare dogs. Naturally, this service does not fall into the "cheap" category, but for a fine painting or work of art, or any other item you deem valuable and important, give them a call.

DO CHINA IN A DAY

When the brochure says "Do China in a Day," it is talking about Stoke-on-Trent, the china and crystal bargain capital of England. Here is where you can stock up on seconds, overruns, and pieces you never can find at home if your pattern happens to be English. You can take the train from Euston Station for around $85 round trip. Better yet, if there are at least two of you, rent a car and drive from London. It is an easy day trip, and the car makes life much easier once you arrive in Stoke. The trip is not worth the effort and money spent on transportation if you just want to browse and pick up a vase or two. But, for brides and serious china shoppers, it is.

If you do take the train, when you arrive in Stoke go directly to the Pottery Centre next door to the station. Here you can load up on information about whatever brand you are interested in, and from there you can take a taxi into town. If you walk, you will have to hike a mile and why waste shopping energy on a dull walk?

What's here? Coalport, Johnson Brothers, Minton, Portmeirion, Royal Doulton, Royal Stafford, Spode, Staffordshire enamels and ceramics, Wedgwood, and more. Shipping is possible, although some outlets do not mail seconds—*you* can.

DEPARTMENT STORES

Whatever you need or want, or never imagined you should have, can be found in one of London's many department stores. These large emporiums make good shopping sense if your time is limited and you have only a few hours to power shop. All of the stores are known for their January and July sales. Only people who have earned a black belt in shopping should attempt opening day at a Harrods sale. If you do brave this onslaught, you will need superhuman stamina and patience to withstand the merciless crowds clamoring and clawing for bargains that come only once or twice a year.

Debenhams
334–38 Oxford Street, W1
TELEPHONE: 071-580-3000
TUBE: Oxford Circus or Bond Street
CREDIT CARDS: AE, DC, MC, V
For the working man and woman. Good prices overall and a step up from Marks & Spencer. Some kicky fashions along with name brands.

D. H. Evans
318 Oxford Street, W1
TELEPHONE: 071-629-8800
TUBE: Oxford Circus
CREDIT CARDS: AE, DC, MC, V
Large department store with a good selection of their own labels and many designers. Some up-and-coming designers featured. Nothing too far out, but generally sturdy, good stuff.

Dickens & Jones
224 Regent Street, W1
TELEPHONE: 071-734-7070
TUBE: Oxford Circus
CREDIT CARDS: AE, DC, MC, V
Clothes aimed toward the smartly dressed working person who can't afford bespoke clothing. A good selection with lots of designers: Yves St. Laurent, Jaeger, Aquascutum, etc.

Fortnum & Mason
181 Piccadilly, W1
TELEPHONE: 071-743-8040
TUBE: Piccadilly or Green Park
CREDIT CARDS: AE, DC, MC, V

Famous for its grocery department with clerks wearing morning coats. Opened in 1701 as a grocery store, it has been selling food items ever since and is a supplier to Buckingham Palace and the Queen. In addition to food, there is a china and crystal department and a clothing section that can best be described as dumpy. The Fountain Restaurant is open for breakfast, lunch, and dinner and recommended for Cheap Eaters in London (see *Cheap Eats in London*).

Harrods
Knightsbridge, SW1
TELEPHONE: 071-730-1234
TUBE: Knightsbridge
CREDIT CARDS: AE, DC, MC, V

The first stop on the yellow brick road of London shopping usually is Harrods. It is not to be missed, if you only see the famous food halls and stand in awe of the sheer size and magnitude of this world-class department store. Harrods boasts that it can take care of you from the cradle to the grave (they have a funeral department). They offer excellent half-day tours of London in their own air-conditioned buses with tea and cookies served after the tour. You can get either a morning or afternoon tour right in front of the main entrance.

Harvey Nichols
109 Knightsbridge, SW1
TELEPHONE: 071-235-5000
TUBE: Knightsbridge
CREDIT CARDS: AE, DC, MC, V

This is the most luxurious department store in London. If I could afford it, I would never shop anyplace else. If you are in London during the January sales, this is an absolute *must*. On the top floor, they have opened a food market that sells every exotic piece of produce you ever heard of and some you never have. It is far less overwhelming than the food halls at Harrods, and a nice place to browse and pick up a fancy jam, unusual tea, or special ground coffee. There are also two restaurants here, and a bar. If you love homewares, don't miss the fourth floor, a treasure trove of home fashion ideas ranging from the traditional and useful to the completely wacky.

Liberty
Regent Street, W1
TELEPHONE: 071-734-1234
TUBE: Oxford Circus
CREDIT CARDS: AE, DC, MC, V

Liberty is known worldwide for their fine Liberty prints. A Liberty tie or scarf makes a perfect gift even the most demanding person on your list will recognize and enjoy. It is easy to get lost in the maze of departments and boutiques, but what a wonderful place to wander.

Lilywhite
Piccadilly Circus, W1
TELEPHONE: 071-930-3181
TUBE: Piccadilly Circus
CREDIT CARDS: AE, DC, MC, V
The largest sporting goods store in England. All brand names represented including American. Good sale prices; otherwise, no breathtaking savings.

Marks & Spencer
458 Oxford Street, W1
TELEPHONE: 071-935-7954
TUBE: Marble Arch or Bond Street
CREDIT CARDS: None, only their own
Marks & Spencer (or "Marks and Sparks" to the locals) is a British shopping institution. There are hundreds of branches throughout the British Isles and probably twenty in London. It is considered "discount shopping" by most Britishers. Best buys? Silk lingerie, sweaters, children's clothing, and the food in the basement. There are no dressing rooms, but you can return for a full refund. To get the VAT refund, check with the Marks & Spencer you are in to be sure they participate. *All* of your purchases must be made from the same store to get the VAT refund.

Peter Jones
Sloane Square, SW1
TELEPHONE: 071-730-3434
TUBE: Sloane Square
CREDIT CARDS: Only its own
Known for fine linen, lighting, fabric, kitchen, and housewares departments. Sloane Rangers (British yuppies) are here in full force on Saturday mornings. The clothing departments are boring.

Selfridges
400 Oxford Street, W1
TELEPHONE: 071-629-1234
TUBE: Marble Arch
CREDIT CARDS: AE, MC, V

After Harrods, this is the best all-around department store in London. At Selfridges you will find a huge cosmetic and perfume department, a theater booking agent, fabulous food halls, good-looking fashions, a big household section, and a pleasing staff. Miss Selfridge on Duke Street (TELEPHONE: same; TUBE: Bond Street) stocks trendy yet affordable fashions for anyone under 35.

MARKETS

INDOOR MARKETS

The indoor markets have regular hours and are open almost every day. The difference between these markets and regular stores is that the markets are made up of stalls specializing in certain collectables. Here you will find Art Deco jewelry, buttons, old books and maps, retro handbags, dolls, prints, boxes, firearms, and much, much more. If you are a collector, do not miss a trip through one of these mazes of sellers.

Antiquarius
135 King's Road, SW3
HOURS: Mon–Sat 10 A.M.–6 P.M.
TUBE: Sloane Square, then bus #19 unless you don't mind a long walk.

There are over one hundred and fifty stalls selling everything from clocks and lace to porcelain and watches. A relaxed atmosphere and good affordability.
AREA: Chelsea

Chelsea Antiques Market
253 King's Road, SW3
HOURS: Mon–Sat 10 A.M.–6 P.M.
TUBE: Sloane Square, then a long walk unless you take the #19 bus.

A chaotic mix of junk and good stuff distributed among one hundred stalls.
AREA: Chelsea

Chenil Galleries
181–183 King's Road, SW3
HOURS: Mon–Sat 10 A.M.–6 P.M.
TUBE: Sloane Square, then #19 bus unless you like to walk.

High quality, reputable, and serious. Art Nouveau, dolls, toys, furniture, and scientific instruments are some of the specialties you will find here.

AREA: Chelsea

Covent Garden & Jubilee Market

See write-up on page 230.

Grey's Antique Markets

58 Davies Street and 17 Davies Mews, W1

HOURS: Mon–Fri 10 A.M.–6 P.M.

TUBE: Bond Street

One hundred and eighty stalls selling top-quality antiques from around the world. Prices run high, but you can hunt down a small piece of jewelry or another trinket for a modest outlay.

AREA: Bond Street

Hyper-Hyper

See write-up on page 212.

Kensington Market

See write-up on page 213.

OUTDOOR FLEA MARKETS

London markets are entertaining and fun for everyone, even the die-hard couch potato whose idea of shopping is to thumb through a mail-order catalog and dial an 800 number. For serious antiques shopping enthusiasts, a pre-dawn visit to one of London's big outdoor flea markets is something you will never forget. While you probably will not unearth a rare Minton vase for a few pence, you will find something and have fun in the bargain.

At all the flea markets, bargaining is expected and part of the game. There are always two prices for everything, the "punter's" and the dealer's. You can guess who you are. There are two things to remember to say to the seller: "What is the best you can do?" and "What is the trade on that?" which means what is the dealer price.

You *must* go early—I am talking 4 A.M. for Bermondsey and by 6 A.M. for Portobello Road. These are the times for hard-core bargaining and buying. I do not recommend the wee hours at Petticoat Lane; the neighborhood is just too dicey.

No matter which market you go to, it is better to travel in pairs for these early morning safaris. Dress simply. Dealers will charge what the market will bear, and if you are clad in designer togs and high visibility jewelry, the prices will not go down. Don't wear shorts and tank tops, but jeans and a clean shirt are fine. Take cash, because credit cards won't get you the best price breaks.

Bermondsey Market (also called New Caledonian Market)
Bermondsey Square south of the Tower Bridge, SE1
TUBE: London Bridge and walk south
HOURS: Friday 5:30 A.M.–1 P.M., but the good stuff is gone by 9 A.M.
This is the most serious and professional antiques market. Over 500 stalls sell silver, glass, dolls, jewelry, clocks, and old prints.

Brixton Market
Electric Avenue, Brixton Station Road and Popes Road, SW2
TUBE: Brixton
HOURS: Mon–Sat 8 A.M.–5:30 P.M.; Wed closed after 1 P.M.
The market is located in the heart of African London. Electric Avenue has stalls selling exotic fruits and vegetables, and at the end, a big selection of second-hand clothing. Go through the enclosed Granville Arcade for African fabrics, reggae records, and other items geared toward the African-British community.

Camden Lock and Camden Stables
Camden High Street—Chalk Farm Road, NW1
TUBE: Chalk Farm
HOURS: Sat–Sun 8 A.M.–5 P.M.
Not to be confused with Camden Passage Market. Camden Lock is a true flea market, loaded with castoffs of various worth and artistic merit. It is a great way to wile away a Saturday or Sunday, wandering among the stalls, munching on street food, and maybe finding something you can't live without. It is very crowded and pickpockets are out in full force. When you have had enough of the market, walk along the peaceful Regent's Canal, or hop on one of the boats that ply the canal.

Camden Passage
Camden Passage, Islington, N1
TUBE: Angel
HOURS: Wed and Sat 7 A.M.–3 P.M.; Thurs 8:30 A.M.–4 P.M.
The focus is on small items, but there are also some shops open daily that sell antique furniture. For the street market, it is antiques on Wednesday and Saturday, and books on Thursday.

Covent Garden & Jubilee Market
Covent Garden Piazza, WC2
TUBE: Covent Garden
HOURS: Daily 10 A.M.–6 P.M., later for restaurants

The original Covent Garden fruit and vegetable market building is now a mall of shops and restaurants. Around the outside are stalls that make up the Jubilee Market. Here you will shop for antiques on Monday, bric-a-brac from Tuesday through Friday, and crafts on the weekend. Every day you can listen to singers and musicians or watch artists and other entertainers performing outside. It is alive, busy, and always fun, and going strong on Sunday when most of London is shuttered tight.

Petticoat Lane
Middlesex Street, E1
TUBE: Aldgate or Liverpool
HOURS: Sun 9 A.M.–2 P.M.

Located in London's East End, this is the best market for inexpensive, *au courant* fashions, which are hanging on racks along the street. The antiques section is on Goulston Street and is called the New Cutler Street Market. It is known for its scrap gold and silver, coins, medals, and stamps. A morning spent at the Petticoat Lane Market is an experience: a wild kaleidoscope of color, noises, and smells . . . including jellied eels sold from carts. If you are a foodie who will try anything, here is another chance for you.

Portobello Road
Portobello Road off Westbourne Park, W11
HOURS: Sat 7 A.M.–4 P.M., but best early until about 1 P.M.
CREDIT CARDS: Depends on dealer. Better deals for cash.

On Saturday, Portobello Road is one of Britain's most famous antiques markets. The best part is the five-block strip running north from Chepstow Villas to the Lonsdale Road intersection. Farther north, the sidewalk and indoor shops progress to vegetable and fruit sellers, and then it all deteriorates into a chaotic mess of trashy clothing and cheap housewares. Beware of pickpockets.

MUSEUM SHOPS

Most of London's major museums have interesting shops. These are worth a look because they often sell reproductions from their own collections that you will not find anyplace else. Quality is always high, the items are unusual and represent good value for money. In most of the museum stores, you can shop without having to pay admission to get into the museum itself. The following is a list of some of the better museum shops in London.

Bank of England Museum Shop
Threadneedle Street, entrance on Bartholomew Lane, EC2
TELEPHONE: 071-601-5792
TUBE: Bank
CREDIT CARDS: MC, V
HOURS: Mon–Fri 10 A.M.–5 P.M.; Sat–Sun 11 A.M.–5 P.M.

British Museum Shop
Great Russell Street, WC1
TELEPHONE: 071-636-1555
TUBE: Russell Square
CREDIT CARDS: AE, DC, MC, V
HOURS: Mon–Sat 10 A.M.–4:30 P.M.; Sun 2:30–5:30 P.M.

Courtland Institute Shop
Somerset House, The Strand, WC2
TELEPHONE: 071-872-0217
TUBE: Charing Cross or Temple (closed Sunday)
CREDIT CARDS: AE, DC, MC, V
HOURS: Mon–Sat 10 A.M.–6 P.M.; Sun 2–6 P.M.

Imperial War Museum Shop
Lambeth Road, SE1
TELEPHONE: 071-416-5000, 071-820-1683
TUBE: Elephand & Castle
CREDIT CARDS: MC, V
HOURS: Daily 10 A.M.–6 P.M.

Museum of London Shop
150 London Wall, EC2
TELEPHONE: 071-600-3699
TUBE: Barbican or St. Paul's
CREDIT CARDS: MC, V
HOURS: Tues–Sat 10 A.M.–6 P.M.; Sun 2–6 P.M.; closed Mondays, but open on Bank Holidays 10 A.M.–6 P.M.

Museum of the Moving Image Shop
Southbank Centre, SE1
TELEPHONE: 071-928-3535
TUBE: Waterloo
CREDIT CARDS: MC, V
Hours: Daily 10 A.M.–6 P.M.

National Gallery Shop
Trafalgar Square, WC2
TELEPHONE: 071-839-3321
TUBE: Charing Cross, Leicester Square
CREDIT CARDS: MC, V
HOURS: Mon–Sat 10 A.M.–6 P.M.; Sun 2–6 P.M.

Natural History Museum Shop
Cromwell Road, SW7
TELEPHONE: 071-938-9062
TUBE: Gloucester Road
CREDIT CARDS: MC, V
HOURS: Mon–Sat 10 A.M.–5:30 P.M.; Sun 11 A.M.–5:30 P.M.

Royal Academy Shop
Burlington House, Piccadilly, W1
TELEPHONE: 071-439-7438
TUBE: Piccadilly
CREDIT CARDS: MC, V
HOURS: Daily 10 A.M.–6 P.M.

Science Museum Shop
Exhibition Road, SW7
TELEPHONE: 071-589-3456
TUBE: South Kensington
CREDIT CARDS: AE, DC, MC, V
HOURS: Mon–Sat 10 A.M.–6 P.M.; Sun 11 A.M.–6 P.M.

Tate Gallery Shop
Millbank, SW1
TELEPHONE: 071-821-1313
TUBE: Pimlico
CREDIT CARDS: MC, V
HOURS: Mon–Sat 10 A.M.–5:30 P.M.; Sun 2–5:30 P.M.

Victoria & Albert Museum Shop & Crafts Council Shop
Cromwell Road, SW7
TELEPHONE: 071-938-8500
TUBE: Gloucester Road
CREDIT CARDS: AE, DC, MC, V
HOURS: Mon noon–5:30 P.M.; Tues–Sun 10 A.M.–5:30 P.M.

INDEX

A

Aaron House	126
Abbey House	62
Abcone Hotel	135
Academy Hotel	75
Accommodation Express	99
Adare House	47
Albert Hotel	135
The Amber Hotel	63
Arran House Hotel	76
Ashley Hotel	47
Aster House Hotel	136
Avalon Private Hotel	76

B

Baden-Powell House	137
Balmoral Hotel	48
The Beaver Hotel	127
Bed and Breakfast in a Private Home	151
Blair House Hotel	120
Bonnington	77
Border Hotel	49
Brown's Hotel	37–38
Bryanston Court Hotel	35
The Burns Park Hotel	127
The Byron Hotel	50

C

Cambria House	78
Camelot Hotel	50
Camping	156
Celtic Hotel	78
The Claverly	121
Collin House	101
Hotel Concorde	36
The Cranley	128
Crescent Hotel	79
The Cumberland	37–38

D

Dean Court Hotel	51
The Delemere Hotel	52
Demetriou Guest House	64

Diplomat Hotel	101
Dorset Square Hotel	147
E	
Eaton House Hotel	102
Ebury House	102
Elizabeth Hotel & Apartments	103
Elmwood Hotel	80
Embassy House Hotel	138
Enrico Hotel	104
Europa House	53
F	
Fairways Hotel	53
The Fielding Hotel	91
Five Sumner Place Hotel	139
Forte Hotel Leisure Breaks	37, 65, 80, 92, 105
Forte Crest Bloomsbury	80
Forte Crest Regent's Park	37–38
Forte Crest St. James's	105
G	
Garden Court Hotel	54
Gate Hotel	67
Georgian House Hotel	38
The Gore	140
The Gresham Hotel	54
Grosvenor House	37–38
H	
Hallam Hotel	39
Hamilton House Hotel	105
Harcourt House	106
Harlingford Hotel	80
Harrington Hall	141
Hart House Hotel	40
Hazlitt's	41
Henley House Hotel	129
Hogarth Hotel	130
Hotel 167	130
Hotel Russell	80
Hotels with Flats to Rent	160
Hyde Park Hotel	105
I	
Imperial London Hotels Limited	81
Bedford Hotel	82
Imperial Hotel	82
Royal National Hotel	83
Tavistock Hotel	83

The Ivanhoe Suites 42

J
The James Cartref House 106
Jenkins Hotel 84

K
Kensbridge Hotel 142
The Kensington Close 65
Kensington Gardens Hotel 55

L
Hotel Lexham 65
London Homes 153
Luna & Simone Hotel 108

M
Mabledon Court Hotel 84
Magnolia Hotel 122
Manzi's Hotel 92
Melbourne House 108
Mitre House Hotel 56
Morgan Hotel 85
Mornington Hotel 56

N
Nevern Hotel 131
Norfolk Court and St. David's Hotel 57
Number Sixteen 143

O
Oak House Hotel 109
Oakley Hotel 122
One Cranley Place 144
Other Options 150
Oxford House Hotel 110

P
The Park International Hotel 145
The Pastoria 93
Pembridge Court Hotel 58
The Phoenix Hotel 59
The Portland Bloomsbury 86
The Portobello Hotel 68
Pyms Hotel 110

Q
Queensway Hotel 60

R
Ravna Gora 69
Regent Palace Hotel 37–38, 42
Regent's Park Hotel 148
Renting a London Flat 159

Richmond House Hotel   111
Ridgemount Private Hotel   87
Royal Adelphi Hotel   94
Royal Norfolk Hotel   60
Royal Trafalgar Thistle Hotel   94
Rushmore Hotel   132
Ruskin Hotel   88
Russell House Hotel   88

S

St. George's Hotel   37–38
St. Margaret's Hotel   89
Searcy's Roof Garden Bedrooms   111
Shopping: Cheap Chic   196
The Strand Palace   92
Strictly for Students   172
Swiss House Hotel   132

T

Thanet Hotel   90
Tophams Ebury Court   112

U

University Dormitory Accommodations   174
Uptown Reservations   155

V

Vandon House   114
Vicarage Private Hotel   66
The Victoria Inn   114

W

The Waldorf   92
The Westbury   37–38
Westminster House   115
Wilbraham Hotel   116
Winchester Hotel   116
Windermere Hotel   117

Y

Ys   184
York House Hotel   133
Youth Hostels   188

READER'S COMMENTS

While every effort has been made to provide accurate information in this edition of *Cheap Sleeps in London,* the publisher and author cannot be held responsible for changes in any of the listings due to rate increases, inflation, dollar fluctuation, the passage of time, or management changes.

Cheap Sleeps in London is updated and revised on a regular basis. If you find a change before I do, or make an important discovery you want to pass along, please send me a note stating the name and address of the hotel or shop, the date of your visit, and a description of your findings. Your comments are very important to me. I investigate every complaint and pass on every compliment you send me. Thank you in advance for taking the time to write.

Send your comments to Sandra A. Gustafson (*Cheap Sleeps in London*), c/o Chronicle Books, 275 Fifth Street, San Francisco, CA 94103.